CALIFORNIA'S IMMIGRANT CHILDREN

Theory, Research, and Implications for Educational Policy

U.S.-MEXICO CONTEMPORARY PERSPECTIVES SERIES, 8
CENTER FOR U.S.-MEXICAN STUDIES
UNIVERSITY OF CALIFORNIA, SAN DIEGO

Contributors

Wayne A. Cornelius
David Durán
Margaret A. Gibson
Kenji Ima
Laurie Olsen
Amado M. Padilla
Alejandro Portes
Richard Rothstein
Rubén G. Rumbaut
Karen Shaw
Carola E. Suárez-Orozco
Marcelo M. Suárez-Orozco
Mia Tuan

California's Immigrant Children

Theory, Research, and Implications for Educational Policy

Edited by

RUBÉN G. RUMBAUT

AND

WAYNE A. CORNELIUS

Center for U.S.-Mexican Studies
University of California, San Diego

PRINTED IN THE UNITED STATES OF AMERICA BY
THE CENTER FOR U.S.-MEXICAN STUDIES,
UNIVERSITY OF CALIFORNIA, SAN DIEGO

1995

Cover photos: courtesy of Erica Hagen, Intercultural Communication Resources

ISBN 1-878367-17-X

For Irene, daughter of immigrants/Para Irene, hija de inmigrantes—RGR

For Craig, an often lonely defender of enlightened social policies—WAC

Contents

Acknowledgments   ix

1   Educating California's Immigrant Children: Introduction and Overview   1
Wayne A. Cornelius

2   The New Californians: Comparative Research Findings on the Educational Progress of Immigrant Children   17
Rubén G. Rumbaut

3   Segmented Assimilation among New Immigrant Youth: A Conceptual Framework   71
Alejandro Portes

4   Additive Acculturation as a Strategy for School Improvement   77
Margaret A. Gibson

5   Korean and Russian Students in a Los Angeles High School: Exploring the Alternative Strategies of Two High-Achieving Groups   107
Mia Tuan

6   The Psychological Dimension in Understanding Immigrant Students   131
Amado M. Padilla and David Durán

7   The Cultural Patterning of Achievement Motivation: A Comparison of Mexican, Mexican Immigrant, Mexican American, and Non-Latino White American Students   161
Marcelo M. Suárez-Orozco and Carola E. Suárez-Orozco

8   Testing the American Dream: Case Studies of At-Risk Southeast Asian Refugee Students in Secondary Schools   191
Kenji Ima

9   School Restructuring and the Needs of Immigrant Students   209
Laurie Olsen

10   Are Our Schools Really Failing?   233
Richard Rothstein

Commentary—Politics, Education, and Immigrant Children in New York City: Is Nothing Sacred?   263
Karen Shaw

Contributors   269

Acknowledgments

We gratefully acknowledge the financial support for this publication, and the project from which it emerged, provided by the California Policy Seminar (a joint program of the University of California and the State Government of California) and the Ford Foundation. Editorial and administrative support was made possible by an unrestricted grant to the Center for U.S.-Mexican Studies at the University of California, San Diego by the William and Flora Hewlett Foundation. Diana Platero provided most of the staff support for the project, and Sandra del Castillo edited the resulting papers for publication.

We would also like to thank Lorraine M. McDonnell of the RAND Program for Research on Immigration Policy; Hugh B. Mehan, Coordinator of the Teacher Education Program at UCSD; Alejandro Portes, of Johns Hopkins University; and Karen Shaw, of the New York City Community Development Agency, all of whom served as expert commentators on the original drafts of the papers published herein.

The illustrations appearing on the cover were produced from Erica Hagen's vibrant photographs, which so beautifully capture the spirit of our immigrant students. We thank Erica for making her photo archive available to us.

Wayne A. Cornelius
Rubén G. Rumbaut

La Jolla, California
July 25, 1995

1

Educating California's Immigrant Children: Introduction and Overview

Wayne A. Cornelius

Defining the Problem

This volume addresses one of the most significant challenges facing California today: educating a large, new, highly diverse wave of immigrant children, in resource-short public schools that are, in general, poorly prepared to understand and respond effectively to the special needs of such students, within a political and public opinion context that has become overtly hostile to immigrants and their offspring.

Until recently, the presence of large numbers of immigrant children (of whatever legal status) in the state's public school systems was a marginal element of the growing public debate over immigration in general. While the costs of providing public education to immigrant children represent, by far, the "big ticket" item in any overall estimate of the fiscal impacts of immigration in California, immigrant education was discussed only tangentially, in the context of the long-running controversy over bilingual education—the need for it, its goals ("cultural maintenance" versus rapid transitioning to all-English instruction), its efficacy in keeping immigrant children in school and improving their performance, and its cost to taxpayers. In recent years, however, the "immigrant invasion" of California public schools has gained greatly in political salience. How did this redefinition of a long-standing social phenomenon as one of California's major public problems occur?

First, the proportion of immigrant children—whom officials usually classify at least initially as LEP (limited-English-proficient) students—in the state's total population of school-age children has been rising rapidly since the 1970s.[1] This was an inevitable consequence of depressed birth rates among the native-born population, coinciding with a great new wave of immigration, especially from Mexico and Central America, beginning in the late 1970s. According to the best available estimates, for at least half of Mexican immigrants entering the United States—legally and illegally—in the 1980s, California was the preferred destination (Cornelius 1992: 165–71). During that decade, the state's population of limited-English-proficient students grew by 150 percent, to 861,531, of whom more than 268,000 were immigrant students who had been in the United States for three years or less (McDonnell and Hill 1993: 4). From 1990 to 1995, the state's LEP student population grew by more than 40 percent. California now enrolls some 45 percent of the nation's immigrant student population. More than one out of ten school-age Californians are foreign-born, and over a third of the state's schoolchildren speak a language other than English at home.

The rapid growth of the state's immigrant children population during the past decade was fueled by an usual conjunction of factors: an economic boom in California and structural changes in the state's economy, which together created hundreds of thousands of low-skill, low-wage, nonseasonal jobs, many of which were eagerly filled by new immigrants; a profound economic crisis in Mexico, running from 1982 to 1989, which pushed many "nontraditional" migrants into the U.S.-bound flow (city dwellers, nonagriculturally employed persons, women, persons originating in Mexican states that had not sent many migrants to the United States in previous eras); civil strife and violent repression in Central America (Guatemala, El Salvador, and Nicaragua), which produced substantial refugee communities in California's three largest metropolitan areas (Chinchilla et al. 1993); and the enactment of two major legalization ("amnesty") programs for illegal immigrants, as part of the 1986 U.S. Immigration Reform and Control Act (IRCA).

Perhaps more than any other single factor, the changes in migration patterns—especially in Mexican migration to the United States—brought about by the 1986 immigration law stimulated the growth of the immigrant student population in California. IRCA made it possible for approximately 1.5 million long-term illegal immigrants in California to regularize their status. Imbued with a new sense of security and stability, newly legalized household heads sought to move their wives and children to California as quickly as possible, whether or not their dependents could qualify for the IRCA amnesty programs. The 1986 law

---

[1] This standard equation of the "immigrant children" population with the "LEP" student population is convenient but imprecise, because many of those designated as LEP are, in fact, native-born U.S. citizens rather than first-generation immigrants. Nationally, over one-third of the fourteen million people (children and adults) who could be classified as LEP on the basis of 1990 census data were native-born (Fix and Passel 1994: 31).

thus encouraged permanent settlement of whole family units in California cities (see Cornelius 1989b: 695–99; 1992: 172–77).

The large volume of IRCA-induced family reunification immigration from Mexico, beginning in 1988 and continuing strongly into the 1990s, was bound to swell the numbers of immigrant children in California public schools. A nationwide Current Population Survey conducted by the U.S. Census Bureau found that, among Mexican nationals who had migrated to the United States between January 1990 and March 1994, 45 percent were women and children—more than double the proportion of women and children reflected in INS apprehension statistics during the 1980s. "Lone male," short-term migrants from Mexico (single men or married men who leave all their dependents in the place of origin) have by no means disappeared from California labor markets; but they are much less significant as a proportion of total legal and illegal immigration from Mexico than ten or fifteen years ago. Because the migration flow from Mexico to California has become more diversified in terms of gender, age, family structure, and settlement intentions, the state's immigrant population today is much more likely to be making use of public schools.

Even more important than the growth of the immigrant student population in absolute terms or relative to native-born Californians has been its high degree of concentration in a handful of counties and predominantly big-city school districts. In 1994, some 42 percent of all LEP students in California were attending schools in Los Angeles County alone. Moreover, within urban areas, immigrant children are clustered in inner-city school districts, a consequence of the low incomes of recent immigrant families and the extremely limited supply of low-cost housing available outside of the central cities.[2]

The spatial concentration of immigrant children strains the school districts where they enroll, in terms of financial resources, class size, and staffing with bilingual personnel. It also increases the immigrant students' visibility to the nonimmigrant population and strengthens natives' objections to their presence. It is no coincidence that the epicenter of California's anti-immigrant movement of the 1990s is the Los Angeles metropolitan area. As Alejandro Portes points out in his chapter in this volume, overconcentration of immigrant students in inner-city schools can have another negative consequence: it brings the children of immigrants into sustained contact with U.S.-born minority students who have developed an adversarial subculture—one that

---

[2]The phenomenon of overconcentration of recent immigrants in inner cities is not specific to California. The 1980 census revealed that 39.5 percent of children in households throughout the nation with at least one foreign-born parent lived in central city neighborhoods, compared with 17.4 percent of children in households with native-born parents (Portes 1995: 252).

denies the usefulness of education and discourages achievement in school.

Apart from the size and distribution of California's burgeoning immigrant student population, there is considerable evidence that many children of immigrant origin are not performing well academically in the state's public schools. To be sure, conspicuous exceptions exist. Researchers, including several of the contributors to this volume, have found that some immigrant children do amazingly well, considering the linguistic, economic, and family- and community-related handicaps under which they must perform in school. First-generation immigrants who obtain most of their education in the United States perform particularly well. Immigrant students of some ethnic and nationality groups (e.g., Vietnamese, Chinese, Koreans, Sikh immigrants from the Indian state of Punjab) achieve better academic performance than majority "Anglo" students, despite the widespread discrimination that they experience and, in the case of the Vietnamese and Punjabi students, their families' poverty upon arrival in California (see the chapters by Rumbaut, Gibson, and Tuan in this volume).

Despite these success stories of "high-achieving" immigrants, dropout rates for the most numerically important segments of California's immigrant student population—particularly Mexico-origin and other Latino students—remain unacceptably high. In the Los Angeles Unified School District, for example, the dropout rate among Latino students hovers around 40 percent and has reached 73 percent in one large, immigrant-dominated high school. Despite some commonalities, the reasons for poor academic performance and high dropout rates among children of immigrants vary considerably, as the empirical evidence and explanatory hypotheses presented in this volume suggest; but for too many of these students in California today, there is clearly a problem of low educational attainment that could sharply limit their lifetime earnings and occupational mobility prospects.

The recent growth of the state's immigrant student population also represents a problem because of the public schools' diminished capacity to pay for bilingual education, English as a Second Language (ESL) instruction, remedial education, psychological counseling, and other special services that some immigrant children need. The immigrant student population is expanding rapidly at a time when school budgets are being squeezed by a combination of factors: reduced financial aid from the federal government, the skewing of state government expenditures toward law enforcement (a direct result of the passage of the 1993 "three strikes and you're out" anticrime ballot proposition, which greatly increases resource requirements for prison construction and incarceration costs), and the school districts' inability to raise local property taxes to cover the funding gaps (the legacy of Proposition 13, another enormously popular voter initiative, approved in 1978).

The federal government has chosen to treat the funding of immigrant education as a state and local responsibility. Only one specialized federal program exists to support immigrant education, and in recent years it has spent only about $42 per student. In 1992, Congress even chose to withhold $812 million in previously approved federal funding to help heavily impacted states and localities pay for education and health services for immigrants who were legalized under the 1986 Immigration Reform and Control Act. This outcome is not surprising, given the fact that the top six immigrant-receiving states (California, New York, Texas, Florida, Illinois, and New Jersey), accounting for 73 percent of the foreign-born U.S. population in 1990, control just 12 percent of the votes in the Senate and 37 percent of the votes in the House of Representatives.

While the federal government has essentially shifted the fiscal burden of providing immigrant services to the most heavily impacted states and localities (Fix and Zimmermann 1993), state spending on immigrant education varies dramatically. California spends far less per pupil for LEP students than most other key immigrant-receiving states. For example, in 1990 California provided $100 million to schools throughout the state that could be spent on programs for LEP students— $118 per student.[3] This compares with 1990 spending of $361 per LEP student in New York State and $1,581 per student in Florida.[4]

The acute shortage of bilingual teachers represents another major constraint on the public schools' ability to cope with rapid growth in the immigrant student population. As of 1995, California had fewer than 11,000 fully certified bilingual teachers—approximately one for every 112 LEP students in the state. The shortage of bilingual teachers is national in scope, but its effects are felt most acutely in California. During the last ten years, the number of bilingual teachers employed in the state increased by only 30 percent, while the population of LEP students grew by 150 percent. The result, in schools with large LEP enrollments, is a fundamental mismatch between students and teaching staff. As one Los Angeles district high school teacher put it,

> We now have a majority or near-majority student body
> in which the primary language is Spanish. The teach-
> ing staff, in Los Angeles at least, is aging and is primar-
> ily non-Spanish speaking. So the demographics are all
> wrong.[5]

---

[3]Not all of these funds were actually spent on LEP students, since there was no state requirement that the money be used in this way; it could also be spent on other (nonimmigrant) disadvantaged students.

[4]Calculated from data in McDonnell and Hill 1993: table 2.1, pp. 39–40.

[5]George Woods, teacher, Venice High School, quoted in the *Los Angeles Times,* July 24, 1995.

Another consequence of the current shortage of bilingual teachers is that instruction in the student's native language can be provided mainly at the elementary level, and only in the principal languages represented among a school's immigrant students. California's fourteen-year-old bilingual education policy, which requires school districts with large numbers of LEP students to teach those children primarily in their native language for at least several years, is the most stringent in the nation.[6] It is obvious, however, that many California schools fall considerably short of full compliance. In the six California counties most affected by the latest wave of immigration, less than half of the LEP students at elementary and secondary levels receive any instruction in their native language. Slightly more than one-quarter of the LEP students in these counties have access to English as a Second Language classes (although the figure for Los Angeles is only 18 percent), and the remainder receive little or no instruction that the state of California qualifies as bilingual education.[7]

Numerous school districts attempt to close the gap between the teacher supply and demand by using bilingual teachers' aides and teachers-in-training in the classroom to backstop fully certified teachers who lack foreign language skills. However, as the gap continues to widen, it is increasingly likely that an immigrant child arriving in California will be taught only by teachers who are monolingual English speakers, or who do not meet the state's stringent certification requirements for bilingual teachers, who must be able to teach the same subjects in both English and a foreign language.[8] In California and other states heavily impacted by the most recent wave of immigration, "Scholarly and political debates over how long language-minority children should remain in bilingual classrooms or what instructional strategies should be used there are no more than hypothetical exercises, as long as bilingual-teacher shortages remain so acute" (McDonnell and Hill 1993: 103).

---

[6]This policy derives from a state bilingual education law that expired in 1987. In recent years the Democratic-controlled state legislature has passed two bills backed by pro-bilingual education groups, the purpose of which was to reinstate the basic provisions of the 1987 law, which emphasized instruction in the student's native language. Both bills were vetoed by Governor Pete Wilson, who favors a shift to English-only instruction. However, the state bilingual education policy based on the expired law is still operative.

[7]Statistics for 1994, from the Bilingual Education Office, California Department of Education.

[8]For example, in a 1993 audit of the Los Angeles Unified School District's bilingual education programs, conducted by the state Department of Education, more than 75 percent of the schools surveyed lacked qualified staff. In a typical secondary school classroom full of LEP students, auditors found a monolingual English-speaking teacher, using English-language texts and lacking a bilingual aide to translate material into the students' native languages (Chávez 1993).

The Changing Political Context of Immigrant Education

Unfortunately for the cause of rational discourse and constructive problem solving, immigrant children have been swept up in the generalized anti-immigrant hysteria and political demagoguery of California in the 1990s. Whipped up by prominent members of the state's political class, the electronic media, and a handful of highly vocal special-interest groups promoting greater restrictions on immigration, the latest in a succession of anti-immigrant movements so prominent in California history reached a fever pitch during the recession of 1990–1993.[9]

One of the milestones in the politicization of immigrant education in California was the 1993 initiative of a little known State Assembly member from San Diego County, who dispatched one of his aides to videotape Mexican-origin children boarding school buses at stops just across the border, near the Mexican border town of Tecate—buses that would carry them to public schools in a U.S. school district adjacent to the international border. That videotape, shown endlessly on local and national television, provoked a predictably angry public response. It made little difference that many of the children depicted were actually U.S. citizens, born in the United States to Mexican immigrants. In most of these cases, the schoolchildren and their parents were living on the Mexican side of the border because they could not afford housing on the California side. Whatever the circumstances, the children were not physical residents of the school district in which they were attending school—a violation of state law. The school district was promptly investigated by state officials and ordered to expel several hundred children who could not prove physical residency within the district.

A considerably more important milestone was the successful effort to secure voter approval of ballot Proposition 187 in the November 1994 state election, coupled with the decision of Governor Pete Wilson to make his support for Proposition 187 the centerpiece of his campaign for reelection.[10] Proposition 187—touted by its advocates as the "Save Our State" (SOS) initiative—was approved by 59 percent of California voters, winning among all significant demographic, eth-

---

[9]Such movements date back to the anti-Chinese movement of the 1880s, which was spearheaded by Californians. See Chan 1991; Heizer and Almquist 1971; Miller 1969; Saxton 1971. One of the best accounts of the anti-Mexican nativist movement of the 1920s in California and other parts of the U.S. Southwest is provided in Reisler 1976.

[10]Wilson's strategy worked remarkably well. Attaching his candidacy firmly to the "Pro-187" campaign, Wilson was able to overcome a large deficit in early preelection polls and win reelection by a substantial margin. Wilson's pollster has revealed that, according to the campaign's internal tracking polls, more than 90 percent of prospective voters knew Wilson's position on Proposition 187—a higher proportion than those who could identify Sacramento as the state capital (Sherwood 1995).

nic, and racial groups except Latinos. If it survives court tests of its constitutionality,[11] Proposition 187 would make illegal immigrant children ineligible to attend public schools and compel the schools to report such children and their parents to state and federal authorities, if school officials "reasonably suspect" that a student is in the United States illegally. Proponents of the measure argued, without corroborating evidence, that it would deter further illegal immigration and cause illegals already living in California with their children to "self-deport" themselves en masse.[12]

Thus in the 1990s, the need to educate immigrant children—which U.S. public schools had been doing on a large scale since the first decade of this century—came to be seen as an intolerable burden on the state of California, along with the provision of health care and all other kinds of social services that immigrants or their children may use. Beginning in 1992 the Governor's Office of Finance issued a series of highly publicized reports in which California's newest immigrants were classified as "tax receivers" (whom the state can no longer afford to subsidize), as contrasted with "tax payers." This categorization conveniently ignores the income, Social Security, and sales taxes that most immigrants—legals as well as illegals—pay to the state and federal treasuries, as well as the property taxes paid by the growing number of immigrant home owners (Fix and Passel 1994: 57–62). Such rhetoric helped to strengthen the angry, zero-sum mentality that was already being fed by the recession of the 1990s and job insecurity caused by massive structural changes in the state's economy (e.g., post-Cold War downsizing of California's defense-related industries). The comfortable margin of victory for Proposition 187 suggests that many native-born Californians had been persuaded that they or their children were being deprived of high-quality public services because of the money being spent to educate and provide other social services to immigrants "not entitled" to receive them.

---

[11]Ultimately, for the public education provision of Proposition 187 to be implemented, the U.S. Supreme Court would have to reverse the precedent that it set in 1982, in the case of *Plyer v. Doe.* In that 5-to-4 decision, the Court declared that public school districts in Texas (and, by implication, all other states) were obligated by the equal protection clause of the U.S. Constitution to provide tuition-free education to all children who are physical residents of the district, regardless of their immigration status. The proponents of Proposition 187 deliberately sought to provoke litigation that could lead the Supreme Court to reverse its decision in *Plyer v. Doe.*

[12]There is no evidence from studies of prospective Mexican migrants to the United States, returned migrants interviewed in their places of origin, nor detained illegal immigrants indicating that appreciable numbers of them have migrated or seek to migrate to California or other parts of the United States in order to take advantage of free or better-quality education, health care, or other social services. On the other hand, there is evidence from field research suggesting that the passage of Proposition 187 already has yielded some unintended, negative consequences (for example, encouraging further permanent settlement of Mexican immigrant families in California), while failing to deter more than a tiny fraction of prospective illegal entrants who seek employment or to join relatives already living in the state (see Cornelius n.d.).

Given this climate of opinion, it was a natural progression to move from steps to reduce immigrants' access to basic human services (Proposition 187) to renewed attacks on bilingual education and other programs seen as benefiting immigrants and other minorities, and to attempts to create a more exclusionary concept of U.S. citizenship. In July 1995, at Governor Wilson's insistence, the Regents of the University of California voted to end a thirty-year-old policy of giving preference to the state's Latino and African American minorities in student admissions. Borrowing his terminology from a tract by historian Arthur Schlesinger that makes much of the cultural threat allegedly posed by uncontrolled Third World immigration (Schlesinger 1992), the governor successfully argued that such preferences threatened to infect California and the nation with "the deadly virus of tribalism."

In the U.S. Congress, the new Republican majority, inspired by a member representing a San Diego County district, has committed itself to the goal of stripping "citizen children" (the term used by immigration authorities to denote the U.S.-born children of illegal immigrants) of their U.S. citizenship. This could be done either by constitutional amendment or, less plausibly, through legislation that would "reinterpret" the Fourteenth Amendment to the Constitution.[13] The rationale offered by proponents of this drastic change is to reduce government outlays—particularly Aid to Families with Dependent Children, or AFDC—for benefits for which "citizen children" are eligible, although their undocumented parents are not (Cleeland and Young 1995). There is also growing enthusiasm in Congress for denying federally funded health and other benefits to *legal* immigrants and refugees.

Thus the political groundwork has been laid for a wholesale rollback of immigrants' human, labor, and civil rights, with the state of California leading the way. Immigrant children seem to have been specially targeted for punitive treatment; unquestionably, the negative consequences of the actions already taken or being contemplated by officials at the state and federal levels will fall most heavily upon them. In the long term, the costs will be borne by California society as a whole.

If the challenge of educating the current and subsequent generations of immigrant children is to be met, in ways that will benefit California as a whole as well as immigrant families, it must be reconceptualized as a problem of human capital development. Californians whose lifetime earnings and chances for upward mobility have been stunted by an inappropriate, poor-quality, or prematurely truncated education will lack the capacity to contribute as much as they might have to the state's

---

[13]The Fourteenth Amendment was enacted in 1868 to grant full citizenship to the children of former slaves. It declares as citizens "all persons born or naturalized in the United States, *and subject to the jurisdiction thereof.*" Pending legislation would exclude illegal immigrant parents from U.S. "jurisdiction," so that children born to them on U.S. soil would not automatically gain U.S. citizenship.

economic development and to its tax base. Indeed, limited formal education and rudimentary job skills set up a self-fulfilling prophecy: such human capital deficits obviously increase the likelihood that the children of immigrants will end up contributing less to government revenues than they take out, through welfare and other financial assistance programs, as today's new immigrants are widely suspected of doing already.

The California economy suffers from a steadily shrinking manufacturing base, while predominantly low-skill, low-wage employment in the service and retail sectors continues to expand. If the state is to have a labor force sufficiently skilled to enable it to compete effectively for the kinds of investments by national and transnational companies that will replenish the "good job" base and create the new, higher-technology industries on which future economic growth will be based, it can hardly afford to ignore the basic education and job-training needs of such a large segment of its youngest residents. Quite simply, today's immigrant children represent the workers and taxpayers of the future. If the immigrant education challenge is recast in this way, the key question becomes: how can we prevent the *underdevelopment* of the human capital that is being received by California through international migration?

The Purpose of This Book

With this overarching, policy-oriented question in mind, the Center for U.S.-Mexican Studies at the University of California, San Diego in 1991 began to assemble a multidisciplinary group of experts on immigrant education who had been conducting pioneering, fieldwork-based studies of the subject in California. They included scholars as well as nonacademic policy analysts, who had had extensive contact with all major fractions of the state's contemporary immigrant population: Mexicans, Central Americans, Indochinese (Vietnamese, Cambodians, Laotians), Koreans, Filipinos, and other Asian immigrant groups. Our collective goals were to synthesize existing knowledge, reinterpret these findings in light of more recently conducted field research and with the aid of new theoretical insights, and identify strategies for improving educational outcomes among immigrant-origin children. A research workshop involving all but one of the contributors to this volume was held at the Center for U.S.-Mexican Studies in January 1993, at which first-draft papers were summarized and critiqued.

We conceived the workshop and the book resulting from it as a blend of state-of-the-art, fieldwork-based empirical research; innovative theoretical perspectives, to make sense of the emerging data; and hard-headed policy analysis. The project brought to bear a broad range of disciplinary perspectives (from anthropology, political science, psychology, and sociology) as well as methodological techniques (from quantitative survey research to qualitative ethnographic methods). Participants focused on different levels of analysis, ranging from the micro (individuals, families, classrooms, specific schools and immigrant communities) to macro-level structures and processes (efforts to restructure public school systems; changes in the larger demographic, economic, and political contexts that are transforming California; international trade and other facets of the global political economy that shape migration flows into California).

While the geographic focus of this volume is squarely on California, several of the contributors (especially Portes, in his references to the experiences of Cuban and Haitian immigrant children in Miami, and Shaw, in her analysis of the impacts of immigration on schools in New York City) introduce a valuable comparative perspective. These brief treatments of East Coast cases illustrate that the issues addressed in this volume are by no means unique to California.

The research assembled in this volume highlights the great diversity of the state's population of immigrant-origin children, in terms of nationality, race, ethnicity, gender, age upon arrival in the United States, family structure and socialization processes, socioeconomic status, generational status, pre-migration schooling, and other experiences that influence post-migration educational outcomes. What emerges is a complex mosaic that deflates many conventional stereotypes (of "Latino" students as a monolithic group, of Asians as "model minorities," and so forth). Several of the contributors (see especially the chapters by Rumbaut, Portes, Suárez-Orozco and Suárez-Orozco) stress the importance of generational differences in educational attainment within the same national-origin groups, and they advance compelling hypotheses to explain these often troubling differences.[14]

Just as we cannot assume homogeneity among the major groups of immigrant-origin children present in California schools, neither can we assume uniformity in the extra-familial contexts in which their acculturation and economic integration is occurring. This variation in the "contexts of reception" that immigrants encounter upon arrival in the United States is the essence of Portes's very useful concept of "segmented assimilation" (chapter 3). The differing vulnerabilities and coping resources exhibited by various immigrant student groups reflect, among other things, different patterns of exposure to racial discrimination, proximity to educationally dysfunctional inner-city subcultures, chang-

[14]For example, among eighth- and ninth-grade children of Latino immigrants attending schools in the San Diego and Miami metropolitan areas, *lower* self-esteem was found to be associated with being U.S.-born (i.e., second-generation status; see Rumbaut 1994: 783). However, in a national sample of eighth graders, both first- *and* second-generation students were outperforming *third*-generation youth on various indicators of scholastic attainment. Second-generation youth were found to be best positioned to achieve academically (Kao and Tienda 1995).

ing economic conditions (e.g., the disappearance of traditional occupational mobility ladders for the second generation, in an "hourglass"
economy created by economic restructuring), and the legal and policy
context affecting undocumented immigrants. In other words, a narrow
focus on the individual attributes of immigrant children ("human
capital" variables such as total years of education upon arrival) and how
such attributes may shape their paths of adaptation and educational
trajectories is inadequate. As Portes urges, we must also ask, *"to what"*
will a particular immigrant group assimilate? We can no longer assume a
relatively uniform "mainstream" into which immigrant-origin students
are being assimilated.

The case Gibson and several other contributors to this volume also explore the
politically sensitive question of how *much* acculturation or assimilation
among immigrant-origin students is desirable or necessary for optimal
performance in school (see also Portes 1995; Rumbaut 1990; Suárez-Orozco
and Suárez-Orozco 1995). The answer is by no means straightforward, nor
necessarily consistent with the general public's apparent preference for
"fast-track," complete assimilation. In 1981, a federal government commission on immigration policy reform expressed concern that "the generation
of children born in the United States will perhaps be *too* eager to cast away
their cultural inheritances" (Select Commission on Immigration and Refugee Policy 1981: 149). In light of more recent data, especially on generational
differences in educational performance, the Commission's warning seems
prophetic. As advocated by Portes and Gibson in this volume, a strategy of
well-paced, "selective" or "additive" acculturation (in which, for example,
learning English does not mean *un*learning the student's native language)
may prove to be the best path for immigrant minorities in California today.

The case studies and comparative analyses presented in this volume
show quite clearly that school context also makes an important difference
in educational outcomes among immigrant students. Excessive class size,
"tracking" practices that may stunt educational aspirations, basic teaching
practices insensitive to cultural diversity, shortages of personnel and
materials for providing bilingual and ESL instruction, the limited availability of in-school psychological counseling and health care services, and the
manner in which "school restructuring" programs are implemented in
most schools serving immigrant students (largely bypassing the specific
needs of these children) are among the key school-context variables
discussed in this volume (see especially the chapters by Rumbaut, Gibson,
Padilla and Durán, Ima, Olsen, and Rothstein).

We present no comprehensive blueprint for reforming the educational
policies affecting immigrant children in California. Indeed, considering the
extreme diversity of the state's immigrant-origin student population that is
documented in this volume, it is clear that no single model of policy reform
or school restructuring will suffice. We have sought to assemble enough
pieces of the complex mosaic to enable policy makers, educators, and the

general public to define more accurately the problems to be confronted, and to identify some of the most promising approaches to intervention and problem solving in this area. Indeed, the careful reader will find in the pages that follow a wealth of specific suggestions for improving the performance of California's immigrant students and the schools that they attend.

We also hope to provoke more wide-ranging thinking about this subject—thinking that goes beyond the arena of public education and focuses on the interface between what happens in the schools and what is occurring in the state and national economies. The concluding chapter by Rothstein explicitly seeks to place the problems of educating immigrant children within the broader context of economic restructuring, job creation, wage stagnation, and the jobs/skills mismatch that is increasingly evident in California today. The perception of schooling found among many academically low-achieving students—as a treadmill having no real payoff, given the limited availability of "good job" opportunities—may be all too correct.

Certainly, the bleak post-high school job prospects of many immigrant and second-generation students are a key factor in the high dropout rates among these groups. A large body of educational research, done in many parts of the United States and in other countries around the world, shows that students' perceptions of the post-school opportunity structure are a crucial determinant of their and their parents' willingness to continue investing in education. More—and better—jobs for which students are appropriately trained must be a major part of the solution.

In the midst of the strongest anti-immigrant backlash since the 1920s, it may be difficult to get public policy makers to focus on the needs of immigrant children in public schools. Indeed, in "post-Proposition 187" California, the thrust of public debate is to reduce the immigrant population, by whatever means may be necessary, rather than to facilitate its integration and help it achieve income and occupational parity with native-born residents. Nevertheless, the number of immigrant children "at risk" in California public schools will continue to grow rapidly in the foreseeable future, whatever new immigration controls are imposed at the federal and state levels.

Short of mass roundups and deportations, the stock of undocumented immigrants—parents and their children—is not likely to be reduced, even by draconian punitive measures like those mandated by Proposition 187. Some painful adaptations may be necessary for immigrant families containing undocumented members, if Proposition 187 should ever be fully implemented.[15] But returning to the home country is a viable option for

---

[15]It is entirely possible that the U.S. Supreme Court may uphold the constitutionality of most provisions of Proposition 187 but strike down the clause denying access to public education, thereby reaffirming its decision in the case of *Plyer v. Doe*. In that event, public schools would remain responsible for educating children who are physical residents of their districts, regardless of immigration status.

only a small minority of settled illegal immigrants, because their economic base has shifted completely to California; they have no assets and no employment prospects in their places of origin. The profound economic crisis that erupted in Mexico in late 1994 inevitably will intensify pressures from new emigration from that overwhelmingly important source country, including whole-family migration. Even if California's other immigrant communities grow much more slowly, or not at all, the heavier flow from Mexico alone will be sufficient to cause continued rapid growth of the immigrant student population. And even if legal immigration ceilings are sharply reduced, as recommended in 1995 by the U.S. Commission on Immigration Reform and enthusiastically endorsed by the Clinton administration and most members of Congress, the state's stock of legal immigrants and refugees is already large enough to assure robust growth of the school-age, immigrant-origin population well into the next century.

Other developments in state educational policy also point to the long-term significance of the issues explored in this volume. The California State University system is moving toward elimination of its extensive remedial education programs for students admitted with deficits in basic academic skills. And as noted above, the University of California system has been required to abandon the use of race and ethnicity as preferences for admission. If gaining access to higher education will be more difficult for the children of today's and tomorrow's immigrants, and if remedial courses will no longer be readily available to those who are admitted, these circumstances make it doubly important that immigrant-origin students be better prepared at the elementary and secondary school levels.

Achieving much higher levels of preparation will require major new resources, not just (or even primarily) for programs aimed at the special needs of immigrant students, but to address the larger, systemic problems afflicting the big-city school districts—problems that would exist even in the absence of the current influx of immigrant students (see McDonnell and Hill 1993: 101–11). It will also require greatly expanded adult education programs, especially those offering ESL classes, for which the demand vastly exceeds current capacity in all large cities where immigrants are clustered. Basic literacy in English is an obvious prerequisite for adequate parental involvement in children's schooling, as well as for increasing family incomes to the level necessary to discourage children from dropping out of school for economic reasons. Studies of adult, undocumented Mexican immigrant workers have found that lack of English proficiency is among the most important obstacles to upward job mobility, and those lacking English competence incur a substantial wage penalty (Cornelius 1989a; Tienda and Singer 1995). This key limitation is overlooked in most discussions of immigrant children's educational problems.

This book does not, of course, exhaust all aspects of such a complex and controversial topic. It does, however, begin to fill some of the major gaps in our knowledge, and it provides a solid, factual context for the emotionally charged public debates concerning immigration and educational policy under way in California today. We hope that these essays will stimulate more constructive attention to the immigrant education challenge by the policy-making community and encourage the sustained, rigorous academic research effort that will be necessary to assess the appropriateness, costs, and benefits of emerging policy options in this high-stakes issue area.

References

Chan, Sucheng, ed. 1991. *Entry Denied: Exclusion and the Chinese Community in America, 1882–1943*. Philadelphia: Temple University Press.

Chávez, Stephanie. 1993. "Los Angeles Schools' Bilingual Program Failing, State Says," *Los Angeles Times*, September 3, pp. A1, A29.

Chinchilla, Norma, et al. 1993. "Central Americans in Los Angeles: An Immigrant Community in Transition." In *In the Barrios: Latinos and the Underclass Debate*, edited by J. Moore and R. Pinderhughes. New York: Russell Sage Foundation.

Cleeland, Nancy, and Eric Young. 1995. "Citizen Children: Offspring of Illegal Immigrants Face an Uncertain Future," *San Diego Union-Tribune*, June 2, pp. A-1, A25.

Cornelius, Wayne A. 1989a. "The U.S. Demand for Mexican Labor." In *Mexican Migration to the United States: Origins, Consequences, and Policy Options*, edited by W. Cornelius and J. Bustamante. La Jolla, Calif.: Center for U.S.-Mexican Studies, UCSD, for the Bilateral Commission on the Future of United States-Mexican Relations.

———. 1989b. "Impacts of the 1986 U.S. Immigration Law on Emigration from Rural Mexican Sending Communities," *Population and Development Review* 15 (4): 689–705.

———. 1992. "From Sojourners to Settlers: The Changing Profile of Mexican Immigration to the United States." In *U.S.-Mexico Relations: Labor Market Interdependence*, edited by J.A. Bustamante, C.W. Reynolds, and R.A. Hinojosa Ojeda. Stanford, Calif.: Stanford University Press.

———. n.d. "Appearances and Realities: Controlling Illegal Immigration in the United States." In *Japanese and U.S. Immigration, Refugee, and Citizenship Policies*, edited by M. Weiner and T. Hanami. Forthcoming.

Fix, Michael E., and Jeffrey S. Passel. 1994. *Immigration and Immigrants: Setting the Record Straight*. Washington, D.C.: The Urban Institute.

Fix, Michael E., and Wendy Zimmermann. 1993. "After Arrival: An Overview of Federal Immigrant Policy." Immigrant Policy Program, Working Paper. Washington, D.C.: The Urban Institute.

Heizer, Robert F., and Alan J. Almquist. 1971. *The Other Californians*. Berkeley: University of California Press.

Kao, Grace, and Marta Tienda. 1995. "Optimism and Achievement: The Educational Performance of Immigrant Youth," *Social Science Quarterly* 76 (1): 1–19.

McDonnell, Lorraine M., and Paul T. Hill. 1993. *Newcomers in American Schools: Meeting the Educational Needs of Immigrant Youth*. Santa Monica, Calif.: RAND.

Miller, Stuart C. 1969. *The Unwelcome Immigrant: The American Image of the Chinese, 1785–1882*. Berkeley: University of California Press.

Portes, Alejandro. 1995. "Children of Immigrants: Segmented Assimilation and Its Determinants." In *The Economic Sociology of Immigration*, edited by A. Portes. New York: Russell Sage Foundation.

Reisler, Mark. 1976. *By the Sweat of Their Brow: Mexican Immigrant Labor in the United States, 1900–1940*. Westport, Conn.: Greenwood Press.

Rumbaut, Rubén G. 1990. *Immigrant Students in California Public Schools: A Summary of Current Knowledge*. Report No. 11. Baltimore, Md.: Center for Research on Effective Schooling for Disadvantaged Students, Johns Hopkins University.

————. 1994. "The Crucible Within: Ethnic Identity, Self-Esteem, and Segmented Assimilation among Children of Immigrants," *International Migration Review* 28 (4): 748–94.

Saxton, Alexander. 1971. *The Indispensable Enemy: Labor and the Anti-Chinese Movement in California*. Berkeley: University of California Press.

Schlesinger, Arthur, Jr. 1992. *The Disuniting of America*. New York: Norton.

Select Commission on Immigration and Refugee Policy. 1981. *U.S. Immigration Policy and the National Interest*. Staff Report of the Select Commission on Immigration and Refugee Policy. Washington, D.C., April 30.

Sherwood, Ben. 1995. "For Pete Wilson, His Political Ambition Is Never Blind," *Los Angeles Times*, July 23, p. M6.

Suárez-Orozco, Carola, and Marcelo Suárez-Orozco. 1995. *Transformations: Migration, Family Life, and Achievement Motivation among Latino Adolescents*. Stanford, Calif.: Stanford University Press.

Tienda, Marta, and Audrey Singer. 1995. "Wage Mobility of Undocumented Workers in the United States," *International Migration Review* 29 (1): 112–38.

2

The New Californians: Comparative Research Findings on the Educational Progress of Immigrant Children

Rubén G. Rumbaut

Introduction

No state has felt the impact of the new immigration more than California, and no institution more than its public schools. Fully a third of the nation's twenty million immigrants are concentrated in California, and over a third of California's K–12 public school children speak a language other than English at home. These new Californians are extraordinarily diverse; they hail largely from Asia and Latin America, and they include at once the most educated and the least educated ethnic groups in the United States today. Their children are growing up in a context where economic restructuring, a prolonged recession, and accompanying fiscal woes have exacerbated a deep public discontent particularly aimed at immigrants, as evidenced by the passage of Proposition 187 in 1994. Yet for all of the political controversy surrounding the public education of immigrant children—and even though they will become a crucial component of the larger economy and society in the years to come—very little is in fact known about their educational progress and adaptation patterns to date. This chapter aims to contribute to the development of that knowledge base.

The author gratefully acknowledges the financial support provided by research grants from the Office for Educational Research and Improvement, U.S. Department of Education, for the project "Immigrant Students in San Diego: School Contexts and the Educational Achievement of LEP/FEP Language Minorities"; and by the Andrew W. Mellon Foundation for the project "Children of Immigrants: The Adaptation Process of the Second Generation." Results from these two studies are reported in this chapter.

The import of the course of this new second generation's adaptation goes far beyond its immediate impacts on school systems, state budgets, and fiscal policies. It will ultimately be the measure by which the long-term national consequences of the present wave of immigration are gauged (Portes 1994, 1995). Will they move into the middle class or into an expanded multiethnic underclass? Will their social mobility be enabled by the structure of opportunities or blocked by racial discrimination and a changed economy? What will be the ratio of immigrant success stories compared to the tales of urban woe? The answers to those questions will determine, more than anything else, how this era of mass migration will change American society; but the fate of the new second generation remains a mystery which is only now beginning to be unraveled by new research (cf. Fernández-Kelly and Schauffler 1994). As Alejandro Portes (1994: 633, and this volume) and Herbert Gans (1992) have argued, conventional expectations of a linear generational process of assimilation into mainstream American life, extrapolated from the historical experience of earlier waves of European immigrants, are seriously open to question, for a variety of reasons. Furthermore, if we can learn something from that checkered past, it may be to harbor few illusions about the value of gazing into crystal balls. Roberto Suro (1994: 82) recently put it this way: "As immigrants disembarked at Ellis Island in 1910, who could have foreseen what the world would be like for their children in 1935 and grandchildren in 1960?" Indeed, from the vantage of 1995, even as we are beginning to learn more about the children of the newest wave, who can foresee what the world will be like for their descendants in 2020 and in 2045?

To be sure, the challenge posed to California schools by contemporary immigration is not unprecedented. In the early part of the century, concerns over the mass immigration of "non-English-speaking races" from Southern and Eastern Europe were expressed in an equivalently massive 42-volume report by the U.S. Immigration [Dillingham] Commission (1911) to the U.S. Congress. Among these were five volumes on *The Children of Immigrants in Schools*, reporting the results of an investigation of more than two million schoolchildren in thirty-seven cities during the 1908–09 school year. Of all the children enrolled in these schools, 58 percent had immigrant parents. The study analyzed factors that impeded school progress for the different "races" and found that 40 percent of the children of immigrants were "retarded" (defined as a pupil who was two or more years older than the normal age for his or her grade), with rates exceeding three-fourths of the foreign-born Polish, "Hebrew" (Jewish), and Italian children, compared to just over one-fourth of the older "English-speaking races." Retardation decreased with younger age at arrival, longer residence in the United States, and the English-speaking ability and naturalization of the fathers—in short, as a function of ability and assimilation. At that time New York City schools enrolled a total of 569,000 students, of whom 72 percent had foreign-born fathers (34 percent Hebrew); Chicago had 235,000, of whom 67 percent had foreign-born fathers (16 percent German, 11 percent Hebrew). Los Angeles and San Francisco had only 33,000 each, and the tally for Los Angeles showed a student body that consisted mainly of native-born whites of native-born fathers (65 percent), while only 32 percent had immigrant parents (6 percent German, 4 percent English). The times, needless to add, have changed.

The aim of this chapter is to provide a point of departure for the book and to review current research findings about immigrant students in California public schools. It is organized in five parts. First, 1990 census data on the size, national origins, and sociodemographic characteristics of the foreign-born population are presented to document the current diversity and its concentration in California. This is followed by a profile of both LEP (limited-English-proficient) and FEP (fluent-English-proficient) language-minority students enrolled statewide in K–12 public schools in California. Next I report results from two new comparative research studies of the educational performance of children of immigrants in San Diego schools (including dropout rates, GPAs, achievement test scores, and educational aspirations), focusing on the largest groups: Mexicans, Filipinos, Vietnamese, Laotians, Cambodians, and East Asian-origin groups. Finally, the findings of four case studies of the adaptation of immigrant high school students in different parts of California are discussed, focusing on Southeast Asians, Punjabi Sikhs from India, Mexicans, and Central Americans. These are discussed as a prelude to issues raised by the authors of the chapters that follow in this book, several of whom are also the authors of the case studies examined herein.

The New Immigration and the New Californians

The 1990 U.S. census counted a foreign-born population of 19.8 million, about 8 percent of the total population (see tables 2.1–2.3 for a detailed demographic portrait). As table 2.1 shows, most are recent arrivals; most of the recent arrivals come from Asia and the Americas; and most of those have settled in California. Nearly half (8.7 million) immigrated to the United States during the 1980s alone, and another 25 percent came in the 1970s; given current trends, more will come during the 1990s than in any other decade in U.S. history.[1] Their recency, as well as the undocu-

---

[1] The immigrant population has continued to grow and diversify during the 1990s. The Immigration Act of 1990 increased worldwide legal immigration limits by about 40 percent, to 700,000 per year; of these, employment-based visas (reserved largely for professionals) nearly tripled to 140,000, and family-sponsored admissions also expanded to about half a million annually. Ironically, since the end of the Cold War in 1989 and the breakup of the Soviet Union in 1991, refugee admissions have also increased, adding well over 100,000 to

mented status of many (particularly from El Salvador, Guatemala, and Mexico), is reflected in currently low rates of naturalization. For the first time, Latin Americans replaced Europeans as the largest immigrant population by far in the country, and the total born in Asia also surpassed the total born in Europe. Mexicans alone accounted for a huge share of the total foreign-born population (22 percent, or 4.3 million) and represented 26 percent of all immigrants arriving since 1970. In fact, there were more immigrants from Mexico in the United States in 1990 than from all of Europe combined, or from the rest of Latin America and the Caribbean combined, or from nearly all of Asia combined. Filipinos ranked a distant second, with close to one million immigrants (5 percent of the total). Mexicans and Filipinos comprise, as a result, the largest "Hispanic" and "Asian" immigrant groups in the United States today. The Southeast Asians (Vietnamese, Cambodians, and Laotians) predominate among refugee admissions—over one million have resettled in the United States since the end of the Vietnam War in 1975—and they also have exhibited the highest fertility rates among ethnic groups in the United States. Taken together, the Indochinese had grown in just over a decade to form the third largest Asian-origin population in the country, behind the Chinese and Filipinos (cf. Rumbaut 1991a, 1994a, 1995).

These groups—and many others, as table 2.1 underscores—now reside primarily in California. Patterns of concentration have been increasing over time, reflecting the way in which immigration is a network-driven process. The 1980 census had counted 3.6 million immigrants in California (25 percent of the national total). That number nearly doubled by 1990 to 6.5 million (33 percent of the national total), helping to increase the state's population from 23.7 million to 29.8 million over the decade. Thus, while only 10 percent of the U.S.-born population resided in California in 1990, fully a third of the foreign-born contingent lived there, including about 40 percent of all Asians and Latin Americans. A whopping 2.9 million lived in the Los Angeles metropolitan area alone (easily surpassing the 2.1 million in the New York City metropolitan area); Orange and San Diego counties, just south of Los Angeles, added one million immigrants, while the San Francisco-Oakland-San Jose corridor in northern California accounted for 825,000 more. Whereas in 1980 15 percent of all Californians were foreign-born, that proportion had climbed to 22 percent by 1990—and it has continued to rise ever since. Their U.S.-born children are not included in these

---

the regular annual flows. And the illegal immigrant population has not only grown but diversified. Excluding the nearly three million formerly undocumented immigrants whose status was legalized under the Immigration Reform and Control Act of 1986 (over two million were Mexican nationals, followed by Salvadorans and Guatemalans), the U.S. Immigration and Naturalization Service estimated that by the end of 1992 the illegal resident population totaled about 3.2 million and was growing at a rate of perhaps 300,000 annually, with approximately half of the total located in California (cf. Rumbaut 1994a).

figures, but they add significantly to this general picture.[2] Indeed, as table 2.2 makes clear, many (but certainly not all) of the groups that are most heavily concentrated in California tend to be the youngest and to have the highest fertility rates, characteristics that are also associated with lower socioeconomic status. This is particularly the case for Southeast Asians, Mexicans, and Central Americans. As a consequence of sharply increased immigration combined with higher fertility, these populations of newcomers are growing much more rapidly than native-born groups—a phenomenon that is redefining the state's ethnic mosaic, and especially that of its school system.

Today's immigrants not only differ greatly in their English language skills, age/sex structures, patterns of fertility, and forms of family organization. As table 2.3 shows, they also include by far the most educated groups (Asian Indians, Taiwanese) and the least educated groups (Mexicans, Salvadorans) in U.S. society, as well as the groups with the lowest poverty rates in the United States (Filipinos) and with the highest (Laotians and Cambodians)—a reflection of polar-opposite types of migrations embedded in very different historical and structural contexts. Although they are drawn from some of the poorest countries of the world, it is not the case that the United States—or California—is thereby importing poor or surplus populations. International migration requires resources and resourcefulness, and the poorest of the poor are least apt to be in a position to migrate (Portes and Rumbaut 1990). In fact, the United States is importing some of the best and brightest from all over the world. This "brain drain" (or "brain gain" for the United States) is partly a function of scarce opportunities in source countries and partly the result of professional occupational preferences built into U.S. immigration laws. For example, among immigrant adults in the United States in 1990, over 60 percent of those from India and Taiwan had college degrees, as did between one-third and one-half of those from Iran, Hong Kong, the Philippines, Japan, South Korea, and China, and about 50 percent of all immigrants from Africa. Those figures are well above the corresponding norms (20 percent) for native-born Americans. Yet by contrast, only 3.5 percent of adult Mexican immigrants had college

---

[2]Because the 1980 and 1990 censuses stopped collecting data on parental nativity, it is impossible to identify U.S.-born children of immigrants unambiguously—i.e., the second generation. Two recent papers have reported 1990 census data, using the 5 percent Public Use Microdata Samples, which do the next best thing: matching the data records of children under age eighteen to information on the parents and household of each child (though this restricts the analysis to the own children of household heads still residing with their parents). Jensen and Chitose (1994), for example, found that while only 8 percent of native-born children of native-born parents live in California, 40 percent of foreign-born children live in California, as do 32 percent of the U.S.-born children of immigrant parents. Landale and Oropesa (1995) noted that 15 percent of all children in the United States are immigrants or native-born children of immigrants. While only about 5 percent of non-Latino whites and blacks are first or second generation, over half of all Latino children and fully 90 percent of Asian-origin children are in the first or second generation.

TABLE 2.1

SIZE, STATES OF PRINCIPAL SETTLEMENT, YEAR OF IMMIGRATION, AND U.S. CITIZENSHIP OF MAJOR IMMIGRANT GROUPS IN THE U.S. IN 1990, BY REGION AND COUNTRY OF BIRTH, IN RANK ORDER BY THEIR PROPORTION IN CALIFORNIA

Region/Country of Birth	Persons (N)	(%)	States of Principal Settlement			Year of Immigration to the U.S.				Naturalized U.S. Citizen	
			California (%)	New York/ New Jersey (%)	Florida (%)	1980s (%)	1970s (%)	1960s (%)	Pre-1960 (%)	Yes (%)	No (%)
Asia:	4,979,037	25.2	40.2	15.7	2.3	57	29	9	5	41	59
Iran	210,941	1.1	54.7	9.1	2.3	50	41	6	3	27	73
Philippines	912,674	4.6	52.8	9.8	2.4	51	31	13	5	54	46
Vietnam*	543,262	2.7	49.9	3.9	2.4	64	35	1	0	43	57
Cambodia*	118,833	0.6	47.5	3.0	1.1	86	14	0	0	20	80
Laos*	171,577	0.9	42.0	1.8	1.3	73	27	0	0	17	83
Hong Kong	147,131	0.7	43.9	24.5	1.8	44	33	19	4	55	45
Taiwan	244,102	1.2	42.9	16.8	1.9	65	27	8	1	39	61
China	529,837	2.7	39.9	27.5	1.5	55	21	13	11	44	56
Korea	568,397	2.9	35.2	17.5	1.5	55	37	6	2	41	59
Japan	290,128	1.5	33.6	14.2	2.3	53	16	14	17	28	72
India	450,406	2.3	18.6	26.4	2.7	58	30	10	2	35	65
Latin America/Caribbean:	8,416,924	42.6	38.7	17.9	12.8	50	28	15	7	27	73
El Salvador	485,433	2.4	60.3	10.5	2.1	76	19	4	1	15	85
Guatemala	225,739	1.1	60.2	10.7	5.1	69	22	7	2	17	83
Mexico	4,298,014	21.6	57.6	1.3	1.3	50	31	11	8	23	77
Nicaragua	168,659	0.9	34.6	7.1	42.7	75	16	5	4	15	85
Colombia	286,124	1.4	10.7	43.0	23.3	52	27	18	3	29	71
Cuba*	736,971	3.7	6.7	15.6	67.5	26	19	46	9	51	49
Jamaica	334,140	1.7	3.4	50.2	22.1	47	33	15	5	38	62
Haiti	225,393	1.1	1.2	45.7	36.9	61	26	11	2	27	73
Dominican Republic	347,858	1.8	1.0	79.9	6.7	53	27	17	3	28	72

TABLE 2.1 (CONTINUED)

SIZE, STATES OF PRINCIPAL SETTLEMENT, YEAR OF IMMIGRATION, AND U.S. CITIZENSHIP OF MAJOR IMMIGRANT GROUPS IN THE U.S. IN 1990, BY REGION AND COUNTRY OF BIRTH, IN RANK ORDER BY THEIR PROPORTION IN CALIFORNIA

Region/Country of Birth	Persons (N)	(%)	States of Principal Settlement			Year of Immigration to the U.S.				Naturalized U.S. Citizen	
			California (%)	New York/ New Jersey (%)	Florida (%)	1980s (%)	1970s (%)	1960s (%)	Pre-1960 (%)	Yes (%)	No (%)
Africa:	363,819	1.8	18.1	22.2	4.1	61	28	7	4	34	66
Europe and Canada:	5,095,233	25.8	16.1	24.6	7.5	20	13	19	48	63	37
Soviet Union*	333,725	1.7	23.2	35.3	5.3	34	17	3	46	59	41
United Kingdom	640,145	3.2	21.2	16.0	9.5	25	15	20	40	50	50
Canada	744,830	3.8	21.0	9.6	10.4	17	12	20	51	54	46
Portugal	210,122	1.1	17.1	23.4	1.8	25	36	29	10	44	56
Germany	711,929	3.6	14.6	18.9	7.8	11	8	22	59	72	28
Ireland	169,827	0.9	11.1	40.0	4.5	19	8	16	57	68	32
Greece	177,398	0.9	9.5	32.6	5.1	13	28	28	31	71	29
Italy	580,592	2.9	8.3	44.9	4.9	5	14	23	58	76	24
Poland*	388,328	2.0	7.5	32.8	6.8	33	11	13	43	62	38
Total Foreign-Born:	19,767,316	100.0	32.7	19.3	8.4	44	25	14	17	41	59
Total Native-Born:	228,942,557	100.0	10.2	9.6	4.9	–	–	–	–	–	–

*Denotes country from which most recent migrants to the U.S. have been officially admitted as refugees.

Sources: U.S. Bureau of the Census, 1990 Ethnic Profiles for States, CPH-L-136, 1993; The Foreign Born Population in the United States 1990, CP-3-1, July 1993, tables 1,3; and The Foreign Born Population in the United States 1990, CPH-L-98, 1993, table 13. Data on year of immigration are drawn from a 5% Public Use Microdata Sample (PUMS) of the 1990 Census, and subject to sample variability; decimals are rounded off.

TABLE 2.2

DEMOGRAPHIC CHARACTERISTICS AND ENGLISH PROFICIENCY OF PRINCIPAL IMMIGRANT GROUPS IN THE U.S. IN 1990, BY COUNTRY OF BIRTH, IN RANK ORDER BY (YOUNGER) AGE

Region/Country of Birth	Persons (N)	Age		Gender	Fertility[1]	Family Contexts[2]		Speaks English[3]	
		Median Age (yrs)	60 Yrs. or Older (%)	Female (%)	Children Born per Woman 35 to 44	Female H'holder (%)	Children < 18 with 2 Parents (%)	English Only (%)	Not Well or At All (%)
Much Younger than U.S. Average:									
Laos*	171,577	27	4.9	48.3	4.2	11.9	81	2	43
Cambodia*	118,833	29	5.1	52.4	3.3	24.3	71	2	43
El Salvador	485,433	29	3.9	46.3	2.7	21.4	61	3	49
Hong Kong	147,131	30	3.2	49.9	1.7	9.7	84	7	15
Guatemala	225,739	30	4.2	48.7	2.6	19.5	66	3	45
Vietnam*	543,262	30	5.3	47.4	2.5	15.3	73	4	31
Mexico	4,298,014	30	7.0	44.9	3.3	14.1	73	4	49
Nicaragua	168,659	30	7.1	51.8	2.5	21.0	66	4	41
Near U.S. Average:									
Taiwan	244,102	33	3.6	53.0	1.7	10.2	81	5	17
Dominican Republic	347,858	34	7.9	54.5	2.5	41.3	47	4	45
Haiti	225,393	35	7.3	50.2	2.4	27.6	56	6	23
Korea	568,397	35	8.1	57.0	1.8	11.1	87	7	30
Iran	210,941	35	9.1	41.9	1.8	7.6	86	8	12
India	450,406	36	6.4	45.1	2.0	3.3	92	12	9
Colombia	286,124	35	8.2	53.6	1.8	21.5	65	5	34
Jamaica	334,140	36	12.0	55.2	2.2	34.6	53	94	0
Japan	290,128	38	12.5	62.6	1.6	14.7	95	16	25
Philippines	912,674	39	14.7	56.7	1.9	15.1	78	11	7
Portugal	210,122	40	17.3	50.0	2.1	8.0	89	6	34

TABLE 2.2 (CONTINUED)
DEMOGRAPHIC CHARACTERISTICS AND ENGLISH PROFICIENCY OF PRINCIPAL IMMIGRANT GROUPS IN THE U.S. IN 1990, BY COUNTRY OF BIRTH, IN RANK ORDER BY (YOUNGER) AGE

Region/Country of Birth	Persons (N)	Age		Gender	Fertility[1]	Family Contexts[2]		Speaks English[3]	
		Median Age (yrs)	60 Yrs. or Older (%)	Female (%)	Children Born per Woman 35 to 44	Female H'holder (%)	Children < 18 with 2 Parents (%)	English Only (%)	Not Well or At All (%)
Much Older than U.S. Average:									
China	529,837	45	25.1	50.5	1.8	8.2	87	3	44
Greece	177,398	49	26.6	46.2	2.1	7.4	89	11	20
Cuba*	736,971	49	30.1	51.6	1.8	16.2	72	5	40
United Kingdom	640,145	50	33.9	59.8	1.8	13.9	85	93	0
Germany	711,929	53	37.0	64.6	1.8	16.4	75	41	2
Canada	744,830	53	40.7	58.7	1.8	12.3	86	80	1
Soviet Union*	333,725	55	45.8	54.8	1.7	10.8	88	20	24
Ireland	169,827	56	43.6	60.0	2.4	17.1	88	90	0
Poland*	388,328	57	46.9	52.8	1.6	11.1	83	20	20
Italy	580,592	59	48.3	51.8	2.1	9.8	85	22	16
Total Foreign-Born:	19,767,316	37	18.0	51.1	2.3	14.8	74	21	26
Total Native-Born:	228,942,557	33	16.7	51.3	1.9	16.1	73	92	1

[1]Children ever born per woman aged 35 to 44 years regardless of marital status (an approximate measure of completed fertility).

[2]Percent of family households headed by a female householder with no husband present; and of children under 18 living with two parents.

[3]English proficiency of persons aged 5 years or older.

*Denotes country from which most recent migrants to the U.S. have been officially admitted as refugees.

Sources: U.S. Bureau of the Census, *The Foreign Born Population in the United States*, CP-3-1, July 1993, tables 1,2; *Persons of Hispanic Origin in the United States*, CP-3-3, August 1993, tables 1, 2; *Asian and Pacific Islanders in the United States*, CP-3-5, August 1993, tables 1,2; and data drawn from a 5% Public Use Microdata Sample (PUMS) of the 1990 U.S. Census, and subject to sample variability.

TABLE 2.3
SOCIOECONOMIC CHARACTERISTICS OF PRINCIPAL IMMIGRANT GROUPS IN THE U.S. IN 1990, BY COUNTRY OF BIRTH, IN RANK ORDER OF COLLEGE GRADUATES

Country of Birth	Persons (N)	Education[1] College Graduates (%)	Labor Force and Occupation[2] In Labor Force (%)	Self-Employed (%)	Upper White-Collar (%)	Lower Blue-Collar (%)	Income[3] Poverty Rate (%)	Public Assistance (%)	Own Home (%)
Well Above U.S. Average Education:									
India	450,406	64.9	74.6	6.3	48	8	8.1	3.4	54
Taiwan	244,102	62.2	64.9	7.5	47	4	16.7	3.7	66
Iran	210,941	50.6	67.9	12.0	42	6	15.7	7.7	55
Hong Kong	147,131	46.8	75.1	5.5	41	7	12.7	3.5	62
Philippines	912,674	43.0	76.3	3.3	28	11	5.9	10.4	61
Japan	290,128	35.0	54.2	7.9	39	7	12.8	2.2	46
Korea	568,397	34.4	63.9	18.0	25	13	15.6	7.9	48
China	529,837	30.9	62.3	7.8	29	16	15.7	10.6	56
Near U.S. Average Education:									
Soviet Union*	333,725	27.1	39.7	10.1	31	11	25.0	16.7	47
United Kingdom	640,145	23.1	57.3	8.3	40	6	6.6	3.7	69
Canada	744,830	22.1	52.1	9.5	38	8	7.8	4.8	71
Germany	711,929	19.1	54.7	9.1	33	9	7.7	4.3	73
Poland*	388,328	16.3	50.4	7.9	21	20	9.7	5.4	64
Vietnam*	543,262	15.9	64.4	5.8	17	21	25.5	26.2	47
Cuba*	736,971	15.6	64.1	7.3	23	18	14.7	16.2	56
Colombia	286,124	15.5	73.7	6.6	17	22	15.3	7.5	38
Jamaica	334,140	14.9	77.4	4.0	22	11	12.1	7.8	44
Greece	177,398	14.8	60.9	14.7	29	12	9.1	5.3	67
Nicaragua	168,659	14.6	73.1	4.7	11	24	24.4	8.4	26
Ireland	169,827	14.6	51.5	7.3	29	9	8.4	4.1	60

TABLE 2.3 (CONTINUED)
SOCIOECONOMIC CHARACTERISTICS OF PRINCIPAL IMMIGRANT GROUPS IN THE U.S. IN 1990, BY COUNTRY OF BIRTH, IN RANK ORDER OF COLLEGE GRADUATES

Country of Birth	Persons (N)	Education[1] College Graduates (%)	Labor Force and Occupation[2]				Income[3]		
			In Labor Force (%)	Self-Employed (%)	Upper White-Collar (%)	Lower Blue-Collar (%)	Poverty Rate (%)	Public Assistance (%)	Own Home (%)
Well Below U.S. Average Education:									
Haiti	225,393	11.8	77.7	3.5	14	21	21.7	9.3	37
Italy	580,592	8.6	46.4	10.1	20	18	8.0	5.5	81
Dominican Republic	347,858	7.5	63.8	5.1	11	31	30.0	27.8	16
Guatemala	225,739	5.8	75.7	5.2	7	28	25.8	8.3	20
Cambodia*	118,833	5.5	48.4	5.2	9	23	38.4	49.5	23
Laos*	171,577	5.1	49.7	2.2	7	41	40.3	45.5	26
Portugal	210,122	4.6	71.6	5.1	9	36	7.0	8.4	62
El Salvador	485,433	4.6	76.3	4.7	6	27	24.9	7.1	19
Mexico	4,298,014	3.5	69.7	4.5	6	32	29.7	11.3	36
Total Foreign-Born:	19,767,316	20.4	64.3	6.9	22	19	18.2	9.1	49
Total Native-Born:	228,942,557	20.3	65.4	7.0	27	14	12.7	7.4	65

[1]Educational attainment for persons aged 25 years or older.

[2]Labor force participation and occupation for employed persons 16 years or older; Upper White-Collar = professionals, executives, and managers; Lower Blue-Collar = operators, fabricators, and laborers.

[3]Percent of persons below the federal poverty line, and of households receiving public assistance income.

*Denotes country from which most recent migrants to the U.S. have been officially admitted as refugees.

Sources: U.S. Bureau of the Census, The Foreign Born Population in the United States, CP-3-1, July 1993, tables 3-5; Persons of Hispanic Origin in the United States, CP-3-3, August 1993, tables 3-5; Asian and Pacific Islanders in the United States, CP-3-5, August 1993, tables 3-5; and data drawn from a 5% Public Use Microdata Sample (PUMS) of the 1990 U.S. Census, and subject to sample variability.

educations—the lowest proportion of any ethnic group in the country—
as did only 4 to 5 percent of Southeast Asian refugees from Laos and
Cambodia and largely undocumented immigrants from El Salvador and
Guatemala. All of these internal characteristics can be expected to
interact in complex ways with external contexts of reception—government policies, existing ethnic communities, employer preferences, the
color line—to mold divergent adaptation outcomes among both the first
and second generations. We turn to a consideration of educational
outcomes in what follows.

LEPs and FEPs: Language-Minority Students in California Public Schools

The limitations of available official data to assess the educational status of
immigrant students should be noted at the outset. Because California
school districts do not collect data on the national origin or immigration
status of their students, precise figures on the size of the state's immigrant student population do not exist. The schools do collect data on
enrollments by broad panethnic or racial categories (such as "Hispanic"
and "Asian"), but these classifications lump together students of diverse
national origins and histories without regard to their nativity or that of
their parents. They include U.S.-born students whose parents may also
be U.S.-born, confounding especially, for example, those of Mexican and
Japanese descent, the majority of whom are third generation or beyond.
Also, the number of immigrant children who do *not* enroll in school
remains undocumented, but it is believed to be fairly sizable among low-
socioeconomic-status children who immigrate to the United States
during their teenage years (Olsen 1988).

The best (if necessarily inexact) statewide estimate of the immigrant
student population can be derived from data collected through the
annual Home Language Census, reported by all schools to the California State Department of Education. Partly as a consequence of Title VI of
the federal Civil Rights Act of 1964 and the U.S. Supreme Court's 1974
decision in *Lau v. Nichols*—which govern guidelines to ensure equal
educational opportunity for language-minority students—the California public schools are required to assess the English language proficiency of students who speak a language other than English at home to
determine their ability to learn successfully in classrooms where English
is the only language of instruction. In general, based on various criteria,
those students are classified either as "limited-English-proficient" (LEP)
or as "fluent-English-proficient" (FEP). The FEP classification does not
necessarily indicate actual "fluency" in English, but rather marks an
arbitrary threshold of English language proficiency (typically the 36th
percentile on a standardized test) which school authorities can then use

to "mainstream" those students from bilingual or ESL classrooms to regular classes. Indeed, bilingual education in California consists largely of "transitional" programs whose goal is to place LEP students in the English-taught curriculum as quickly as possible. The State Department of Education has reclassified an average of 55,000 students from LEP to FEP each year since the early 1980s, with most of the reclassifications taking place within three years after a student enters the school system. Although immigrant children gain proficiency in English at different rates—depending on such factors as age at arrival, parental social class of origin, literacy in another language, familial and community contexts, and other situational and psychocultural characteristics (see Hakuta and García 1989; Portes and Rumbaut 1990)—it has been reported that very few remain designated as LEP beyond five years (Olsen 1988).

In 1993 the Home Language Census found that 1,778,310 (34.2 percent) of California's K–12 public school children spoke a primary language other than English at home. Of those, 1,151,819 (22.2 percent) were designated as LEP and 626,491 (12.1 percent) as FEP. Of the LEP total, over two-thirds (68 percent) were concentrated in the elementary grades (K–6), with 31 percent in grades 7 through 12. In fact, the number of LEPs decreases at every grade level, from 133,000 in kindergarten to only 36,000 in twelfth grade. Looked at another way, of all K–3 students in California in 1993, 29 percent were classified as LEP, as were 21 percent of those in grades 4–8, and 16 percent in grades 9–12. Among the FEPs, only 46 percent were in K–6, while 54 percent were in grades 7–12 (California State Department of Education 1993).

Given the well-established immigrant pattern of a shift from the mother tongue to English monolingualism within three generations in the United States (Portes and Rumbaut 1990), the overwhelming majority of students who speak a primary language other than English (whether classified as LEP or FEP) may be reasonably assumed to be either immigrants or native-born children of immigrants. Moreover, many students who report speaking English as their primary home language may themselves be children of immigrants whose primary language *is* English or whose home environment has been effectively anglicized over time. Among these, children of well-educated immigrants from the Philippines (a former U.S. colony) and India (a former British colony) are most likely to be overrepresented since English remains an official language of instruction in those countries.

Table 2.4 presents trend data on the enrollments of LEP and FEP students in California public schools over the twelve-year period from 1981 to 1993, during which their numbers tripled from 376,794 to 1,151,819. These data tell, as well as any others, the story of the impact of contemporary immigration on the state's school system. A decade earlier, in 1973, there had been a total of only 168,159 students classified as LEP in the state. That number climbed sharply to 290,082 by 1976, reflecting the sudden influx of the first-wave Vietnamese who were evacuated to California in the aftermath of the Vietnam War. Each year since, their numbers have increased dramatically. One of the sharpest increases, from 1979 to 1983, coincided with the flood of second-wave "boat people" from Vietnam and the survivors of Cambodia's "killing fields," the concomitant decision of the U.S. government to admit large numbers of Laotian highlanders such as the Hmong for resettlement, the beginning of the mass exodus of Salvadorans and Guatemalans fleeing civil wars in their countries, the increase in the number of Iranians who came after the 1978 revolution and the fall of the Shah, and the continuing movement of undocumented immigrants from Mexico to California—all alongside the increasing numbers of regular immigrants (especially from Mexico, the Philippines, Korea, and China) who are admitted into California under the occupational preferences and family reunification provisions of U.S. immigration law. Even sharper increases can be noted in table 2.4 for the 1989–92 period, which encompassed not only the beginning date for the legalization of formerly undocumented immigrants (predominantly Mexican nationals) under the amnesty provisions of the 1986 Immigration Reform and Control Act, but also the end of the Cold War and a sudden (if ironic) increase in Russian and Armenian LEP enrollments.

LEP students represent the closest approximation to the number of the *most recently arrived* immigrant children enrolled in California schools (although again, a substantial if unknown number of LEP students may be U.S.-born). Although these students speak about one hundred different languages—reflecting the extraordinary diversity of contemporary immigration to California from all over the world—Spanish is by far the single largest language group, reflecting the predominance of Mexico-origin groups, whose numbers are augmented by Central American and other Spanish-speaking immigrants. As table 2.5 shows, in 1993 over three-fourths of the LEP population (and almost two-thirds of the FEP population) consisted of Spanish speakers. Another 9.8 percent of the LEPs were Southeast Asians (4.2 percent Vietnamese, 2.7 percent Hmong and Mien, 1.8 percent Cambodians, 1.0 percent Lao), followed by 5.2 percent East Asians (3.3 percent Chinese, 1.4 percent Koreans, 0.5 percent Japanese), and 2.1 percent Filipinos (speakers of Tagalog and several other Filipino dialects). Within the Chinese group are found mainly Cantonese and Mandarin speakers from Taiwan, Hong Kong, and mainland China, but also ethnic Chinese from throughout Southeast Asia who speak several other distinct Chinese dialects. The remaining LEP students represented a wide variety of other language groups, including Farsi, from Iran; Hindi, Urdu, Punjabi, Gujarati, and other Indian dialects; Arabic and Hebrew; Thai, Afghan, Armenian, Russian, and a polyglot range of European, Afri-

Table 2.4

Trends in California Public School Enrollments (K–12) of LEP and FEP Students[1] Who Speak a Primary Language Other Than English at Home, 1981–1993

Year	Total Students N	Total LEP Students N	%	Total FEP Students N	%	Total LEP + FEP N	%
1993	5,195,777	1,151,819	22.2	626,491	12.1	1,778,310	34.2
1992	5,107,145	1,078,705	21.1	624,515	12.2	1,703,220	33.3
1991	4,950,474	986,462	19.9	620,655	12.5	1,607,117	32.5
1990	4,771,978	861,531	18.1	621,505	13.0	1,483,036	31.1
1989	4,618,120	742,559	16.1	614,670	13.3	1,357,229	29.4
1988	4,488,398	652,439	14.6	598,302	13.3	1,250,741	27.9
1987	4,377,989	613,222	14.0	568,928	13.0	1,182,150	27.0
1986	4,255,554	567,564	13.3	542,362	12.7	1,109,926	26.1
1985	4,078,743	524,082	12.8	503,695	12.3	1,027,777	25.2
1984	4,014,003	487,835	12.2	475,203	11.8	963,038	24.0
1983	3,984,735	457,542	11.5	460,313	11.6	917,855	23.0
1982	3,976,676	431,443	10.8	437,578	11.0	869,021	21.9
1981	3,941,997	376,794	9.6	434,063	11.0	810,857	20.6

[1]LEP: Limited English Proficient; FEP: Fluent English Proficient. The overwhelming majority of LEP *and* FEP students are immigrants or children of immigrants. These students speak over 100 different primary languages at home.

Sources: California Department of Education, Educational Demographics Unit, "Language Census Report for California Public Schools," 1990–1993; and Bilingual Education Office, DATA BICAL series, 1981–1993 (Sacramento: California Department of Education).

TABLE 2.5

LEP AND FEP STUDENTS[1] IN CALIFORNIA PUBLIC SCHOOLS, BY PRIMARY
LANGUAGES SPOKEN AT HOME, 1993

Primary Home Language	LEP Students		FEP Students		Total LEP + FEP		FEP-to-LEP Ratio
	N	%	N	%	N	%	
Spanish:	887,757	77.1	393,783	62.9	1,281,540	72.1	0.444
Indochinese:	112,766	9.8	45,710	7.3	158,476	8.9	0.405
Vietnamese	48,890	4.2	28,613	4.6	77,503	4.4	0.585
Hmong, Mien	30,910	2.7	5,177	0.8	36,087	2.0	0.167
Cambodian	21,040	1.8	7,219	1.2	28,259	1.6	0.343
Lao	11,926	1.0	4,701	0.7	16,627	0.9	0.394
East Asian:	60,210	5.2	75,244	12.0	135,454	7.6	1.250
Chinese[2]	38,215	3.3	47,481	7.6	69,064	5.1	1.252
Korean	16,496	1.4	21,766	3.5	31,755	2.3	1.319
Japanese	5,499	0.5	5,617	0.9	11,691	0.9	1.021
Filipino:[3]	23,986	2.1	64,544	10.3	88,530	5.0	2.691
All Other Languages:[4]	67,190	5.8	47,120	7.5	114,310	6.1	0.701
STATE TOTALS	1,151,819	100.0	626,491	100.0	1,778,310	100.0	0.544

[1]LEP: Limited English Proficient; FEP: Fluent English Proficient; primary home language other than English.

[2]Chinese languages include Cantonese, Mandarin, and other Chinese.

[3]Filipino languages include Tagalog, Ilocano, Visayan, and others.

[4]Three language groups account for about half (3%) of "all other languages" represented in California public schools: Armenian, Farsi, and Indian languages (Hindi, Punjabi, Gujarti, Urdu). The remainder include dozens of other languages from Europe, the Middle East, and around the world, plus a variety of Native American languages.

Source: Educational Demographics Unit, "Language Census Report for California Public Schools, 1993" (Sacramento: California Department of Education, 1993), tables 6–7. FEP-to-LEP ratios were calculated from the raw data.

can, and other immigrant languages. In general, these proportions reflect fairly well the relative size of recently arrived immigrant groups in the state.

Table 2.5 also provides a ratio of the number of FEP to LEP students for each ethnic group. Ratios above 1.0 indicate a greater level of overall proficiency in English, while those below 1.0 are indicative of LEP-dominant populations that are likely to be recent arrivals of low socio-economic status. Not surprisingly, Filipinos exhibit the highest ratio (2.69), followed by East Asian groups (all above 1.0). By contrast, very low ratios are evident among the Spanish speakers (0.44) and the Indochinese (0.40), with the latter ranging from a high of 0.58 for the Vietnamese to a dismally low 0.167 for the Hmong and the Mien (Laotian highlanders).

Reflecting immigrant patterns of spatial concentration, the impact of the influx of these limited-English students has not been evenly felt throughout the state. LEP students have been most numerous in the school districts of Southern California—in Los Angeles, Orange, and San Diego counties; those three counties account for 60 percent of the statewide LEP total, and Los Angeles alone absorbs 44 percent. They are followed by the northern metropolitan areas of Santa Clara (which includes the "Silicon Valley" city of San Jose), Alameda, and San Francisco counties. In recent years, school districts in California's Central Valley—especially in Fresno and San Joaquin counties (the latter including the city of Stockton, site of the 1989 massacre of Indochinese children at an elementary school)—have experienced a sharp increase in language-minority students. Within counties, specific school districts in turn vary in the degree to which they have been impacted by the enrollment of LEP newcomers. The greatest impact is on smaller elementary school districts in areas with large immigrant populations. For example, by 1989 LEP students constituted 83 percent of the enrollment in the San Ysidro schools (in San Diego County) and 79 percent in Calexico (in Imperial County), both school districts adjacent to the Mexican border. Among the largest school districts, 56 percent of total K–12 enrollments in 1989 in the Santa Ana Unified School District (in Orange County) were LEP, compared to 43 percent of the students in Glendale schools, 31 percent in Los Angeles, 28 percent in San Francisco and Stockton, 25 percent at Long Beach, 22 percent at Oakland and Fresno, and 17 percent in San Diego and San Jose (California State Department of Education 1993). The number of language-minority FEP students nearly doubled those proportions, such that in districts like Santa Ana's, over 90 percent of the students were of immigrant origin. These shifts have generally been accompanied by "white flight" from the most impacted public schools, producing an extraordinary mix of new immigrants and native-born ethnic minorities; for example, in the huge Los Angeles Unified School District (the second largest in the nation), the proportion of native white students declined sharply from 65 percent in 1980 to only 15 percent in 1990.

Especially in those districts, the overwhelming diversity of the LEP population presents tough challenges to the public school system. The most immediate problem faced by the schools is that teachers who know second languages are rare: in 1993 only a handful of the dozens of languages spoken by the LEP students were served by certified bilingual teachers, and statewide there was only one bilingual teacher for every 118 LEP students. Of the 10,000 bilingual teachers in California in 1993, 96 percent spoke only Spanish as their second language. The remaining 4 percent of bilingual teachers consisted of 206 Cantonese speakers, 83 Vietnamese, 44 Filipino, 38 Armenian, 36 Korean, 7

Mandarin, 5 Punjabi, 3 Japanese, 2 Hmong, and 1 Cambodian, Lao, and Russian each—statewide (California State Department of Education 1993). There are thousands of LEP students speaking a Babel of languages for whom not a single bilingual teacher is available. Moreover, as noted earlier, such students become proficient in English at different rates: in Los Angeles schools, higher-socioeconomic-status native speakers of Farsi and Japanese have been the quickest to be transferred to the all-English curriculum, while lower-socioeconomic-status native speakers of Spanish and Khmer (Cambodian) have transferred at the lowest rates. Under these circumstances the nature and availability of "bilingual education" programs for limited-English students become widely uneven and inequitable (cf. U.S. General Accounting Office 1994a).[3]

LEPs and FEPs: Patterns of Educational Progress

Assuming that LEP and FEP status (referring to students who speak a primary language other than English at home) are rough proxies for immigrant or second-generation status, we turn now to an examination of trend data on various indicators of the educational performance of language-minority students in San Diego high schools. The impact of the new immigration has been reflected in the rapidly changing ethnic composition of students in the San Diego Unified School District (SDUSD): ethnic "minorities" are now in the majority. Of the 121,000 students enrolled during 1976–77, 66 percent were majority whites while 34 percent were ethnic minorities. But of the 125,000 students enrolled during the 1992–93 school year, the figures were exactly reversed: only 34 percent were native whites while 66 percent were ethnic minorities (Smollar 1992). As is the case in other impacted districts in

---

[3]School districts in California may offer several basic types of programs for LEP students, from standard bilingual classrooms to ESL (English as a Second Language). In the bilingual classrooms (92 percent of which are in elementary schools), LEP students learn reading and writing in their primary language and math, science, and social studies in simplified (or "sheltered") English, while gradually learning to speak, read, and write in English. In an individualized program (especially when fewer than ten students at one grade level need bilingual help), the teacher speaks in English while the students are helped by a bilingual aide (who is not a certified teacher), if one is available. This is the only way to serve young immigrants who speak the less common languages, and a quarter of all LEP students are placed in this type of program. In the secondary school grades, LEP students are placed in an ESL program in which instruction during the entire day is conducted primarily in English, although the teachers are trained to speak more slowly and use more body language and other illustrations to carry out a lesson. Other approaches to instruction include the "Eastman Program," which segregates Spanish-speaking from English-speaking students for much of the school day (thus using bilingual instructors more efficiently) and "immersion" programs in which youngsters are taught entirely in Spanish through the third grade and 50 percent in English in grades four to six (which have been used by the San Diego Unified School District).

California, an increasing proportion of those ethnic minorities are classified as LEP or FEP.

We collected data on educational achievement from the school district for the entire high school student cohorts (that is, all sophomores, juniors, and seniors) for two periods: the 1986–87 and 1989–90 school years. These data included both "active" (currently enrolled) students and "inactive" students, those who *entered* their respective high school cohort in the ninth grade but later dropped out of school or left the district. Thus the data are not biased in favor of only "active" students. This is important because dropout rates vary widely by ethnicity. Ethnicity, in turn, is based on two classificatory schemes used by the school district. First, all students, regardless of language status, are classified by broad racial-ethnic categories (white, black, Hispanic, Filipino, Indochinese, [East] Asian, Pacific Islander, American Indian). Second, if a student speaks a primary language at home other than English, that language will be identified (e.g., Vietnamese, Korean, Arab, Italian, permitting a more detailed measure of ethnic identity), and the student is tested and assigned a LEP or FEP status; a student who speaks English only will have only a broad racial-ethnic identity in school records. For ethnic categories such as "Hispanic" and "Filipino" which coincide with a mother tongue, it is thus possible to compare the proportion of such students who speak "English only" to those who are LEP or FEP Spanish or Filipino bilingual speakers.

Table 2.6 shows comparative data on 1986–87 and 1989–90 cumulative academic GPAs (grade point averages), in rank order, for the major language-minority groups in these high school cohorts: Hispanics (who in San Diego are preponderantly of Mexican origin, but there is no way of determining country of origin from available school data), Filipinos, Indochinese (including Vietnamese, Lao, Hmong, and Cambodian speakers), and East Asians (Chinese, Korean, and Japanese). In addition, table 2.6 provides the percentages of each ethnolinguistic group who were classified as LEP, FEP, or English-dominant at the two time periods. For ease of presentation, data on native (English-only) whites and blacks, as well as much smaller immigrant groups (Europeans, South Asians, Middle Easterners, Africans, etc.), are not included.[4]

In 1986–87, 30 percent of these students—most likely U.S. born—spoke English as their primary home language, with the proportion ranging from almost 60 percent among East Asians to less than 6 percent among the Indochinese. The other 70 percent spoke a language other than English at home. Of these, 37 percent were classified as FEP and 33 percent as LEP. Most likely, these students are immigrants or children of

---

[4]However, data for the entire 1986–87 cohort (N = 38,820) have been reported elsewhere (see Rumbaut and Ima 1988; Rumbaut 1990; Portes and Rumbaut 1990: chap. 6). Data for the 1989–90 cohort have not been previously released.

TABLE 2.6

ACADEMIC GPA[1] OF TWO COHORTS OF SAN DIEGO HIGH SCHOOL
STUDENTS, IN RANK ORDER, AND PERCENTAGE CLASSIFIED AS LEP, FEP,
AND ENGLISH-DOMINANT,[2] BY SELECTED ETHNIC GROUPS AND ENGLISH
LANGUAGE STATUS, 1986–87 AND 1989–90

(N [1986] = 12,288 AND [1989] 15,656 HIGH SCHOOL SENIORS, JUNIORS, AND SOPHOMORES,
SAN DIEGO UNIFIED SCHOOL DISTRICT)

Ethno-linguistic Group	Year	LEP Students		FEP Students		English Only		Total	
		GPA	%	GPA	%	GPA	%	GPA	N
East Asian:	1986	2.83	13.7	3.05	26.6	2.38	59.7	2.62	826
	1989	2.86	10.7	3.02	39.0	2.58	50.4	2.78	1,050
Chinese	1986	2.94	41.0	3.40	59.0	—	—	3.21	166
	1989	2.95	21.4	3.26	78.6	—	—	3.19	248
Korean	1986	2.76	41.1	3.00	58.9	—	—	2.90	56
	1989	2.90	33.0	2.81	67.0	—	—	2.84	88
Japanese	1986	2.56	19.8	2.70	80.2	—	—	2.67	111
	1989	2.69	12.8	2.80	87.2	—	—	2.79	156
Indochinese:	1986	2.30	68.7	2.88	25.4	2.66	5.9	2.47	2,388
	1989	2.35	52.0	2.94	42.5	2.72	5.5	2.62	3,102
Vietnamese	1986	2.38	61.9	2.96	38.1	—	—	2.60	1,184
	1989	2.47	43.9	3.02	56.1	—	—	2.78	1,618
Hmong	1986	2.27	73.5	2.66	26.5	—	—	2.37	113
	1989	2.42	57.1	2.84	42.9	—	—	2.60	170
Cambodian	1986	2.30	91.8	2.77	8.2	—	—	2.34	391
	1989	2.21	77.8	2.82	22.2	—	—	2.35	415
Lao	1986	2.18	83.2	2.63	16.8	—	—	2.26	560
	1989	2.26	66.5	2.72	33.5	—	—	2.41	728
Filipino:	1986	2.02	11.4	2.53	50.1	2.33	38.5	2.39	2,064
	1989	1.94	6.6	2.49	56.6	2.38	36.8	2.41	3,311
Hispanic:	1986	1.71	29.7	1.85	37.5	1.81	32.8	1.79	7,007
	1989	1.74	20.1	1.91	54.1	2.01	25.8	1.90	8,193
TOTALS	1986	2.00	33.1	2.21	36.6	2.03	30.3	2.09	12,288
	1989	2.06	22.9	2.27	51.3	2.23	25.8	2.21	15,656

[1]GPA = Cumulative grade point average since 9th grade, excluding Physical Education; A = 4, B = 3, C = 2, D = 1, F = 0.

[2]LEP: Limited English Proficient; FEP: Fluent English Proficient; primary home language other than English. Groups are classified by ethnicity and (for mostly immigrant students) primary language spoken at home if other than English.

Source: Rubén G. Rumbaut, "Immigrant Students in San Diego: School Contexts and the Educational Achievement of LEP/FEP Language Minorities" (San Diego State University, 1993).

immigrants because, as noted, speaking another language at home is a good indicator of second-generation status. However, there is considerable variance in the percentage of LEPs from group to group. Over two-thirds of the Southeast Asians (and among them, over 90 percent of the

Cambodians) were classified as LEP, reflecting the fact that they were the most recently arrived immigrant group. By contrast, less than a third of the Hispanics were LEP, as were less than 15 percent of the East Asians and Filipinos. Half of the Filipinos were FEP, however, pointing to their homegrown advantage in English proficiency relative to other major immigrant groups. In general, these data suggest the recency of the migration of these groups and the relative extent to which they are currently handicapped in their command of English. For the 1989–90 cohort, the proportion of FEPs increased notably and the proportion of LEPs decreased for all groups without exception, while the relative rank order of the ethnic groups remained stable.

The data on GPAs are cumulative grade point averages earned by the students in high school academic courses since the ninth grade. As a point of reference, the mean GPA for native white students in these high school cohorts was 2.24. Lower GPAs were found for Pacific Islanders, Hispanics, and blacks, whereas all other groups exhibited higher GPAs. Female students of every ethnic group and language status, without exception, systematically outperformed male students. Remarkably, in 1986–87 and again in 1989–90, with the main exception of Hispanics (who are generally of lower socioeconomic status), *all of the non-English immigrant minorities were outperforming their English-only co-ethnics as well as majority white students*. This applied in most cases for FEP and LEP students alike, despite their language handicaps, although clearly FEP students do significantly better than their LEP co-ethnics. The highest GPAs were found among immigrant Chinese (exceeding the district average by a full grade point), Korean, Japanese, Vietnamese, and Filipino students. More remarkable still, even the Hmong, whose parents were largely preliterate peasants from the Laotian highlands, and the more recently arrived Cambodians, who were mostly rural-origin survivors of the "killing fields" of the late 1970s, were outperforming all native-born American students; and again this pattern applied for both FEP and LEP students among these refugee groups. This finding held for GPAs in both ESL (English as a Second Language) and mainstream courses; that is, the refugees' GPAs were not an artifact of the curriculum (cf. Rumbaut and Ima 1988).

For all ethnic groups virtually without exception, English monolinguals (who tend to be U.S.-born) have significantly lower GPAs than their bilingual FEP co-ethnics (who tend to be foreign-born).[5] One important implication of these findings is that educational achievement, at least as measured by GPA, appears to decline from the first to the

[5]The sole and curious exception involves the Hispanic cohort in 1989–90, where the English monolingual Hispanics surpassed the average GPA of both their FEP and LEP co-ethnics. This may be related, based on interviews with high school principals at the time, to the sudden entrance into several high schools of ill-prepared Mexican immigrant students in the wake of the IRCA legalization program.

second and third generations. These findings also lend strong support to previous research showing a significant positive association between "true" bilingualism (most closely approximated by FEP students in this analysis) and educational achievement, in contrast to the lower GPA registered by either of the essentially monolingual types (LEP and English-only).

TABLE 2.7

ANNUAL DROPOUT RATES[1] FOR THE 1989–90 COHORT OF SAN DIEGO HIGH SCHOOL STUDENTS, IN RANK ORDER, BY SELECTED ETHNIC GROUPS AND ENGLISH LANGUAGE STATUS[2]

(N [1989-90] = 15,656 HIGH SCHOOL SENIORS, JUNIORS, AND SOPHOMORES, SAN DIEGO UNIFIED SCHOOL DISTRICT)

Ethno-linguistic Group	LEP Students %	FEP Students %	English Only %	Total %	Total N
East Asian:	10.7	2.2	5.3	4.7	1,050
Chinese	5.7	1.0	—	2.0	248
Korean	17.2	1.7	—	6.8	88
Japanese	15.0	3.7	—	5.1	156
Filipino:	15.4	4.5	5.5	5.6	3,311
Indochinese:	11.0	3.5	7.0	7.6	3,102
Vietnamese	10.7	3.4	—	6.6	1,618
Hmong	5.2	5.5	—	5.3	170
Cambodian	14.9	5.4	—	12.8	415
Lao	9.9	2.5	—	7.4	728
Hispanic:	17.9	10.9	9.9	12.1	8,193
TOTALS	14.4	7.7	7.8	9.3	15,656

[1]The annual dropout rate is the percentage of students in grades 10–12 who dropped out of school during a given academic year. The data reported are for the academic year 1989-1990. The California State Department of Education defines a dropout as any student in grades 10, 11, or 12 who left school before graduating or completing formal education or its legal equivalent (e.g., a GED) and did not return to school or other educational program by mid-October of the following academic year, as evidenced by a transcript request or other reliable documentation.

[2]LEP: Limited English Proficient; FEP: Fluent English Proficient; primary home language other than English. Groups are classified by ethnicity and (for mostly immigrant students) primary language spoken at home if other than English. English Only refers to students whose primary home language is English.

Source: Rubén G. Rumbaut, "Immigrant Students in San Diego: School Contexts and the Educational Achievement of LEP/FEP Language Minorities" (San Diego State University, 1993).

Table 2.7 adds to this general picture by providing a breakdown, by ethnicity and language status, of dropout rates for the 1989–90 high school cohort. Overall rates for the Cambodians actually exceeded the overall rate for Hispanics, while the rate for the Hmong was the lowest of all Indochinese groups, continuing patterns we had observed a few years earlier for both groups (Rumbaut and Ima 1988). LEP students were far more at risk of leaving school than FEP students or English monolinguals. More importantly, FEPs had much lower dropout rates than English monolinguals (again with the sole exception of the Hispanic students in the 1989 cohort) (cf. U.S. General Accounting Office 1994b).

In the mid-1980s the SDUSD began a career counseling program that required students in the tenth grade to complete a comprehensive questionnaire about their educational and occupational aptitudes and goals. In the process, students were asked to select their top two career choices from a list of about two hundred occupations. Available data on occupational aspirations were collected for all sophomores and juniors in our cohorts (N = 13,778), and mean prestige scores for their career selections were calculated based on Treiman's Standard International Occupational Prestige Scale (SIOPS). It should be noted that because the career questionnaire required an adequate level of English proficiency, it was not given to most LEP students. The mean SIOPS score for non-Hispanic whites was 49.8, and Pacific Islanders, Hispanics, and blacks reflected aspirations slightly below that norm. By contrast, East Asians, Southeast Asians, and Filipinos had higher average prestige values that generally paralleled their patterns of academic achievement noted earlier, and their selections of higher-status professions were disproportionately in science, engineering, health care, and math-based fields, where their relative English language handicaps would be least likely to place them at a competitive disadvantage. Among U.S.-born students and especially majority whites, those aspiring to the professions were much more likely to select careers in arts and letters rather than in math or science. Among the Indochinese students, the Vietnamese and the Hmong had SIOPS scores above 50, while the Cambodians and the Lao reflected notably lower aspirations. Over 40 percent of the Vietnamese chose math-based professions and another 15 percent selected high-status professions in the arts and letters, while two-thirds of the Cambodians and the Lao chose lower-status blue-collar, clerical, or personal services jobs. These data also show sharply different types of career selections between males and females for all ethnic groups, reflecting traditional patterns of occupational segregation by gender.

As with FEP versus LEP status, GPAs, test scores (not here discussed), dropout rates, and now occupational aspirations, these findings raise some intriguing issues about ethnicity, bilingualism, and achievement, and they underscore the complex internal diversity that exists even within the "Indochinese" refugee population, or the still broader "Asian" and for that matter "Hispanic" categories of immigrant students. It is still not clear, save for the testing of English language ability, what are the characteristics of students assigned to LEP and FEP statuses (cf.

Ima and Rumbaut 1989). Official data from school districts do not permit a systematic analysis of causal factors, however, because the schools do not collect information on such key variables as immigration status, time and age of arrival in the United States, parents' social class of origin, their modes of exit from the homeland and of incorporation in the local economy, level of and attitudes toward acculturation into American life, psychological factors, patterns of social relationships, or the nature of existing ethnic communities. All of these variables may influence directly or indirectly the observed differences in the educational adaptation of immigrant students, and they need to be studied through detailed surveys and contextualized case studies. It is to those studies that we now turn.

Children of Immigrants: Predictors of Educational Progress

For a more systematic analysis of the educational progress and prospects of the new Californians, we will turn to a new data set from the recently completed first phase of a survey of over 5,200 children of immigrants enrolled in schools located in San Diego and South Florida.[6] The students surveyed were in the eighth and ninth grades, a level at which dropout rates are still relatively low, to avoid the potential bias of differential dropout rates between ethnic groups at the senior high school level. To be eligible for inclusion in the study, a student had to be either foreign-born or U.S.-born with at least one foreign-born parent. Since the schools do not collect information on the nativity of parents, a brief initial survey of *all* eighth and ninth graders in the district was first done to determine their eligibility. Eligible students were then administered the survey questionnaire at school during the spring 1992 semester.

The final sample in San Diego—which will be our focus here— totaled 2,420 Mexican, Filipino, Vietnamese, Cambodian, Laotian, and other Asian and Latin American students. Most of the respondents were fourteen or fifteen years old. The sample is evenly split by gender and grade level. By generation, 44 percent are U.S.-born children of immigrant parents (the "second" generation), and 56 percent are foreign-born youths who immigrated to the United States before age twelve (the "1.5" generation). Among the foreign-born, the sample is also evenly split by age at arrival: about half had lived in the United States for ten years or more (they were pre-school-age at arrival), while the other half had lived

[6]The project, "Children of Immigrants: The Adaptation Process of the Second Generation," is being carried out in collaboration with Alejandro Portes and Lisandro Pérez, and is funded by the Andrew W. Mellon, Spencer, Russell Sage, and National Science Foundations. Several papers reporting results from the first phase of this survey have recently been published in a special issue of the *International Migration Review* (see Portes 1994).

in the United States nine years or less (they had reached elementary school age in their native country but arrived in the United States before adolescence). In this sense, time in the United States for immigrant children is not only a measure of length of exposure to American life, but it is also an indicator of different developmental stages at the time of migration. The survey gathered data on respondents' demographic characteristics, family, socioeconomic status, ethnic self-identity, peers, language, hours spent on homework and television, educational and occupational aspirations, perceptions of discrimination, self-esteem, and depression (see the appendix to this chapter for further details on measures used). In addition, school data on grade point averages, Stanford reading and math achievement test scores, LEP/FEP classification, gifted status, and related variables were obtained from the respective school systems for all the students in the sample. Selected results by national origin groups are displayed in table 2.8.

As table 2.8 shows, levels of parental education are lowest for the Mexicans and the Indochinese, especially the Laotians and the Cambodians; and the Indochinese also have the highest proportions by far of parents who are not in the labor force, a reflection of the fact that they exhibit the highest rates of poverty and welfare dependency in the United States (cf. Rumbaut 1995). The Filipinos and the "Other Asians" (mainly Chinese, Japanese, Koreans, and Indians) show the highest proportions of college graduates among mothers and fathers, and their families are much more likely to own rather than rent their homes. As a reflection of this, Mexican and Indochinese youth (especially the Cambodian, Hmong, and Lao) were most likely to be attending inner-city schools, while the Filipinos were the least likely to be doing so. Asian-origin groups have a higher proportion of families with both natural parents at home; the somewhat higher incidence of father absence among the Hmong and especially the Cambodians is due less to divorce than to the death of the father prior to arrival in the United States, a reflection of extraordinarily harsh contexts of exit (Rumbaut 1991b).

Nearly two-thirds of the sample said they *preferred* to speak English, including substantial majorities in every group and nearly nine out of ten Filipinos; the single exception was the Mexicans, who are the most loyal to their mother tongue, although even among them 45 percent already preferred English. The Laotians and the Cambodians, two-thirds of whom were classified as LEP by the schools, also have the lowest scores in both the four-item English Language Index and the Stanford reaching achievement test (the data in table 2.8 reflect national percentiles). In contrast, the "Other Asians" show a level of ability in the Stanford math achievement test that is well above national norms, followed by the Vietnamese and Filipinos; the high proportions of these students who are classified as "gifted" by the schools are also well above

TABLE 2.8

SOCIAL CHARACTERISTICS OF CHILDREN OF IMMIGRANTS IN SAN DIEGO, 1992, BY NATIONAL ORIGIN OF PARENTS[1]

(N = 2,420 EIGHTH AND NINTH GRADERS IN SAN DIEGO CITY SCHOOLS WITH FOREIGN-BORN PARENTS)

Social Characteristics	Mexico (727)	Philippines (807)	Vietnam (361)	Laos		Cambodia (95)	Other Asian (134)	Other Latin (89)	Total (2,420)
				Lao (154)	Hmong (53)				
Nativity and Time in U.S.:									
% Less than 10 years in U.S.	23.1	26.0	42.7	44.8	34.0	48.4	27.6	32.6	30.2
% U.S.-born	60.4	55.3	15.2	1.3	5.7	2.1	53.0	49.4	43.9
% One parent is U.S.-born	17.6	19.3	2.5	0.7	0	0	34.3	27.0	15.0
Family Socioeconomic Status:									
% Father is college graduate	6.3	29.1	14.4	10.4	1.9	4.2	40.3	30.3	18.0
% Mother is college graduate	3.7	38.2	8.3	3.9	0	4.2	26.1	24.7	17.9
% Father ≤ 8 years education	55.7	10.4	52.6	57.1	79.3	69.5	17.2	18.0	37.8
% Mother ≤ 8 years education	59.2	16.0	59.6	70.1	92.5	80.0	17.2	19.1	43.3
% Father in white-collar job	12.4	39.2	15.8	11.7	9.4	3.2	40.3	36.0	23.8
% Mother in white-collar job	16.6	56.3	12.2	9.1	0	6.3	32.1	49.4	30.0
% Father not in labor force	21.6	17.6	46.3	67.5	75.5	79.0	17.2	25.8	30.2
% Mother not in labor force	45.0	14.0	60.4	74.7	88.7	87.4	35.8	27.0	40.3
% Own home	31.2	73.6	33.8	24.0	1.9	10.5	66.4	40.5	46.1
% Both natural parents at home	59.0	79.4	72.9	72.1	77.4	68.4	72.4	46.1	69.8
% Father absent from home	35.6	15.0	19.4	16.2	18.9	25.3	19.4	41.6	23.6
Language:									
% Prefers English	44.3	88.4	51.3	52.0	64.2	65.3	75.4	69.7	64.4
English Knowledge Index (1-4)	3.45	3.85	3.35	3.27	3.13	3.36	3.66	3.73	3.57

TABLE 2.8 (CONTINUED)

SOCIAL CHARACTERISTICS OF CHILDREN OF IMMIGRANTS IN SAN DIEGO, 1992, BY NATIONAL ORIGIN OF PARENTS[1]

(N = 2,420 EIGHTH AND NINTH GRADERS IN SAN DIEGO CITY SCHOOLS WITH FOREIGN-BORN PARENTS)

Social Characteristics	Mexico (727)	Philippines (807)	Vietnam (361)	Laos — Lao (154)	Laos — Hmong (53)	Cambodia (95)	Other Asian (134)	Other Latin (89)	Total (2,420)
Schooling:									
% In inner-city schools	62.5	5.6	49.6	66.9	83.0	92.6	23.1	40.4	40.5
% School-classified as LEP	43.7	6.8	39.4	49.4	66.0	69.5	16.4	21.4	30.3
% School-classified as Gifted	5.4	21.2	16.1	5.2	0	1.1	35.8	24.7	14.3
Activities:									
Hours daily on homework	1.16	1.88	2.00	1.84	2.32	1.73	1.97	1.56	1.67
Hours daily watching TV	2.44	2.64	2.05	2.15	1.85	2.21	1.95	2.22	2.37
Achievement:									
Grade point average (GPA)	2.23	2.94	3.04	2.86	2.95	2.71	3.18	2.68	2.73
Stanford Math test (%ile)	30.7	58.9	60.3	41.9	29.7	35.0	69.4	46.4	48.2
Stanford Reading test (%ile)	25.7	51.2	37.4	21.9	15.2	13.6	62.1	50.4	38.3
Aspirations:									
% Expect to finish college	60.8	82.0	76.2	52.6	39.6	60.0	88.8	82.0	71.5
% Get upper-white-collar job	38.4	53.9	48.8	42.2	22.6	37.9	47.8	57.3	46.2
Psychological Status:									
Self-esteem scale (1–4)	3.16	3.25	3.10	3.07	2.99	3.07	3.35	3.40	3.19

[1] All differences between national-origin groups are significant beyond the .001 level for all variables. See text and the appendix for details on measurement.

district norms. The Hmong, Mexicans, and Cambodians are well below national math norms, followed by the Lao. The students' math rankings generally reflect the socioeconomic status of their parents.

The association between social class and educational attainment outcomes does not, however, extend to GPAs. For example, despite their poor performance on achievement tests, the Hmong had earned the highest academic GPAs of all the groups except for the high-achieving Vietnamese and "Other Asians." One measure of effort in table 2.8 suggests the reason: the Hmong devote far more hours per day to homework than any other group. In general, Asian-origin students put in the most homework time, and Latin American students the least. Students with the highest ratios of homework-to-television-watching hours had the highest GPAs. Significantly, over time and generation in the United States, reading achievement test scores go up, but the number of hours spent on homework goes down, as do GPAs—a finding that confirms similar findings among immigrant students in California and elsewhere (Caplan et al. 1991; Gibson 1989; Olsen 1988; McNall, Dunnigan, and Mortimer 1994; Rumbaut 1990, 1995; Rumbaut and Ima 1988; Suárez-Orozco 1989).

Most of the national origins groups report very high educational aspirations, led by the "Other Asians"; the Hmong, Lao, Cambodians, and Mexicans, on the other hand, exhibit notably lower occupational aspirations than the other groups. The Mexican students and especially the Indochinese showed the lowest global self-esteem scores, with the lowest score in the sample found for the Hmong (for an analysis of determinants of self-esteem and depressive symptomatology in the full sample, see Rumbaut 1994b; see also Padilla and Durán, this volume).

Earlier we noted that little is known about the characteristics that distinguish students who are classified as LEP and FEP by the schools, although that is a critical status assignment, governing as it does the inclusion or exclusion of the student from the mainstream school curriculum—and the access to resources, teachers, peers, and opportunities that goes with it (see Stanton-Salazar and Dornbusch 1995). In the social system of the school, a LEP identity is also a stigmatized status that carries a heavy dose of social opprobrium. Our data set permits us to explore the question in some detail, as sketched in table 2.9. These status assignments are based on tested levels of English proficiency, and that is reflected in the fact that LEP students scored below the 10th percentile on the Stanford reading achievement test, compared to the 46th percentile for the FEPs and just above the 50th percentile for those classified as English-dominant. It is also to be expected that English-only students are preponderantly U.S.-born and especially likely to have a U.S.-born parent, whereas LEPs are relatively recent arrivals.

TABLE 2.9

SOCIAL CHARACTERISTICS OF CHILDREN OF IMMIGRANTS IN SAN DIEGO, 1992, BY THEIR LANGUAGE-STATUS CLASSIFICATION AT SCHOOL (LEP, FEP, ENGLISH ONLY)[1]

(N = 2,420 EIGHTH AND NINTH GRADERS IN SAN DIEGO CITY SCHOOLS WITH FOREIGN-BORN PARENTS)

Social Characteristics	LEP Students %	FEP Students %	English Only %	Total %
Nativity and Time in U.S.:				
% Less than 10 years in U.S.	59.5	20.1	11.0	30.2
% U.S.-born	19.1	47.9	71.3	43.9
% One parent is U.S.-born	3.5	10.4	43.6	15.0
Family Socioeconomic Status:				
% Father is college graduate	9.0	20.2	26.1	18.0
% Mother is college graduate	6.0	22.4	24.4	17.9
% Father ≤ 8 years education	60.0	34.5	12.4	37.8
% Mother ≤ 8 years education	67.0	39.0	18.1	43.3
% Father in white-collar job	11.9	26.4	35.2	23.8
% Mother in white-collar job	10.0	34.2	49.7	30.0
% Father not in labor force	48.2	23.3	20.2	30.2
% Mother not in labor force	64.5	32.6	22.6	40.3
% Own home	15.4	58.2	62.7	46.1
% Both natural parents at home	62.4	75.4	67.0	69.8
% Father absent from home	30.2	19.9	23.0	23.6
Schooling:				
% In inner-city schools	72.0	30.5	17.7	40.5
% School-classified as Gifted	1.8	19.5	20.6	14.3
Activities:				
Hours daily on homework	1.59	1.71	1.72	1.67
Hours daily watching TV	2.21	2.45	2.43	2.37
Achievement:				
Grade point average (GPA)	2.54	2.86	2.71	2.73
Stanford Math test (%ile)	20.0	55.1	55.0	48.2
Stanford Reading test (%ile)	9.9	45.8	50.7	38.3
Aspirations:				
% Expect to finish college	59.9	76.3	77.2	71.5
% Get upper-white-collar job	36.7	51.7	47.0	46.2
Psychological Status:				
Self-esteem scale (1-4)	2.96	3.27	3.31	3.19

[1]All differences between LEP and FEP groups are significant beyond the .001 level for all variables, except for homework hours, which does not differ significantly. See text and the appendix for details on measurement.

But what is striking in table 2.9 is the stark bifurcation that is apparent between LEP students and the other two types in socioeconomic status, educational and occupational aspirations, self-esteem, and other variables. For example, the data show that the parents of English-only types are the most advantaged by every socioeconomic indicator, and the parents of LEP students are the most disadvantaged, with the FEPs in between. But the disparities between FEPs and LEPs are far greater than those between the FEPs and the English-only, especially with regard to home ownership and to the likelihood of attending inner-city schools: while 72 percent of LEP students attended inner-city schools, only 30 percent of the FEPs and 18 percent of the English-only did so. Parenthetically, the data in table 2.8 also support our earlier findings about FEP achievement: despite the socioeconomic advantages of the English monolinguals, FEP bilinguals have significantly higher GPAs (and perhaps also significantly, they are more likely to live in intact two-parent families).

To explore these issues further, I used logistic regression to test the effects, in a multivariate analysis, of an array of likely determinants on the odds of being assigned to a LEP status. In a nutshell, the results (not shown) indicated that net of English ability, time in the United States, and grade level, the odds of being LEP were significantly higher for older boys in the inner city, whose parents are unemployed and uneducated, and do not own their home. Residing with both natural parents washed out of the equation. Of the variables with statistically significant effects, the strongest effect was observed for a contextual variable: an inner-city location (on "segmented assimilation" processes in inner-city social contexts, see Portes, this volume; Rumbaut 1994b). In addition, again net of all other variables, Mexican, Vietnamese, Cambodian, and Laotian ethnicity significantly increased the odds of LEP assignment. That is, despite controlling for socioeconomic status and other individual and contextual variables, the independent effect of national origin or of being a part of Mexican and Indochinese groups or communities was not eliminated. Why that is so is not at all clear.

Finally, given our interest in the question of determinants of educational progress and prospects among children of immigrants, I carried out a series of least-squares multiple linear regression analyses of four key outcomes: GPA, math and reading achievement test scores, and educational aspirations. The results are presented in table 2.10. Controlling for grade in school, and looking first at the effect of age and gender on educational outcomes, it is clear that girls have a significant edge on boys when it comes to academic GPA, and they also have greater aspirations—although gender had no effect on math scores and only a weak effect on reading skills (with the edge, again, to girls). Older age is strongly and negatively associated with all outcomes across the board. Both of these are familiar results in the literature.

An important finding, supporting our earlier reported research, is the *negative* association of length of residence in the United States with

TABLE 2.10
PREDICTORS OF EDUCATIONAL ACHIEVEMENT AND ASPIRATIONS AMONG CHILDREN OF IMMIGRANTS: LEAST-SQUARES MULTIPLE REGRESSIONS FOR SAN DIEGO SAMPLE, 1992[1]

(N = 2,420 EIGHTH AND NINTH GRADERS IN SAN DIEGO CITY SCHOOLS WITH FOREIGN-BORN PARENTS)

Predictor Variables	Academic GPA	Math Scores	Reading Scores	Educational Aspirations
Children:				
Gender (1 = male, 0 = female)	-.342***	-.070NS	-2.530*	-.196***
	(-11.089)	(-0.058)	(-2.304)	(-5.826)
Age	-.118***	-5.812***	-3.572***	-.126***
	(-5.017)	(-6.253)	(-4.234)	(-4.939)
Grade in school	.146***	5.034***	1.532NS	.083*
	(3.780)	(3.326)	(1.116)	(1.962)
Length of residence in U.S.	-.083***	-.118NS	3.024***	-.118***
	(-4.491)	(-0.158)	(4.437)	(-5.835)
Knowledge of English	.046NS	9.703***	17.806***	.282***
	(1.341)	(6.370)	(12.726)	(7.582)
Friends are co-ethnics	.081**	3.328**	1.917NS	.040NS
	(2.604)	(2.723)	(1.732)	(1.171)
Homework (daily hours)	.104***	1.573***	1.062**	.092***
	(8.952)	(3.392)	(2.533)	(7.205)
TV watching (daily hours)	-.024**	-.869*	-.897**	-.042***
	(-2.456)	(-2.311)	(-2.632)	(-4.022)
Parents and Family:				
Education of parents	.010NS	.816***	1.192***	.053***
	(1.519)	(3.314)	(5.276)	(7.708)
Parents are professionals	.135***	2.963*	4.008**	.070NS
	(3.704)	(2.107)	(3.192)	(1.776)
Parents are not in labor force	.011NS	-2.728**	-4.623***	-.087***
	(0.487)	(-2.960)	(-5.544)	(-3.398)
Own home (1 = own, 0 = rent)	.120***	5.731***	6.019***	.144***
	(3.282)	(3.979)	(4.658)	(3.607)
Two natural parents at home	.109**	1.046NS	-1.425NS	-.022NS
	(3.141)	(0.751)	(-1.134)	(-0.577)
One parent is U.S.-born	-.170***	-.788NS	.758NS	-.085NS
	(-3.762)	(-0.455)	(0.486)	(-1.724)
Mexican	-.447***	-15.372***	-10.510***	.023NS
	(-10.999)	(-9.615)	(-7.213)	(0.512)
Vietnamese	.162***	12.861***	4.162**	.159**
	(3.508)	(7.079)	(2.528)	(3.159)
(Constant)	3.163***	45.368***	-4.104NS	4.204***
	(9.792)	(3.486)	(-0.346)	(11.925)
Adjusted R²	.275	.265	.351	.208

[1]Unstandardized regression coefficients (b), with T-ratios in parentheses. See text and appendix for details of measurement.

***p < .001; **p < .01; *p < .05; NS = Not Significant.

both GPA and aspirations. Time in the United States is, as expected, strongly predictive of improved English reading skills; but despite that seeming advantage, longer residence in the United States and second-generation status (that is, being born in the United States) are connected to declining academic achievement and aspirations, net of other factors. That finding does not support a linear assimilation hypothesis. What is more, as table 2.10 shows, having a parent who is also U.S.-born is strongly associated with *lower* GPAs; students whose parents are both immigrants outperform their counterparts whose mother or father is native-born. A similar finding has recently been reported by Kao and Tienda (1995) with national data from the NELS:88 (the National Educational Longitudinal Study, 1988). Further, English language proficiency has no effect on GPA—although it is positively associated with both test scores and aspirations. By contrast, having a peer group made up of co-ethnic friends who are also children of immigrants does have a positive effect on GPA—and the positive influence of such peers who may also be oriented toward an achievement ideology of hard work extends to math scores as well. Clearly, the effort invested in daily homework pays off across the board in higher grades, test scores, and aspirations for the future. By contrast, the hours spent daily watching television are associated negatively with all outcomes across the board. Taken together, these results point rather to the association of achievement outcomes with an immigrant ethos that appears to erode with increasing exposure and assimilation to native norms and contexts, and that seems to be affirmed within the context of co-ethnic peer groups and intact immigrant families.

Turning to parental and family variables, we note that family socioeconomic status, particularly home ownership, has strongly positive effects on all outcomes. Parental education has no effect on GPA, but it does on math and reading test scores as well as on educational aspirations. By contrast, such aspirations plummet when one or both parents are unemployed. Students living in a home with both natural parents are significantly more likely to have higher GPAs—although that is not associated with the other different types of outcomes. It is of particular interest to note that with all of those variables controlled for in these models, Mexican and Vietnamese ethnicity nonetheless retain strong and significant effects on virtually all outcomes, although the direction of the effect differs between them: Mexican origin is *negatively* associated with GPA and test scores (but not with aspirations) net of all other variables in these models, while Vietnamese ethnicity is *positively* linked to all four outcomes. Once again, despite the richness of our data set, the influence of ethnicity on educational achievement and aspirations was not eliminated, raising questions as to why this might be so. What does "Mexican" or "Vietnamese" mean or stand as a proxy for in a statistical analysis of this nature? It might include nothing less than the culture, history, and collective memory of an entire group as embedded in the American context. To gain more insight into these and other possibilities, we will consider the findings of four selected case studies (on taking "context" into account rather than pretending to "control it away" in an analysis of ethnicity, parenting, peer crowds, and high school performance, see Steinberg et al. n.d.).

Four Case Studies

In this final section, four case studies are selected for review: two groups of "Asians" (Southeast Asians and Punjabi Indians) and two groups of "Hispanics" (Mexicans and Central Americans) attending high schools in various areas of California during the 1980s. In terms of their migration motivations, two of these groups consist primarily of "political" refugees (the Southeast Asians and the Central Americans), and two are mainly "economic" immigrants (the Punjabis and the Mexicans). In terms of their actual context of reception in the United States, however, the Southeast Asians were eligible for a variety of refugee assistance programs, while the Central Americans were not. Substantial proportions of the Mexicans and probably a majority of the Central Americans entered clandestinely. Despite the many differences between them, and in contrast to the children of well-educated professional and managerial immigrants, most of these high school students have in common the fact of their families' economic disadvantages and modest social class origins.

Southeast Asian Refugee Students in San Diego Secondary Schools

The "Indochinese Health and Adaptation Research Project" (IHARP) collected survey data in 1983 and again in 1984 through in-depth interviews with a representative sample of Indochinese refugees in San Diego. The sample included 739 adults from the five major Indochinese ethnic groups—Vietnamese, Chinese-Vietnamese, Cambodian, Hmong, and Lao—ranging in age from eighteen to seventy-one, with about equal numbers of men and women. The interviews were conducted in the home and language of the respondent and collected migration histories and data on social background, English proficiency, employment, income, acculturation, and mental health (Rumbaut 1989, 1991b). A follow-up study was done in 1986–87 to examine the educational adaptation of all of the children of these refugees who were enrolled in the San Diego Unified School District. Complete academic histories for this sample of Indochinese students (including GPAs and standardized achievement test scores) were then obtained from the school district in 1986 and again in 1989 and matched with the 1983 data on their parents and households. Combined data were thus collected for 239 (in 1986) and 340 (in 1989) secondary school students, and these were supplemented by intensive ethnographic fieldwork. Thus the design permitted the analysis of the effects of parental and family characteristics measured in 1983 on the children's academic achievement measured three and six years later (Rumbaut and Ima 1988; Rumbaut 1991b, 1995).

This subsample is representative of children who came accompanied by one or both parents; it does not include the relatively small minority of children who came without their parents, nor does it include second-generation children who were born in the United States. Rather, they are members of what I earlier called the "one-and-a-half" or "1.5" generation of refugee youths who were born in Southeast Asia but are being educated and are coming of age in America.[7] The socioeconomic profile of the households in the youth study matched in most essential respects that of the larger parent (IHARP) study. The academic characteristics of the students in the youth subsample also generally corresponded to those noted above for all Indochinese students in San Diego high schools.

As expected, Vietnamese and Chinese students showed the highest levels of educational attainment: they had higher GPAs and higher CTBS (California Test of Basic Skills) test scores in math and reading. Less than half of the Vietnamese and Chinese were classified by the school district as LEP; the majority were classified as FEP. Although their reading scores were below the national average, reflecting their limitations with the English language as recently arrived newcomers, their GPAs were well above those for native whites in the district and their math achievement scores placed them in the top quartile of the nation. Cambodian and Lao students showed the lowest levels of attainment in both GPAs and test scores among these refugee groups, although their GPAs matched the Anglo norm and their math scores were at about the national average. The ranking of these four groups paralleled that of their parents' level of education: Vietnamese parents were the most educated, followed by the Chinese, Cambodians, and Lao. Surprisingly, however, the Hmong occupied an intermediate position in both GPAs and test scores between these four other groups—despite the fact that

---

[7]I had coined the concept in the 1970s in another context, having to do with Cuban rather than Indochinese "1.5ers" and the dynamics of identity formation in adolescence. The idea for the term came from reading W.I. Thomas and Florian Znaniecki's *The Polish Peasant in Europe and America*, in which the authors referred in passing to the "half-second generation." The concept applies best to the situation of children who immigrate after reaching school age in the country of origin but before reaching puberty (roughly ages six through twelve). Teenagers (13–18) and pre-school children (0–5) are at different developmental stages and seem closer to the experience, respectively, of the first and second generations (and might be termed, pursuing the decimal system, 1.25ers and 1.75ers). See Rumbaut 1991b, 1994b; Pérez Firmat 1994.

Hmong parents had by far the least amount of education (just above first-grade level). Thus the refugee students' current educational achievement was not simply a function of their parents' social class of origin.

About 75 percent of all of these students lived in households with incomes below the federal poverty line; indeed, their families were the poorest in the San Diego area. About 90 percent of the Vietnamese and Chinese lived in intact homes with both parents, as did about 83 percent of the Hmong and the Lao. But less than half of the Cambodians lived in two-parent households; most lived with widowed mothers, reflecting the extremely high death rates in Cambodia during the Pol Pot period of the late 1970s. Cambodian mothers also showed the most elevated levels of depressive symptoms, followed by Hmong and Lao mothers, with the Vietnamese and Chinese reflecting the best mental health profiles. The Cambodians and the Lao were the most recently arrived groups and hence had fewer semesters in American schools and a higher proportion of LEP students.

An analysis of the students' GPAs found that several student characteristics except gender showed significant positive effects: the younger the students and the longer in U.S. schools, the higher their GPAs; and FEP students (fluent bilinguals) clearly had an advantage over those classified as LEP (limited bilinguals). Among objective family characteristics, parents' education and English literacy did not affect GPA directly, but income had a strong positive effect, as did the size of the household (and both variables had actually increased in predictive strength by 1989). This latter result goes against the grain of conventional wisdom, which presupposes that the larger the household, the fewer resources parents have to invest in their children. Fieldwork in the Vietnamese community, however, suggested an opposite social capital explanation: the largest families were organized as "mini school systems," with older siblings tutoring the younger ones (often giving them harder practice tests than the ones they got at school) even in the absence of any direct parental involvement in the school or in homework.

In addition, two subjective variables were strongly associated with GPA: (1) the level of psychological distress of the mother (the higher this score, the lower the student's GPA); and (2) the parents' score on an index measuring their sense of ethnic resilience and reaffirmation (the higher this score, the higher the GPA of their children). That score was a summed index of four items, which expressed the degree to which parents felt that (1) their ethnic group must stay together as a community to preserve their own culture and identity even as they adapt to the U.S. economy to "make a living"; (2) they should stick together as a group for social support and mutual assistance; (3) they should live in co-ethnic neighborhoods; and (4) they would *not* return to their homelands even if there were a change in government. This index thus provided a general measure not of assimilation or "Americanization" as such, but rather of accommodation among parents who intend to stay in the United States while affirming their ethnic culture and social networks. Both of these variables (measured in 1983), and especially the latter, remained significant predictors of the child's GPA at both the 1986 and 1989 time periods. The latter finding supports in part results reported by Caplan, Choy, and Whitmore (1991) for Indochinese students in five other cities, but it runs counter to the conventional assumption that the more acculturated and Americanized immigrants become, the greater will be their success in the competitive worlds of school and work. Instead, it suggests an opposite proposition, namely, that "Americanization" processes, all other things being equal and to the extent that they involve "subtractive" rather than "additive" forms of acculturation, may be counterproductive for educational attainment.

In summary, a combination of objective and subjective factors combined to influence educational achievement even after the passage of several years. That the set of more subjective variables—the parents' "psychocultural status"—was strongly predictive of GPA points to the importance for effort-based achievement of subjective factors in parent-child (and especially mother-child) relationships. Of these, the parents' affirmation of ethnic identity and solidarity within family and community structures was of greater import—and indeed, it may also be connected to the generation of social capital in large households. Age and time variables were also quite important. The (younger) age of the student is predictive of higher GPAs and test scores. But time in the United States has a different effect—and meaning—depending on age at arrival. A key difference seems to involve those youth whose age at arrival in the United States was pre-puberty (or roughly younger than twelve) versus those who arrived post-puberty, in their later teens. The older students are more handicapped by language deficiencies, may have "lost" more time from normal schooling during their often prolonged stays in refugee camps overseas, have had less time to learn the ropes of the new system, and must cope simultaneously with the additional developmental stressors of middle and late adolescence. However, the finding that educational achievement improves for younger Indochinese refugees and over time in the United States may reflect a temporary effect that will plateau and then begin to diminish as a function of a process of "becoming American," which ironically may prove counterproductive for educational attainment in competitive school settings. The younger ones, even though their English competency and their knowledge of American society are better, may become less driven and less single-minded in their pursuit of school and work goals, and thus at some point less apt to reach the levels of attainment of their more motivated and harder-working older siblings. The exact transition may depend on the structural ability of Southeast Asian families to develop and maintain bicultural values, norms, and pressures that lead to high achievement net of the parents' social class resources, and that assist them in bridging effectively their native and adoptive worlds (but see also Ima, this volume).

Punjabi Sikh Immigrant Students at "Valleyside High" in Northern California

As seen earlier, over the past two decades immigrants from India have constituted perhaps the most highly educated group of newcomers to the United States, reflecting classic patterns of professional "brain drain" international migration. There is considerable internal diversity among the Indians, however, as illustrated by an ongoing case study of the children of Punjabi Sikhs attending Valleyside High School in an agricultural region of northern California, carried out by Margaret Gibson (1987; 1989; see her chapter in this volume for an update). Most of the Indians in "Valleyside," who in 1981 numbered around 6,000, were Punjabi Sikhs. Unlike the Indochinese refugees discussed above, the Punjabis emigrated primarily for economic reasons; but like the rural-origin Cambodians and Laotians, most of them came from small farming villages. The baseline study, conducted during 1980–82, collected school performance data for all 2,100 students attending Valleyside High (grades 9–12), of whom 231 (11 percent) were Punjabi Sikhs. Intensive ethnographic research then focused on the experiences of a random sample of forty-four Punjabi seniors and a comparison group of forty-two white Anglo seniors.

At the time of fieldwork, the median income for Punjabi families with children enrolled at Valleyside High was about $15,000—roughly half the income of comparable Anglo families. A third of the Punjabis had been in the United States less than five years, a third between five and ten years, and a third over ten years. Half of the Punjabi fathers worked as farm laborers in the nearby fruit orchards, usually for the minimum wage. Another quarter (mostly those who had come by themselves before 1970 and later sent for their wives and children) had become entrepreneurial orchard farmers themselves, and the remaining quarter commuted to factory jobs in Sacramento or the San Francisco Bay area. The majority of the Punjabi mothers (much like the Hmong and the Cambodians) were illiterate or semiliterate. The fathers were more educated, but less than half of them had finished secondary school in India. Punjabi was the language spoken at home, and most parents spoke English only with difficulty.

Compounding these socioeconomic and language handicaps was the situation of "severe prejudice" that the Punjabi students encountered in the school setting, as well as "sharp conflicts" between home values and those promoted by the school. Gibson (1987: 268) describes it this way:

> Valleyside is "redneck" country, and some white residents are extremely hostile toward immigrants who look different, act different, and speak a different language. In school, Punjabi teenagers are told they stink . . . told to go back to India . . . accused of being illegals . . . physically abused by majority students, who spit at them, refuse to sit by them in class or in buses, crowd in front of them in line, stick them with pins, throw food at them, and worse. They are labeled troublemakers if they defend themselves. . . . In one way or another, Punjabi students are told that India and Indian culture are inferior to Western and American ways . . . criticized for their hairstyle, their diet, and their dress . . . faulted because they defer to the authority of elders, accept arranged marriages, and believe in group decision making . . . condemned most especially for not joining in majority-dominated school activities and for resisting as best they can the forces for cultural assimilation.

Despite their relative disadvantages, the Punjabi high school students exhibited a generally more favorable picture of school performance than majority-group Anglo students. The study found that 85 to 90 percent of the Punjabis graduated from high school, compared to 70 to 75 percent of Anglo students. Among the Punjabis, there was a strong relationship between age at arrival in the United States and performance in high school (a pattern also observed among the Indochinese students in the San Diego study); and that variable (along with male gender, a pattern similar only to the Hmong in the Indochinese study) was a stronger determinant of educational attainment than were the parents' income, education, occupation, or level of English proficiency. Upon entering the ninth grade, more Punjabis were classified as LEP and placed into ESL or remedial English classes (overwhelmingly those who had emigrated from India after the fourth grade), while more Anglo students were placed into remedial math. Punjabi students who had received all of their education in the United States were as likely as their Anglo classmates to be placed in college preparatory courses. During high school, Punjabi boys surpassed the GPAs of majority peers, and they were more likely to take advanced math and science classes and to express aspirations for careers in computer science, engineering, and electronics. Punjabi girls tended instead to enroll heavily in business classes in their last two years of high school and to reflect their parents' wishes that the girls should marry first, leaving decisions about higher education and career options to be made later with their husbands and in-laws.

Unlike the Punjabi students, most Anglo students participated in extracurricular activities at school, held after-school jobs, and maintained an active social life. Anglo boys in particular invested little time in homework and held to the view that the senior year was "kickback time," explaining that they could always take advanced classes in math, science, or English later on in college. By contrast, the Punjabis (especially the girls) led extremely restricted social lives, and 75 percent of the boys reported doing more than an hour of homework each day on average. They were rarely absent from school, reportedly created few discipline problems, and were characterized by teachers as "highly motivated, hard working, and coming from households where the parents seemed to value education" (Gibson 1987: 267). Punjabi parents pressured their children against too much contact with non-Punjabi peers, which would "dishonor" their families and community, and defined "becoming Americanized" as "forgetting one's roots and adopting the most disparaged traits of the majority group"—including dancing, dating, leaving home at age eighteen to live independently, and making decisions without parental consent. Their frame of reference was not the Anglo majority group but rather members of their own ethnic group here and in India, and from this comparative point of view the Punjabi immigrants expressed considerable psychological satisfaction with their situation overall. At the same time, the parents urged their children to abide by school rules and to learn useful skills from their teachers, to ignore racist remarks and avoid fights, to look up to successful American adult role models, and to become proficient in English and in the ways of the dominant culture in order to help them deal with the host society—provided that they *also* maintained strong roots within the Indian community. Gibson (1987, 1989) referred to this additive bicultural strategy as "accommodation without assimilation"— a process again reminiscent of the findings of the Southeast Asian case study reported above.

Immigrant and U.S.-Born Mexican-Descent Students at "Field High" in Central California

The Mexico-origin population constitutes by far the largest ethnic minority in California schools, and throughout the twentieth century Mexican immigrants have constituted by far the largest segment of both documented and undocumented immigration to the state. Indeed, Mexican immigration to California has accelerated since the end of the

Bracero program in 1964. However, official data on the educational
performance of Mexican immigrant children are unavailable from school
districts. As noted previously, the "Hispanic" ethnic category used by
the schools lumps all Spanish-speaking students together irrespective
of nativity or country of origin. Also, the presence of a sizable component of U.S.-born children who speak Spanish at home makes it impossible to rely on FEP or LEP classifications as proxies of immigrant status.

However, a comparative study does address the educational performance of Mexican-descent students enrolled at "Field High School" in a
small coastal community in central California (Matute-Bianchi 1986,
1991). The economy of this community (in the Santa Cruz area) has long
been tied to agricultural production and to immigrant farm labor, and
the region has experienced a succession of waves of immigrants over the
years, especially from Mexico. This is reflected in the changing ethnic
distribution of students enrolled at Field High: in 1971, 60 percent of the
total enrollment of 2,507 students were white Anglos and 34 percent
were Spanish-surname students, but by 1984 only 33 percent of the
2,377 students were Anglos while the proportion of Spanish-surname
enrollments had jumped to 57 percent. The Asian student population
(primarily of Japanese and Filipino ancestry) had remained relatively
small, increasing from 5 percent to 10 percent over the same period.

The class of 1985 was selected for analysis in this study. The class
entered Field High as ninth graders in September 1981 (N = 643 students). A first indicator of school performance among these students
concerned their dropout rates. Data maintained by the school showed
that among white Anglo students, 40 percent failed to graduate with
their class in 1985. By comparison, among Japanese Americans, only 13
percent dropped out; while of the Spanish-surname students, 51 percent did not graduate with their class. Significantly, however, only 35
percent of the Spanish-surname students who had been classified as
LEP (primarily immigrants) failed to graduate, whereas the majority of
the Spanish-surname students who had been identified as U.S.-born
had dropped out by 1985. This finding has been supported by another
study in a different community, which found that Mexican-born immigrant students were less likely to drop out from high school than U.S.-
born students of Mexican descent (Valverde 1987).

Intensive ethnographic fieldwork identified five general categories
of ethnic identity into which most Mexican-descent students could be
placed (Matute-Bianchi 1986: 236–41; 1991).

• *Recent Mexican immigrant students.* These are Mexican-born, Spanish-
  speaking students who are most frequently classified by the school as
  LEP and placed in ESL classes, and who are also identified by other
  Mexican-descent students as well as teachers and staff as dressing
  differently from the rest of the student body. In interviews these

students claimed an identity of "Mexicano," and they consider Mexico their permanent home. Students within this group include "legals" versus "illegals" and permanent settlers versus those who migrate seasonally back to Mexico, and they generally make various other distinctions among themselves that are of significance in Mexico, such as their rural versus urban origins and their "mestizo" versus "indio" ethnicity. These students differ significantly in their level of proficiency *in Spanish*, and the most academically successful are those who are most proficient in both oral and written Spanish (reflecting their class origins and level of previous education in Mexico). Almost all of them, however, are described by teachers and staff as more courteous, more serious about their schoolwork, more respectful and eager to please, more industrious and well behaved, as well as more naive and unsophisticated than all other students at Field High.

- *Mexican-oriented students.* These are most often bilingual students with varying degrees of proficiency in English, though they speak Spanish at home and are typically classified by the school as FEP. They have strong bicultural ties with both Mexico and the United States, reflecting the fact that most of them were born in Mexico but have lived in the United States for more than five years. They claim an ethnic identity as "Mexicano" and are very proud of their Mexican heritage, even as they see themselves as different from the Mexican *"recién llegados"* and from the "Mexican-Americans," "Chicanos," and "Cholos." The latter two in particular they see in derogatory terms as people who have "lost" their Mexican culture, while they view "Mexican-Americans" as "arrogant." The students in this group tend to be active in soccer and especially in the Sociedad Bilingüe club, the most visible Mexican-oriented organization on campus, which is involved throughout the year in fundraising events for college scholarships and cultural events such as school dances and the Cinco de Mayo "Semana de la Raza" celebrations in May. Although not all of them are academically successful, most are. Indeed, virtually all of the Mexican-descent students who graduated in the top 10 percent of their class in 1985 were identified by teachers and other students as members of this group.

- *Mexican-American students.* These are native-born students of Mexican parentage who identify themselves as such (or as "Americans of Mexican descent"). They are much more American-oriented than the two types described above, and they clearly distinguish themselves from the "Mexicanos." They often do not speak Spanish well (even when they do, they prefer to speak English in school), and they are frequently described by school personnel as "totally assimilated." At the same time they consider the term "Chicano" offensive and synonymous with "Cholo" and "Low Rider." Some of the most active and academically successful students at Field High are in this group. They participate more than any of the other Mexican-descent groups in mainstream school clubs and in student government (along with the Anglos and Japanese); yet, significantly, few of them get involved in either the Mexican-oriented club (the Sociedad Bilingüe) or in the Chicano-oriented MATA (Mexican-Americans Taking Action) club.

- *Chicanos.* According to Matute-Bianchi, this group is the largest segment of Mexican-descent students at Field High, with perhaps as many as 40 to 50 percent of the Spanish-surname enrollment. They do not find the term "Chicano" offensive, though many of them will also identify themselves as "Mexicano." Instead, they refer derisively to academically successful Mexican-descent students (those who are seen carrying books around the campus, who attend classes regularly and obey school rules) as "schoolboys" and "schoolgirls," and they refer to the more assimilated Mexican-American students as "Wannabees" ("wanting to be" white or Anglo). They reflect an *oppositional* orientation to what they perceive to be mainstream norms and values, and they behave in self-fulfilling ways that promote failure (frequent absences from or disruptive behavior in classes, failure to bring their books or to do their homework when they do attend). These students are most distinguished from the above three groups by their level of alienation from the school. They are much more concerned with "loyalty" to the Chicano group than with school programs or activities, with the exception of their activities in the MATA association. In practice, according to Matute-Bianchi, "to be a Chicano" meant: "to hang out by the science wing . . . *not* eating lunch in the quad where all the *gringos*, 'white folks,' and schoolboys hang out . . . cutting classes by faking a call slip so you can be with your friends at the 7–11 . . . sitting in the back of a class of '*gabachos*' and *not* participating . . . *not* carrying your books to class or doing your homework . . . *not* taking the difficult classes . . . doing the minimum to get by" (1986: 253). In a follow-up paper, Matute-Bianchi (1991) has suggested that recruitment into a Chicano identity begins in elementary school and is confirmed and reinforced by the time the student reaches junior high, when similarly minded peer groups begin to assume much greater influence.

- *Cholos.* This was by far the smallest of the five Mexican-descent groups identified by the study—but also the most easily identifiable by deliberate manner of dress, walk, speech, and other highly visible stylistic cultural symbols. These students were frequently identified by others as gang members or gang sympathizers (though not all students who manifested the sartorial Cholo symbols were gang members) and as "Low Riders." Like the Chicanos, the Cholos too are held in low esteem both by the other Mexican-descent students and by mainstream students. They are marginalized from and disaffected with the school community, do poorly academically, and tend not to be involved in any school activities. Teachers generally perceived the Chicanos and Cholos as more "irresponsible," "disrespectful," "mistrusting," "sullen," "smart-mouthed," "street tough," "apathetic," and "less motivated" than their ethnic counterparts; and they explained their poor school performance as the inevitable result of such attitudes and behaviors (or "secondary cultural differences"). By contrast, teachers explained the poor performance of other Mexican-descent students as based on their difficulties with English or the relative lack of skills and school savvy among those who come from peasant backgrounds in Mexico—in short, on the basis of "primary cultural differences."[8]

Matute-Bianchi interviewed a group of thirty-five "successful" and "unsuccessful" Mexican-descent students over a two-year period to ascertain their educational and occupational aspirations and perceptions of the future. In general, the successful students tended to see a definite connection between their high school education and their adult futures. They expressed an interest in going to college and looked upon adults at Field High as role models of success. "Success" was often defined as "being someone" and having "a nice car, a nice house, a nice job, and enough money that you don't have to worry about it anymore" (1986: 242–43). Many of them were born in Mexico and received their earliest schooling there. They immigrated to the United States voluntarily in search of economic opportunities, and their frame of reference was "back home." Their parents typically showed strong interest in and support for their schoolwork. One junior was quoted as saying: "My mother keeps telling me, 'Ay, mi hija, tienes que sacar buenas calificaciones en la high school para que no te estés chingando igual que yo' [My daughter, you need to get good grades in high school so that you don't have to struggle like I've had to]. And you know, she has a point. I don't want to be doing that. I've been in the cannery before. . . . I've got to do well in school so that I don't have to face this in my future." Among these successful students were primarily Mexican-immigrant and Mexican-oriented students who saw no affective dissonance or contradiction between maintaining an identity as Mexicanos even as they adapted to the American context, which they saw as a prerequisite to getting ahead—recalling the notion of an additive "accommodation without assimilation" among the Punjabis and the Indochinese (see also chapters 4 and 7, this volume).

By contrast, unsuccessful students reportedly lacked positive adult role models, defined success in terms of "working the system," said they came to school mainly to see their buddies, and generally had no clearly

---

[8]For the distinction between "primary" and "secondary" cultural differences as distinguishing features of "immigrant" versus "caste-like" minorities, see also Ogbu 1987; Gibson and Ogbu 1991.

articulated sense of their adult futures. Others focused fatalistically on enduring, external barriers to opportunities: "Mexicans don't have a chance to go on to college and make something of themselves. . . . People like us face a lot of prejudice because there are a lot of people who don't like Mexicans. . . . Some people, no matter how hard they try, just have bad luck" (Matute-Bianchi 1986: 252–53). Most of these students were identified as nonimmigrant Chicanos or Cholos who faced what they perceived as an either–or, subtractive, "forced-choice dilemma" between doing well in school *or* being a Chicano. To "act white" was to be disloyal to the group. Additive accommodation was not seen as an option for the maintenance of collective identity. To the contrary, the construction of this ethnic identity, forged through a "reactive process" and "intensive intragroup reliance . . . as a disadvantaged, disparaged minority group," is interpreted by Matute-Bianchi as a multigenerational product of "historical and structural forces of exclusion and subordination by the dominant group, as well as the vehicle of resistance that the group has made to structured inequality" (1986: 255). Similar observations about the development and maintenance of such an "oppositional identity" have also been made regarding black American high school students (see Fordham and Ogbu 1987).

Central American Refugee Students in Inner-City Schools in the Bay Area

Although Mexican immigration to California has a long history, mass immigration from Central American countries (primarily from El Salvador and Guatemala, with a much smaller number from Nicaragua) is just over a decade old. In that short span of time, hundreds of thousands of Central Americans crossed into California. While they generally share with Southeast Asian refugees many of the psychosocial characteristics of political refugees from war-torn contexts, they also often share with many Mexican immigrants an undocumented status—because the U.S. government deemed them "economic migrants" and has largely refused to grant them political asylum. The recency of their arrival and the clandestine status of a substantial proportion may explain in part the paucity of information about the educational adjustment of young Central Americans in California schools. The leading case study remains a psychosocially oriented investigation carried out in two inner-city high schools in the San Francisco Bay area and recently reported by Marcelo Suárez-Orozco (1987, 1989).

The student body of each school was 90 percent minority, and almost 50 percent of the students were immigrants from Asia or Latin America. Roughly a third of the enrollments were Spanish-speaking students; another third consisted of Filipinos, Chinese, or other Asians; and close to a quarter were blacks. In the two schools there were about six hundred Central American youths who had entered the United States within the five years preceding the start of the research. Of these, some forty students (mostly Nicaraguans) from upper-status family backgrounds were eliminated from the study. From the remainder, a convenience sample of fifty cases was selected for daily contacts, classroom observations, and intensive interviews with the students and their families over the course of a year. The student sample included thirty males and twenty females between fourteen and nineteen years of age; thirty-three were from El Salvador, nine from Guatemala, and eight from Nicaragua. Over four hundred TAT (Thematic Apperception Test) stories were also collected from this sample, scored, and analyzed toward the end of the fieldwork.

The learning environment of these recent arrivals from Central America consisted of "overcrowded, understaffed classes in overcrowded, understaffed, poor inner-city schools . . . a school atmosphere of drugs, violence, low expectations, bitter teachers [who were often very afraid of their students], the seductive offers by more acculturated peers to join the street culture . . . and the need to work to help the family" (Suárez-Orozco 1987: 290). Two-thirds of the sample worked fifteen to thirty hours a week while attending high school full time— work schedules that sometimes affected their school obligations—and shared their salaries with relatives in the United States or in Central America. In addition, as undocumented immigrants, many of the students faced a "legal ceiling" in their post-graduation prospects, especially the *ilegales* who intended to go on to college but were shocked and depressed when they found that (at the time) colleges and universities required them to have legal residency to enroll. Despite all of these problems, the Central American students managed to learn English at a rapid rate—fast enough, in fact, that teachers privately reported to the researcher that the counselors were deliberately keeping the students in lower-level ESL classes longer than required because of lack of space in the regular classrooms. Most of them remained in school; half of the sample made it to the honor roll in high school; and, upon graduation, five of the fifty students were accepted into major American universities. The Central Americans received fewer school suspensions than either Anglo or native-born minority students and, confirming an observation that is consistently repeated in California schools, teachers generally considered them more "respectful" and "nicer to have around." Two experienced bilingual teachers confided at one point that "they could never go back to teaching 'American [minority] students' because their immigrant students [mostly Central Americans and Asians] were so eager to learn, so appreciative, and, above all, so polite that they could not face regular unruly classes in the rough inner-city high school" (Suárez-Orozco 1987: 289). To be sure, however, some of the Central American students—particularly the 14-to-16-year-old recent arrivals—developed specific problems in response to the culture of terror from which they had escaped and the systematic school hostilities they experienced in the new setting. Under the circumstances, the more challenging question that is raised by these outcomes is why these students remained in school at all.

At one level, Suárez-Orozco attributes part of this favorable and highly motivated school performance more to parental expectations than to parental education. Only 6 percent of the mothers and 8 percent of the fathers had completed college. Of the mothers, 57 percent had not completed an elementary education and 78 percent had not completed a secondary education; of the fathers, 39 percent had not completed an elementary education and 55 percent had not completed high school. But the parents often emphasized that a primary factor in their decision to flee their homeland was the welfare of the children (often in terms nearly identical to the statements of Indochinese parents in the San Diego study above). One Nicaraguan mother with five children—who left her native country because she feared that her sixteen-year-old son would be drafted to fight the Contras on the Honduran border—put it this way: "We came here for them . . . so that they may become somebody tomorrow. . . . I am too old, at my age it is too late for me . . . if anything, it is harder for me here than there [Nicaragua]" (Suárez-Orozco 1987: 290). The parents' expectations were defined in the context of a dual frame of reference comparing present opportunities in the United States with past realities of fear and economic scarcity. Their idealized belief in education and individual effort as a key to status mobility in the United States was contrasted with the perceived need to make it in the country of origin through networks of friends, nepotism, or family. As one Salvadoran saw it, "Here [in the United States] is *what* you know, there [El Salvador] is *who* you know" (p. 291). At the same time, life in the inner city offered most of the new arrivals a "crash course in reality" (p. 89). In accommodating to the pace of life in the inner city, an "additive" adaptive strategy was favored (much as in the previous cases considered above): learning the language of the host society and acquiring its requisite behaviors and symbols for "success" without giving up the essence of their shared cultural code (p. 92).

Their children, in turn, were often keenly aware of the degree of parental sacrifice involved in getting out of the country of origin. They saw what their parents endured in the United States so that they could go to school to receive the kind of education that their parents never had. Perceptions of parental sacrifice, in fact, emerged as a key interpersonal concern among the young immigrants' responses to the TAT, which were in turn connected to their strong motivation to achieve—and in this respect they differed significantly from the responses of Anglo, Japanese, or Korean immigrant samples to the same TAT cards (Suárez-Orozco 1989: 85). That is, the Central American students showed a salient sense of duty to their parents and family members for their hardships, and a strong wish to achieve, to do well in school, in order to repay them by "becoming somebody." Achievement motivation for them did not follow the pattern found among more individualistic Anglo Americans but was actually related to "a wish for affiliation and mutual nurturance." That is, the most motivated and successful of the new refugee students from Central America were not individualists seeking independence and self-advancement, but rather were motivated by underlying feelings of guilt (something akin to "survivor guilt") and by the dream of helping those who had sacrificed on their behalf (1989: 143–54). These findings of a unique motivational pattern undercut the often-made assimilationist argument that "Hispanic" students fail to achieve in school because they overemphasize family ties, honor, and "interdependence," values that putatively hinder mobility, while they neglect those that are conducive to "independence." For that matter, these findings undercut the myth of "Hispanic" homogeneity that is implied in such formulations. What they underscore is the need to understand the complex diversity of immigrant student adaptations in the larger social context (including the school context) within which they are situated, invented, tested, negotiated, and accomplished.

Conclusion

The studies reviewed above focused on recently arrived immigrant and refugee groups of widely different sociocultural origins. Despite their relatively modest social class backgrounds, a climate of pervasive prejudice, and initial obstacles in adapting to their new school environments in California, the evidence suggests that most of these children are making a rapid and positive adjustment—and in many instances they are outperforming even native-born majority-group high school students in such basic indicators as grades and graduation rates. These data offer a challenge to conventional theories of educational attainment among ethnic minority groups, particularly those explanations that have attributed the relatively poor school performance of native-born minorities to "cultural deficits," "cultural deprivation," a "culture of poverty," "cultural discontinuity," and "cultural and language differences," and those that, on what is but the other side of the same argument, see educational achievement and success as a function of "straight-line" assimilation processes.

Indeed, these findings add to a mounting body of evidence that suggests that some minority groups do well in school even though they do *not* share the language and culture of the dominant group which is built into the school system (for a review, see Ogbu 1974, 1987, 1991). In fact, some (though not all) of those who are doing exceptionally well in

American schools differ *more* from the dominant group in language and culture than those who are doing less well. Furthermore, other comparative evidence (Ogbu 1987: 316) suggests that a minority group that does poorly in school in its own country of origin or has an involuntary minority status (such as Koreans in Japan) appears to do much better when its members voluntarily immigrate to another country where its language and culture differ even more from those of the dominant group of the host society (such as Koreans in the United States). While suggestive on the face of it, such evidence does not necessarily prove the thesis; self-selection factors, for example, may account for some of the observed differences in the Korean case. Nevertheless, although nearly all immigrant children confront substantial social adjustment and academic learning problems initially, these problems seem to diminish over time for some but seem to persist and to become aggravated over time for others. Why this is so remains an unanswered question.

Among educational anthropologists who have focused on this question, the work of Ogbu and his associates has centered on a minority group's experience in the post-school opportunity structure and on how the members' varying perceptions of dismal future economic opportunities influence in turn their perceptions of and responses to schooling (cf. Gibson and Ogbu 1991). Variability in minority school performance is thus seen in part as a function of the history and structure of subordination of minority groups, especially those groups marked by an "involuntary" entry into the dominant society and their collective memory of a bitter history of racial oppression and blocked opportunities for social mobility—and in part too as a function of the nature of the minority groups' particular instrumental and expressive strategies of response to their situation, which can make them "more or less accomplices to their own school success or failure" (Ogbu 1987: 317). Ogbu thus proposes a dichotomy hinging on a minority group's original mode of entry into the society and argues that the responses of *"immigrant (voluntary) minorities"* differ significantly from those of *"caste-like (involuntary) minorities."* For the former, learning English and other aspects of the culture of the dominant group are seen—from the vantage point of a dual frame of reference—as barriers to be overcome in school through additive learning (at an instrumental level), but not necessarily as a threat to their own collective identity (at an affective or expressive level). Hence, accommodation without assimilation emerges as a feasible definition of the situation and strategy of response. For the latter, however, their responses are marked by an "oppositional" frame of reference which is conducive not to "additive" adaptations but to reactive or passive-aggressive forms of resistance to a school system that they may perceive as ultimately irrelevant to their future adult opportunities. Here there can be no accommodation without assimilation, as illustrated by the case of the Chicanos and Cholos summarized above.

Instead, a forced choice tends to be perceived between "acting white" *or* group loyalty, with self-fulfilling and counterproductive consequences (cf. Vigil 1988; Suárez-Orozco 1991; Hayes-Bautista 1993).

These are valuable and provocative ideas, although the "voluntary/ involuntary" dichotomy is perhaps too Procrustean, formulaic, and riddled with exceptions to do justice to the complexities and dynamics of diverse social contexts. The development of "oppositional" subcultures, in any case, need not hinge on a history of racial oppression and the formation of reactive ethnicities. In MacLeod's (1987) ethnography of leveled aspirations in a mostly white inner-city housing project, for instance, the typecast roles are reversed: it is a peer group of white youths, the Hallway Hangers, who repudiate the achievement ideology, validate an adversarial posture toward school, reject teachers (who are seen as irrelevant and at best a conduit for manual labor jobs), and "keep a lid on hope" to protect their self-esteem. Their pervasive cynicism reflects family histories dominated by failure (some had been on public assistance in the projects for three generations). As white youths they could point to no extenuating circumstances to explain their poverty; and their oppositional subculture was in part a reaction to the stigma they felt as poor whites. Also, the peer group itself attracted those with low aspirations who rejected school, and then deepened and shaped those proclivities to fit the group. By contrast, the Brothers, a group of black teens, developed an entirely different definition of the situation. They accepted and validated as a peer group an outlook that connected hard work to future payoffs, could point to racial discrimination in the past as a way of explaining their families' poverty, and felt themselves part of an upward social trajectory. In addition, their outlook was also a reaction against the Hallway Hangers' penchant for drugs, alcohol, and an adversarial stance toward school ("as long as I don't end up like that"). The (black) Brothers had been taunted and abused by a group of disaffected white boys, so in reaction they dissociated themselves completely from the Hangers and pursued a distinctly different path. Unlike the case of the Hangers, moreover, the Brothers' parents still exercised a good deal of authority over them, and their older siblings could serve as positive role models. Interestingly, although MacLeod glosses over this point, it turns out that the Brothers were mostly children of recent immigrants from Haiti, the Dominican Republic, and the West Indies, as well as of African Americans who migrated up from the South.

For new immigrants in California—and in American schools generally—the findings reviewed above point to a positive association between school performance and a resilient affirmation of collective ethnic identity. But as the case study of native-born Chicanos (and African Americans) also suggests, a mere affirmation of ethnic solidarity cannot by itself explain positive or negative educational outcomes. The issue has to do instead with the specific nature, content, and style of the minority groups' perceptions and adaptive responses to their specific social and historical contexts. Thus, such a focus needs to take into account human agency itself, viewing students—minority and majority, immigrant and nonimmigrant alike—as active subjects who are participants in their own development and not merely passive objects of impersonal circumstances.

References

California State Department of Education. 1993. "Language Census Report for California Public Schools, 1993." Sacramento: Educational Demographics Unit, Program Evaluation and Research Division, California Department of Education.

Caplan, Nathan, Marcella H. Choy, and John K. Whitmore. 1991. *Children of the Boat People: A Study of Educational Success*. Ann Arbor: University of Michigan Press.

Fernández-Kelly, M. Patricia, and Richard Schauffler. 1994. "Divided Fates: Immigrant Children in a Restructured U.S. Economy," *International Migration Review* 28 (4): 662–89.

Fordham, Signithia, and John U. Ogbu. 1987. "Black Students' School Success: Coping with the Burden of 'Acting White'," *Urban Review* 18 (3): 176–206.

Gans, Herbert J. 1992. "Second-Generation Decline: Scenarios for the Economic and Ethnic Futures of the Post-1965 American Immigrants," *Ethnic and Racial Studies* 15 (2): 173–92.

Gibson, Margaret A. 1987. "The School Performance of Immigrant Minorities: A Comparative View," *Anthropology and Education Quarterly* 18 (4): 262–75.

———. 1989. *Accommodation without Assimilation: Sikh Immigrants in an American High School*. Ithaca, N.Y.: Cornell University Press.

Gibson, Margaret A., and John U. Ogbu, eds. 1991. *Minority Status and Schooling: A Comparative Study of Immigrant and Involuntary Minorities*. New York: Garland.

Hakuta, Kenji, and Eugene E. García. 1989. "Bilingualism and Education," *American Psychologist* 44 (2): 374–79.

Hayes-Bautista, David E. 1993. "Mexicans in Southern California: Societal Enrichment or Wasted Opportunity?" In *The California-Mexico Connection*, edited by A.F. Lowenthal and K. Burgess. Stanford, Calif.: Stanford University Press.

Ima, Kenji, and Rubén G. Rumbaut. 1989. "Southeast Asian Refugees in American Schools: A Comparison of Fluent English Proficient (FEP) and Limited English Proficient (LEP) Students," *Topics in Language Disorders* 9 (3): 54–77.

Jensen, Leif, and Yoshimi Chitose. 1994. "Today's Second Generation: Evidence from the 1990 U.S. Census," *International Migration Review* 28 (4): 714–35.

Kao, Grace, and Marta Tienda. 1995. "Optimism and Achievement: The Educational Performance of Immigrant Youth," *Social Science Quarterly* 76 (1): 1–19.

Landale, Nancy S., and R.S. Oropesa. 1995. "Immigrant Children and the Children of Immigrants: Inter- and Intra-Ethnic Group Differences in the

United States." Population Research Group (PRG) Research Paper 95-2. East Lansing: Institute for Public Policy and Social Research, Michigan State University.

MacLeod, Jay. 1987. *Ain't No Making It: Leveled Aspirations in a Low-Income Neighborhood*. Boulder, Colo.: Westview.

Matute-Bianchi, Maria Eugenia. 1986. "Ethnic Identities and Patterns of School Success and Failure among Mexican-Descent and Japanese-American Students in a California High School: An Ethnographic Analysis," *American Journal of Education* 95 (1): 233–55.

———. 1991. "Situational Ethnicity and Patterns of School Performance among Immigrant and Nonimmigrant Mexican-Descent Students." In *Minority Status and Schooling: A Comparative Study of Immigrant and Involuntary Minorities*, edited by Margaret A. Gibson and John U. Ogbu. New York: Garland.

McNall, Miles, Timothy Dunnigan, and Jeylan T. Mortimer. 1994. "The Educational Achievement of the St. Paul Hmong," *Anthropology and Education Quarterly* 25 (1): 44–65.

Ogbu, John U. 1974. *The Next Generation: An Ethnography of Education in an Urban Neighborhood*. New York: Academic Press.

———. 1987. "Variability in Minority School Performance: A Problem in Search of an Explanation," *Anthropology and Education Quarterly* 18 (4): 312–34.

———. 1991. "Immigrant and Involuntary Minorities in Comparative Perspective." In *Minority Status and Schooling: A Comparative Study of Immigrant and Involuntary Minorities*, edited by Margaret A. Gibson and John U. Ogbu. New York: Garland.

Olsen, Laurie. 1988. *Crossing the Schoolhouse Border: Immigrant Students and the California Public Schools*. San Francisco: California Tomorrow.

Pérez Firmat, Gustavo. 1994. *Life on the Hyphen: The Cuban-American Way*. Austin: University of Texas Press.

Portes, Alejandro. 1994. "Introduction: Immigration and Its Aftermath," *International Migration Review* 28 (4). Special issue on "The New Second Generation," edited by Alejandro Portes.

———. 1995. "Children of Immigrants: Segmented Assimilation and Its Determinants." In *The Economic Sociology of Immigration: Essays on Networks, Ethnicity, and Entrepreneurship*, edited by Alejandro Portes. New York: Russell Sage Foundation.

Portes, Alejandro, and Rubén G. Rumbaut. 1990. *Immigrant America: A Portrait*. Berkeley: University of California Press.

Rumbaut, Rubén G. 1989. "Portraits, Patterns and Predictors of the Refugee Adaptation Process." In *Refugees as Immigrants: Vietnamese, Cambodians and Laotians in America*, edited by David W. Haines. Totowa, N.J.: Rowman and Littlefield.

———. 1990. *Immigrant Students in California Public Schools: A Summary of Current Knowledge*. CDS Report No. 11. Baltimore, Md.: Center for Research on Effective Schooling for Disadvantaged Students, Johns Hopkins University.

———. 1991a. "Passages to America: Perspectives on the New Immigration." In *America at Century's End*, edited by Alan Wolfe. Berkeley: University of California Press.

———. 1991b. "The Agony of Exile: A Study of Indochinese Refugee Adults and Children." In *Refugee Children: Theory, Research, and Services*, edited by

Frederick L. Ahearn, Jr. and Jean L. Athey. Baltimore, Md.: Johns Hopkins University Press.

———. 1994a. "Origins and Destinies: Immigration to the United States since World War II," *Sociological Forum* 9 (4): 583–621.

———. 1994b. "The Crucible Within: Ethnic Identity, Self-Esteem, and Segmented Assimilation among Children of Immigrants," *International Migration Review* 28 (4): 748–94.

———. 1995. "Vietnamese, Laotian, and Cambodian Americans." In *Asian Americans: Contemporary Trends and Issues,* edited by Pyong Gap Min. Thousand Oaks, Calif.: Sage.

Rumbaut, Rubén G., and Kenji Ima. 1988. *The Adaptation of Southeast Asian Refugee Youth: A Comparative Study.* Washington, D.C.: U.S. Office of Refugee Resettlement.

Smollar, David. 1992. "Ratio of Whites Hits City Schools Low," *Los Angeles Times,* December 1.

Stanton-Salazar, Ricardo D., and Sanford M. Dornbusch. 1995. "Social Capital and the Reproduction of Inequality: Information Networks among Mexican-Origin High School Students," *Sociology of Education* 68 (April): 116–35.

Steinberg, Laurence, Nancy E. Darling, Anne C. Fletcher, B. Bradford Brown, and Sanford M. Dornbusch. n.d. "Authoritative Parenting and Adolescent Adjustment: An Ecological Journey." In *Linking Lives and Contexts: Perspectives on the Ecology of Human Development,* edited by P. Moen, G. Elder, Jr., and K. Luscher. Washington, D.C.: American Psychological Association. Forthcoming.

Suárez-Orozco, Marcelo M. 1987. "'Becoming Somebody': Central American Immigrants in U.S. Inner-City Schools," *Anthropology and Education Quarterly* 18 (4): 287–99.

———. 1989. *Central American Refugees and U.S. High Schools: A Psychosocial Study of Motivation and Achievement.* Stanford, Calif.: Stanford University Press.

———. 1991. "Immigrant Adaptation to Schooling: A Hispanic Case." In *Minority Status and Schooling: A Comparative Study of Immigrant and Involuntary Minorities,* edited by Margaret A. Gibson and John U. Ogbu. New York: Garland.

Suro, Roberto. 1994. *Remembering the American Dream: Hispanic Immigration and National Policy.* New York: The Twentieth Century Fund.

U. S. General Accounting Office. 1994a. *Limited English Proficiency: A Growing and Costly Educational Challenge Facing Many School Districts.* GAO/HEHS-94-38. Washington, D.C.: USGAO.

———. 1994b. *Hispanics' Schooling: Risk Factors for Dropping Out and Barriers to Resuming Education.* GAO/PEMD-94-24. Washington, D.C.: USGAO.

U. S. Immigration [Dillingham] Commission. 1911. *The Children of Immigrants in Schools.* Vols. 29–33. Washington, D.C.: U.S. Government Printing Office.

Valverde, Sylvia A. 1987. "A Comparative Study of Hispanic High School Dropouts and Graduates: Why Do Some Leave School Early and Some Finish?" *Education and Urban Society* 19 (3): 320–29.

Vigil, James Diego. 1988. *Barrio Gangs: Street Life and Identity in Southern California.* Austin: University of Texas Press.

APPENDIX
COMPOSITION AND RELIABILITY OF SCALES

Scale and Scoring	Cronbach's Alpha	Items and Measures
English Proficiency Index (4 items: scored 1 to 4)	.92	How well do you (speak, understand, read, write) English? 1 = Not at all, 2 = Not well, 3 = Well, 4 = Very Well
Foreign Language Index (4 items: scored 1 to 4)	.93	How well do you (speak, understand, read, write) [foreign language]? 1 = Not at all, 2 = Not well, 3 = Well, 4 = Very Well
Educational Aspirations (2 items: scored 1 to 5)	.80	What is highest level of education you would like to achieve? And *realistically* speaking, what is the highest level of education that you think you will get? 1 = Less than high school, 2 = High school, 3 = Some college, 4 = Finish college, 5 = Finish a graduate degree
Rosenberg Self-Esteem (10 items: scored 1 to 4)	.81	I feel I am a person of worth, at least on an equal basis with others. I feel I have a number of good qualities. I am able to do things as well as most other people. I take a positive attitude toward myself. On the whole, I am satisfied with myself. All in all, I am inclined to think I am a failure *[reverse score]*. I feel I do not have much to be proud of *[reverse score]*. I wish I could have more respect for myself *[reverse score]*. I certainly feel useless at times *[reverse score]*. At times I think I am no good at all *[reverse score]*. 1 = Disagree a lot, 2 = Disagree, 3 = Agree, 4 = Agree a lot

Standardized Math and Reading subtest scores are taken from the Abbreviated Stanford Achievement Test (ASAT) and are expressed as percentiles of national norms.

3

Segmented Assimilation among New Immigrant Youth: A Conceptual Framework

Alejandro Portes

Growing up in an immigrant family has always been difficult as individuals are torn by conflicting social and cultural demands while they face the challenge of entry into an unfamiliar and frequently hostile world. And yet the difficulties are not always the same. The process of "growing up American" oscillates between smooth acceptance and traumatic confrontation depending on the characteristics that immigrants and their children bring along and the social context that receives them. In what follows I explore some of these factors and their bearing on the process of social adaptation of the immigrant second generation, and I propose a conceptual framework for understanding this process.

Changing Contexts of Reception

The great deal of research and theorizing on post-1965 immigration offers only tentative guidance on the prospects and paths of adaptation of the second generation because the outlook of this group can be very different from that of their immigrant parents. For example, it is generally accepted among immigration theorists that entry-level menial jobs are performed without hesitation by newly arrived immigrants, but that they are commonly shunned by the U.S.-reared offspring. This disjuncture gives rise to a "race" between the social and economic progress of first-generation immigrants and the

This essay is excerpted from an article entitled "The New Second Generation: Segmented Assimilation and Its Variants," by Alejandro Portes and Min Zhou, published in the *Annals of the American Academy of Political and Social Science*, volume 530 (November 1993), pp. 74–96. Reprinted by permission of Sage Publications, Inc.

material conditions and career prospects that their American children grow to expect (Gans 1992).

Nor does the existing literature on second-generation adaptation, based as it is on the experience of descendants of pre-World War I immigrants, offer much guidance for the understanding of contemporary events. The last sociological study of children of immigrants was Irving Child's *Italian or American? The Second Generation in Conflict*, published fifty years ago (Child 1943). Conditions at the time were quite different from those confronting settled immigrant groups today. Two such differences deserve special mention. First, descendants of European immigrants who confronted the dilemmas of conflicting cultures were uniformly white. Even if of a somewhat darker hue than the natives, their skin color reduced a major barrier to entry into the American mainstream. For this reason, the process of assimilation depended largely on individual decisions to leave the immigrant culture behind and embrace American ways. Such an advantage obviously does not exist for the black, Asian, and mestizo children of today's immigrants.

Second, the structure of economic opportunities has also changed. Fifty years ago the United States was the premier industrial power in the world, and its diversified industrial labor requirements offered to the second generation the opportunity to move up gradually through better-paid occupations *while remaining part of the working class*. Such opportunities have increasingly disappeared in recent years following a rapid process of national deindustrialization and global industrial restructuring. This process has left entrants to the American labor force confronting a widening gap between the minimally paid menial jobs that immigrants commonly accept and the high-tech and professional occupations requiring college degrees that native elites occupy (see, for example, Sassen 1985). The gradual disappearance of intermediate opportunities also bears directly on the "race" between first-generation economic progress and second-generation expectations, noted above.

Segmented Assimilation: Vulnerabilities and Resources

An emerging paradox in the study of today's second generation is the peculiar form that assimilation has adopted for its members. The process has become segmented. That is, the question today is, *to what sector* of American society will a particular immigrant group assimilate? Instead of a relatively uniform "mainstream" whose mores and prejudices dictate a common path of integration, we observe today several distinct forms of adaptation. One of them replicates the time-honored portrayal of growing acculturation and parallel integration into the white middle class. A second leads straight in the opposite direction to permanent poverty and assimilation to the underclass. Still a third associates rapid economic advancement with deliberate preservation of the immigrant community's values and tight solidarity. This pattern of "segmented assimilation" immediately raises the question of what makes some immigrant groups become susceptible to the downward route and what resources allow others to avoid this course.

Along with individual and family variables, the context that immigrants find upon arrival plays a decisive role in the course that their offspring's lives will follow. To explain second-generation outcomes and their "segmented" character, however, we need to go in greater detail into the meaning of these various modes of incorporation from the standpoint of immigrant youths. There are three features of the social contexts encountered by today's newcomers that create vulnerability to downward assimilation. The first is color, the second is location, and the third is the absence of mobility ladders. The majority of contemporary immigrants are non-white. Although this feature many appear at first glance as an individual characteristic, in reality it is a trait belonging to the host society. Prejudice is not intrinsic to a particular skin color or racial type, and indeed many immigrants never experienced it in their native lands. It is by virtue of moving into a new social environment, marked by different values and prejudices, that physical features become redefined as handicaps.

The concentration of immigrant households in cities—and, in particular, central cities—gives rise to a second source of vulnerability because it puts new arrivals in close contact with concentrations of native-born minorities. This leads to the identification of the condition of both groups—immigrants and the native poor—as the same in the eyes of the majority. More importantly, it exposes second-generation children to the adversarial subculture developed by marginalized native youths to cope with their own difficult situation. This process of socialization may take place even when first-generation parents are moving ahead economically, and their children have no "objective" reasons for embracing a countercultural message. If successful, the process can effectively block parental plans for intergenerational mobility.

The third contextual source of vulnerability has to do with changes in the host economy that have led to the evaporation of occupational ladders for intergenerational mobility. As noted previously, new immigrants may form the backbone of what remains of labor-intensive manufacturing in the cities as well as in the growing personal services sector, but these are niches that seldom offer channels for upward mobility. The new "hourglass" economy created by economic restructuring means that children of immigrants must cross a narrow bottleneck to occupations requiring advanced training if their careers are to keep pace with the U.S.-acquired aspirations. This "race" against a narrowing middle demands that immigrant parents accumulate sufficient resources to allow their children to effect the passage and to simultaneously prove to them the viability of upward mobility aspirations. Otherwise, "assimilation" may not be to mainstream values and expectations, but to the adversarial stance of impoverished groups confined to the bottom of the new economic hourglass.

Different modes of incorporation also make available, however, three types of resources with which to confront the challenges of contemporary assimilation. First, certain groups, notably political refugees, are eligible for a variety of government programs, including educational loans for their children. The Cuban Loan Program, implemented by the Kennedy administration in connection with its plan to resettle Cuban refugees away from South Florida, gave many impoverished first- and second-generation Cuban youths a chance to attend college. The high proportion of professionals and executives among Cuban American workers today, a figure on par with that for native white workers, can be traced at least in part to the success of that program. Passage of the 1980 Refugee Act gave to subsequent groups of refugees—in particular, Southeast Asians and Eastern Europeans—access to a similarly generous benefits package.

Second, certain foreign groups have been exempted from the traditional prejudice endured by most immigrants, hence facilitating a smoother process of adaptation. Some political refugees—such as the early waves of exiles from Castro's Cuba, Hungarians and Czechs escaping the invasions of their respective countries, and Soviet Jews escaping religious persecution—provide examples. In other cases, it is the cultural and phenotypic affinity of newcomers to ample segments of the host population that ensures a welcome reception. The Irish coming to Boston during the 1980s provide a case in point. Although many were illegal aliens, they came into an environment where generations of Irish Americans had established a secure foothold. Public sympathy effectively neutralized governmental hostility in this case, culminating in a change of immigration law, to the direct benefit of the newcomers.

Third, and most important, are the resources made available through networks in the co-ethnic community. Immigrants who join well-established and diversified ethnic groups have access from the start to a range of moral and material resources well beyond those available through official assistance programs. Educational help for second-generation youths may include not only access to college grants and loans but also to a private school system geared to the immigrant community's values. Attending these private ethnic schools insulates children from contact with native minority youths while reinforcing the authority of parental views and plans. In addition, the economic diversification of several immigrant communities creates niches of opportunity that members of the second generation can occupy, often without need for an advanced education. Such community-mediated opportunities provide a solution to the "race" between material resources and second-generation aspirations not available through competition in the open labor market. Through creation of a capitalism of their own, some immigrant groups have thus been able to circumvent outside discrimination and the threat of vanishing mobility ladders.

In contrast to these favorable conditions are those foreign minorities who either lack a community already in place or whose co-ethnics are too poor to render assistance. The condition of Haitians in South Florida provides an illustration of one of the most handicapped modes of incorporation encountered by contemporary immigrants—combining official hostility and widespread social prejudice with the absence of a strong receiving community. From the standpoint of second-generation outcomes, the existence of a large but downtrodden co-ethnic community may be even less desirable than no community at all. This is because newly arrived youths enter into ready contact with the reactive subculture developed by earlier generations. Its influence is all the more powerful because it comes from individuals of the same national origin, "people like us," who can more effectively define the proper stance and attitudes of the newcomers. To the extent that they do so, the first-generation model of upward mobility through school achievement and attainment of professional occupations will be blocked.

Conclusion

Fifty years ago, the dilemma of Italian American youngsters studied by Child consisted of assimilating to the American mainstream (in the process, sacrificing their parents' cultural heritage) versus taking refuge in the ethnic community from the challenges of the outside world. In the contemporary context of segmented assimilation, the options have become less clear. Children of nonwhite immigrants may not even have the opportunity to gain access to middle-class white society, no matter how acculturated they become. Joining those native circles to which they do have access may prove a ticket to permanent subordination and disadvantage. Remaining securely ensconced in their co-ethnic community may, under these circumstances, not be a symptom of escapism but the best strategy for capitalizing on otherwise unavailable material and moral resources. A strategy of paced, selective assimilation may prove the best course for immigrant minorities. But the extent to which this strategy is possible also depends on the history of each group and its specific profile of vulnerabilities and resources.

References

Child, Irving L. 1943. *Italian or American? The Second Generation in Conflict*. New Haven, Conn.: Yale University Press.

Gans, Herbert, 1992. "Second-generation Decline: Scenarios for the Economic and Ethnic Futures of the Post-1965 American Immigrants," *Ethnic and Racial Studies* 15 (April): 173–92.

Sassen, Saskia. 1985. "Changing Composition and Labor Market Location of Hispanic Immigrants in New York City, 1960–1980." In *Hispanics in the U.S. Economy*, edited by George J. Borjas and Marta Tienda. New York: Academic Press.

4

Additive Acculturation as a Strategy for School Improvement

Margaret A. Gibson

Introduction

Of this nation's forty-one million schoolchildren, one in eight attends school in California. One-third of all California students today speak a language other than English at home. One-fifth have been identified as limited-English-proficient (LEP), an increase of 65 percent in the number of LEP students in the last five years. While three-quarters of all LEP children in California speak Spanish at home, the large majority of them from Mexico, the total population of new immigrants comes from 125 different countries.

The pace of immigration will continue through this decade and into the next century. During the 1990s a projected 80 percent of California's population gain will result from foreign immigration (*San Francisco Chronicle*, October 2, 1990). All California schools are feeling the impact of the changing demography and are searching for strategies that respond to their increasingly diverse clientele.

This chapter discusses findings from recent ethnographic research on immigrants and education, including my own work with Asian Indians in California (Gibson 1988) and with West Indians in St. Croix, U.S. Virgin Islands (Gibson 1976a, 1991a). I look first at several key factors that appear to influence the school performance of immigrant children. Second, I describe what may be termed an immigrant orientation to schooling and the immigrant strategy of accommodation and acculturation without assimilation. Third, I present some preliminary findings from my current research project, "Accommodating Diversity: Teachers' Perspectives on Meeting the Needs of Language Minority Students." The final section of the paper addresses issues of educational policy.

Factors Influencing School Performance

Age on arrival, length of residence in the United States, and grade of entry into U.S. schools are all variables that must be carefully considered when sorting out the variability in academic performance among immigrant pupils (see Gibson 1988: 192; Rumbaut 1990: 21). So, too, are family background in the country of origin, including parents' educational and economic status, prior exposure to Western and urban lifestyles, and languages spoken in the family, all of which contribute to the cultural and social capital that newcomers bring with them to this country. Another important variable is the type of schooling that was available to the immigrant child prior to emigration. Some young people arrive during their teenage years illiterate in any language, while others have attended schools in their homelands that are academically equal to if not better than those available to them in the United States. Although most newcomers need special help in learning to read, write, and speak English, others have already studied English in school and can fit directly into mainstream classes. Some immigrants have a wide network of family support available to them on their arrival; others are totally on their own. Some have had prior exposure to Western and urban lifestyles; others have not. These and many other factors interact in ways that contribute to the wide variability in immigrant children's school performance (Gibson 1991b, 1992, 1993b).

There is considerable evidence in this country and abroad to suggest that children who arrive in the new country by age six or seven do better academically during high school than older arrivals (Gibson 1988: 192). There are exceptions, of course, but in general the older arrivals are at greater risk of dropping out or of being promoted year by year without ever obtaining the required skills in academic English (or some other language) to do well academically at the secondary and postsecondary levels.

The point I wish to focus on, however, is not the special needs of the newer arrivals,[1] nor the contrast between their school performance patterns and those of immigrant-origin children raised from early childhood in the United States. Nor is it my intention to focus on differences between the school persistence and performance levels of various minority groups (e.g., Asian, non-Asian; immigrant, nonimmigrant; Cuban, Mexican) that exist in the aggregate, because such a discussion can all too easily lead to inappropriate and harmful stereotypes. Rather, I wish to explore how it is that large numbers of immigrant children are able to transcend the oftentimes very substantial cultural, linguistic, social, and economic barriers that stand in the way of their success in school. I wish to focus on this because I believe the insights

---

[1]See Gibson 1988 for a discussion of within-school barriers encountered by first-generation immigrants.

gained have important implications for improving educational opportunities for all children.

Kenji Ima (this volume) notes that the research questions we ask influence the data we gather and, in turn, the usefulness of our findings for informing educational policy and improving educational programs. More specifically, Ima suggests that research designed to explain *why* certain groups or subgroups of immigrant students are successful in school is not very useful to those who wish to answer the question of *how* schools can be restructured to meet the needs of students who are floundering. I disagree. Answers to the first question may not yield evaluative information on the merits of specific instructional approaches. However, research on why first- and second-generation immigrant youths are often more successful in school than their nonimmigrant peers can yield findings with important implications for school change. In fact, it is the intention of this chapter to show how ethnographic research on immigrant school success can be very helpful in pointing the way to educational reform.

Ima's research, like my own, identifies a bimodal pattern of Asian students' performance, with one subgroup doing very well in school and another experiencing serious difficulties. Immigrant students' average-to-good grades may mask what in fact is a very low level of academic achievement. The Sikh students whom I studied provide one such example. The newer arrivals—those entering U.S. schools after fourth grade—often remained in ESL (English as a Second Language) classes through high school and graduated with no real preparation for jobs or college. Their parents and sometimes the students themselves were unaware that, although they were awarded the same diploma as American-born peers, they had far from the same education.

Research that neglects the variability in school achievement among Asian Americans contributes to a model minority stereotype that can be injurious to Asian and non-Asian students alike. Such research not only glosses over the substantial difficulties that many Asian children face in school, but it also can lead to misleading conclusions about the role of Asian cultures in promoting school achievement. To guard against these shortcomings, we need more studies that look comparatively at Asian and non-Asian students, immigrant and nonimmigrant alike, and that investigate how cultural, structural, and situational variables interact to influence school performance.

Such research can help us answer not only Ima's question regarding the factors that predict success for immigrant students, but also his question regarding how best to educate immigrant students. It can do this by identifying and describing the strategies that the successful first- and second-generation immigrant students employ to overcome the barriers they encounter in U.S. schools, and then drawing on these findings to design instructional environments where such strategies are explicitly acknowledged, encouraged, and rewarded.

Definition of Terms

The term *minority*, as used in this chapter, refers to a group occupying a subordinate position in a multiethnic society, suffering from the disabilities of prejudice and discrimination, and maintaining a separate group identity.

The term *immigrant* refers to the various categories of persons who have moved to this country for work or residence, including refugees, undocumented aliens, and migrant workers, as well as voluntary immigrants who arrive with permanent residence visas in hand. Although a number of recent studies indicate that school success patterns for the children of refugees, undocumented aliens, and temporary workers may be similar to those of voluntary immigrants (Caplan, Choy, and Whitmore 1992; Gibson 1983; Rumbaut 1990, this volume; Suárez-Orozco 1991), further empirical research is needed to determine more fully the nature of the relationship between the parents' legal status and their children's educational needs.

Immigrant minority, in my usage, includes both the first generation—those who themselves immigrated to the United States—and the second and third generations if these children and grandchildren of immigrants continue to maintain a separate ethnic identity and if their group continues in a subordinate position vis-à-vis the dominant group.

Nonimmigrant minority, on the other hand, refers not simply to those who are native born but to groups incorporated into this country involuntarily, most frequently by means of colonization, conquest, or slavery, and assigned a subordinate position within it (Ogbu 1978, 1991a). These groups are sometimes referred to as *involuntary minorities* (Gibson and Ogbu 1991).

Facilitative Orientation to Schooling

Comparative research points to what may be called an *immigrant orientation to schooling*, which appears to contribute directly to immigrant students' success in school (Gibson and Ogbu 1991; Gibson 1993b). Not all immigrant groups or subgroups share this orientation or school-response pattern, but enough do that it merits examination. This pattern might better be termed a *facilitative orientation to schooling* rather than an immigrant orientation because various aspects of it certainly pertain to nonimmigrant minority students as well. It remains a topic for further research, however, to determine the extent to which factors associated with this orientation are characteristic of academically successful nonimmigrant minority students (for one example of such a comparison, see Mehan, Hubbard, and Villanueva 1994).

Educational and Occupational Aspirations

Immigrant parents' high job aspirations for their children and very high expectations for their school success appear to be related to their children's school performance. Parents with dead-end, low-paying, and physically demanding jobs make clear to their offspring that formal education is the route to their escaping a similar fate. Parental expectations and assumptions about the value of schooling appear to have more impact on the immigrant child's decision to persist in school and to take the "tough" classes than either the parents' social class background or the child's actual academic aptitude. Such is their faith in the value of education that many immigrant young people enroll in community colleges following high school even when their scholastic record is weak.

Sanctions Supporting School Success

High expectations alone are not enough. Immigrant parents are often far more insistent than are nonimmigrant parents that their children treat schooling as a job, and they utilize effective sanctions to impel their children to take this job seriously. On the positive side, the children may be told that their accomplishments bring honor to their family and to their community. One South Asian father, a Sikh immigrant to Britain from the Indian state of Punjab, explained the relationship as follows:

> If one *rhistedhar* [relative] . . . gets educated, a whole *kul* [subcaste] raises its status. We can get better matches for our daughters and sons. We will get more respect as well. We can also get help from the educated person and give his or her example to the younger generation to create an even more educated set of people (cited in Gibson and Bhachu 1991: 79).

Conversely, Punjabi Sikh children learn that poor behavior in school shames the family. Their slacking off in academics or deportment may lead to gossip, ridicule, and ostracism. It may even lead to a child being withdrawn from school by his or her parents (Gibson and Bhachu 1991).

"Valleyside," as I call the town where I have carried out research on immigrant students' school adaptations, is a small agricultural community in California's Central Valley. At the present time, the town's single high school has 59 percent white students; 21 percent Mexican students, about two-thirds of them Californians by birth; 16 percent Asian students, most of them Sikh Punjabis; and 4 percent other students of color. At the time of my initial fieldwork (1980–1982), almost all Sikh parents were involved in farming, the majority as unskilled, low-paid orchard laborers. "The fields are waiting," the parents would say, if a child, especially a male child, was wasting time in school. This was no idle threat. Every Sikh youngster knew of at least one teenage boy who had been pulled out of school and put to work doing hard physical labor. When he repented and asked to return to school, his parents said, "Sorry, you lost your chance." Every youngster also knew of at least one young woman who had been withdrawn from high school and her marriage immediately arranged because she was paying more attention to her social life than her books.

Similar sanctions and incentives have been observed in other countries. Eugeen Roosens (1992) notes with respect to the Spanish immigrant community in Antwerp, Belgium, that the parents of successful students not only encourage their children in general terms to do well in school, but they also monitor their work on a daily basis. Conversely, Roosens and his team of anthropologists found that parents of the less successful students offer encouragement for education only in a theoretical way, failing to back this up with the necessary supervision.

Much like the Sikh parents in Valleyside, the Spanish parents in Antwerp often have no clear idea of what the schools are all about, have only a minimal formal education themselves, comparable to the least advantaged members of the Belgian population, and thus can give little or no direct assistance with homework. Nonetheless, they provide close oversight of their children's schoolwork. "It is striking," Roosens writes, "how everything is done to make the children study." As with the Latino youths described by Marcelo and Carola Suárez-Orozco (this volume), guilt can play a major hand in Spanish immigrants' drive to study. Spanish children learn that they "hurt their parents" if they fail to do well in school and that they "owe it to their parents, who are making so many sacrifices for them" (Roosens 1992: 8–9).

Immigrants' aspirations and expectations for their children's success are sometimes so high that they place undue pressure on their young to excel in school and to strive for professional careers. Such pressure may occur even when the academic work required is beyond a child's capacity. In such cases, as Roosens observes, the results can be catastrophic.

A Comparative Frame of Reference

Many immigrant parents, most notably those who have migrated to the United States in search of economic betterment, share a sense of relative satisfaction with the opportunities available to them, or those they anticipate will be available to their offspring. Even if they must struggle for years to make ends meet, sometimes laboring longer and harder than they did in their homelands, they may still believe their family is better off in the United States. Judged through their comparative lens, formal education is more accessible, less expensive, and generally of a higher quality than that available to members of their social class in the old country. Suárez-Orozco (1991, this volume) refers to this aspect of the immigrants' orientation to schooling and life in the United States as a "dual frame of reference." For the Sikhs and other ethnic groups who have settlements in several different countries, the frame of reference is more than dual. Valleyside's Sikhs, for example, compare the social and economic conditions of California to those in Britain, Canada, India, and sometimes Fiji and Uganda.

Terms of Incorporation

If members of a minority group have come to this country voluntarily, they will have a different response to this society and its schools than those minorities who have been incorporated into this society involuntarily (Ogbu 1978, 1991a). Immigrants, at least for a time, have an attitude that "we are guests in a foreign land" and "we must be grateful for the opportunities afforded us" (Gibson 1988). The response patterns of refugees, migrants, and undocumented workers have yet to be compared in any systematic way to the response patterns of those who have come primarily for economic purposes or to reunite with family.

Effort and Persistence over Innate Ability

Immigrant students and their families are more likely than either majority or long-established minority students and parents, or their teachers, to assume that effort and perseverance are the keys to school success. Likewise, immigrants are less inclined to attribute academic success mainly to innate ability or to such variables as race or socio-economic status.

In keeping with their view that effort will be rewarded, immigrants invest more time and energy in schoolwork than nonimmigrants. They generally like school and have positive attitudes about their teachers. They have better attendance and cause fewer discipline problems than their involuntary minority classmates. They devote more hours to homework and are less likely than nonimmigrants, majority as well as minority, to shy away from the tougher classes. It is not uncommon, moreover, for the children of immigrants to recall how their fathers checked everyday even in their final year of high school to see if all homework had been completed. Their fathers had reminded them, too, with equal frequency, that family reputation rested on their shoulders and that they must do nothing that would dishonor the family name.

Respect for Teachers and Trust in the System

There is increasing evidence that students who respect and trust their teachers have an easier time learning what their teachers seek to impart than those who mistrust or disrespect their teachers (Erickson 1987; Sung 1979). Once again, immigrants appear to have an advantage. Immigrants often instill in their children a sense of strong respect for teachers and other educators, and they will discipline a child sternly if they learn that he or she has not been properly attentive or courteous at school. In addition, immigrants tend to believe that the American educational system, unlike the one left behind in the old country, provides all children the same chance to excel in school and to compete for desirable jobs. Moreover, they socialize their children to accept this ideology even though on a concrete level there is much evidence to the contrary (see Handsfield 1993).

In general, immigrant youths comply with school regulations and teachers' requests. They demonstrate an eagerness to learn, abide by the rules set forth by those in authority, and are, for the most part, better behaved than nonimmigrant classmates. In fact, according to Valleyside teachers, becoming Americanized means "becoming as obnoxious as the rest" (de Ortiz 1993). Immigrant children may play by the rules even when the social and cultural milieu at school causes them extreme discomfort (Gibson 1991b). Their deference, combined with diligence, profits them in the classroom because teachers respond positively to those who abide by school rules and who seem eager to learn.

When students do not respect their teachers, they may also have a difficult time respecting the knowledge their teachers seek to impart. Whether consciously or unconsciously, students may even refuse to learn from those they disrespect. In his insightful essay "I Won't Learn from You," Herbert Kohl (1991) makes a distinction between failure to learn and refusal to learn. Failure to learn, Kohl notes, "results from a mismatch between what the learner wants to do and is able to do," while resistance to learning or "willed not-learning consists of a conscious and chosen refusal to assent to learn" (pp. 15, 41). One of the lessons that comparative research on minority youth appears to be teaching us is that immigrants are less likely than American-born students to be the resisters to school and teacher authority, a point I shall return to shortly.

Dealing with Prejudice and Discrimination

Immigrant parents are often reluctant to find fault with the school or to offer suggestions for how the school might better meet the needs of their children. Even when their children experience serious difficulties socially or academically, or as the result of classmates' outright racist attitudes, parents generally instruct their children to try harder, to seek assistance from their teachers, and to accommodate themselves as best they can to the situation. Immigrant parents may also advise their young to avoid being viewed as troublemakers. Should their child get into a fight at school, no matter the cause, the parents may fear that it will reflect poorly on them or the child and in some way jeopardize his or her educational opportunities. They may feel, as was the case with the Valleyside Punjabi parents—Sikh, Hindu, and Muslim alike—that conflict between themselves and school officials will only distract a child from his or her studies. Immigrant parents may believe, therefore, that it is better to try to ignore racial problems unless they are really serious. Such a pattern of accommodation is more characteristic of recent immigrants than those long settled.

It is important to note that not all immigrant groups or subgroups experience prejudice and discrimination in the same way or respond to them in the same way (see Gillborn 1990). Moreover, it is not only the existence and intensity of prejudice and discrimination that influence the minority students' school performance. The way that a student responds to and deals with inequitable treatment has a determinative influence on school performance as well. Studies conducted from the perspective of resistance theory show how students from subordinate groups sometimes participate actively and even deliberately in their own school failure (Giroux 1983; MacLeod 1987; Willis 1977). These studies also reveal great variability of response among students to unfair and inequitable treatment, ranging from accommodation to active resistance or sometimes a combination of both (Daoud 1993; Gillborn 1990).

The comparative literature on immigrant students' school adaptation patterns shows, too, that immigrants frequently continue to invest in schooling even when they are being treated unfairly at school. Although they may resist pressures to conform culturally, they welcome the formal education and the credentials that schools provide. Immigrant parents, thus, often have high regard for the schools' credentialing functions but look with ambivalence and discomfort, and even outright alarm, on the schools' socialization functions (for similar findings in the Netherlands, see Eldering 1992).

Recent immigrants are particularly vulnerable to racism and prejudice. The weakest—often those newcomers who have yet to master English or the culture of their American peers—tend to be preyed upon the most. I found this to be the case in the U.S. Virgin Islands, where the West Indian immigrants were labeled "aliens," teased, accused of being invaders, and told to go home. I also found it in Valleyside, where Punjabi newcomers were subjected to verbal and even physical abuse.

Teachers need most urgently to educate American-born students about the newcomers' histories and cultures rather than, as happened in Valleyside, asking the newcomers (and even the second generation) to be tolerant of their white classmates' ignorance and prejudice. Students and teachers alike need to understand that a successful response to the new demographics requires adaptation and adjustment on everyone's part. No student, moreover, should ever be asked to acquiesce to racial prejudice because of a classmate's ignorance.

ESL and Bilingual Education

Immigrant children often arrive in U.S. schools with little or no knowledge of the English language. They need special support through ESL and bilingual education classes. Most immigrant children who lack proficiency in English welcome ESL instruction when they first arrive. They may even welcome placement in separate classes for a time, especially at the secondary level, but they also want to move out of these classrooms as quickly as possible. This was the case with the Punjabi students attending Valleyside High School.

At Valleyside High, Punjabi newcomers were (and still are) placed in an ESL track for as many as five periods a day. Although such classes give the most recent arrivals an opportunity to strengthen their skills in English while also studying math, science, and social studies, they run the risk of offering watered-down instruction to those who are ready and able to engage in more challenging and age-appropriate academic work. Moreover, they may be viewed as a social as well as an academic ghetto. Recently arrived Punjabis worried that they would never catch up academically or be able to take the courses they knew they needed for college admission. They also observed that by segregating them for much of the day from fluent English speakers, the ESL track actually contributed to racial hostilities on the high school campus (Gibson 1988).

Studies of Hmong and Salvadoran refugees point to similar problems with high school ESL programs (Suárez-Orozco 1991; Walker 1989). In these as well as the Punjabi case, the students wanted a more rigorous curriculum, and they wanted the opportunity to compete in mainstream classes rather than being insulated in an ESL track. The need for ESL instruction is clear, but such instruction must be academically rigorous, guided by teachers with appropriate training in second-language acquisition, and organized in such a way that limited-English speakers have ample opportunity to interact with their American peers.

Bilingual education, like ESL, can be an important instructional strategy for the children of immigrants. The Punjabis whom I studied as high school seniors generally scored poorly on standardized tests in English even when they had received all their education in this country. The large majority of those who entered U.S. schools after fourth grade were still classified as LEP (limited-English-proficient) in high school. These more recent arrivals, as well as those raised from early childhood in the United States, might well have benefited from bilingual instruction, assuming adequate Punjabi-language curriculum materials were available.

The advantages of well-designed bilingual programs go far beyond issues of language development. Bilingual education is an effective strategy for enhancing students' sense of identity and self-esteem, and for teaching children that it is important to become competent in more than one language and culture. When its goal is to develop and reinforce two languages, bilingual education sends a message to all students, majority and minority, that American society encompasses multiple language and ethnic groups and that all students have much to gain through contact with other languages and cultures. Moreover, bilingual teachers provide role models of adults who are proficient in two languages, who demonstrate that bilingualism is an asset, and who show themselves receptive to interethnic reciprocal learning. Through bilingual education, immigrant and nonimmigrant children alike can learn to distinguish proficiency in a second language from their own social identification with a particular ethnic and language group.

Alternative Models for Parental Involvement

Parental involvement in schooling has become much talked about in recent years. My research, like other studies, indicates that strong parental and community support for education is a critical factor in immigrant children's academic success. It also shows that the definitions of parental involvement and parental support for education must be understood within the cultural and social context of each ethnic group. Immigrant parents, especially if they themselves have little formal education and lack proficiency in the dominant language, are hesitant to intervene directly in their children's schooling. They rarely, if ever, visit the school, meet with teachers, or become involved in school affairs. They may, however, create an environment at home that instills in their children a belief that schoolwork is important and that academic diligence will have its rewards. They adopt what British social anthropologist Parminder Bhachu has labeled a *noninterventionist strategy* vis-à-vis the schools. As Bhachu's research indicates, such an approach can be as effective in promoting school success as an interventionist strategy (Bhachu 1985). Immigrant parents who are themselves well educated and who speak English with ease are more likely to become directly involved in instructional issues, but still they may only do so when a child is experiencing some difficulty at school. If their children are progressing satisfactorily, they may see little need for direct involvement.

Let me raise a policy issue here. Many middle-class, mainstream Americans pursue an interventionist strategy with respect to their children's education, and educators frequently assume that other parents need to be encouraged to emulate this strategy. It is assumed without adequate evidence, I believe, that adoption of the mainstream model will help solve the problems that minority children face in school. This is so even though a significant number of minority children do notably well academically without interventionist parents.

In reporting these findings, I do not mean to suggest that parents should not be encouraged to be involved directly in school affairs and given a real role in making the decisions that affect their children's education. In fact, there is evidence that "dramatic changes in children's academic progress" can occur when parents who otherwise feel alienated from the schools are given a sense of empowerment. Jim Cummins explains this relationship: "When educators involve minority parents as partners in their children's education, parents appear to develop a sense of efficacy that communicates itself to children, with positive academic consequences" (Cummins 1986: 26).

Such findings are extremely encouraging, but we need to be cautious about their generalizability or applicability to all minority groups and subgroups. If school programs are so structured that parental intervention becomes a prerequisite for student success, we may actually penalize children with noninterventionist parents. For example, if homework is set up in such a way that parents must take an active part in its accomplishment, the children of poorly educated or non-English-speaking parents may suffer. Many immigrant parents, moreover, are working very long hours to ensure their family's economic survival. Many are also struggling to learn the ropes of life in a new country and culture. If the mainstream, middle-class model of parental involvement is imposed on immigrant families, it may actually become more difficult for their children to use schooling as an avenue for upward mobility. No single model of parent and family participation in the educational process can fit all groups. We need, therefore, to give more attention to alternative models.

The Role of Peer Group

We also need to know more about why the peer group in some instances acts as a force *for* compliance with school rules for success and in others as a force *against* such compliance (De Vos 1975). Among immigrant minorities the peer group frequently, but certainly not always, is supportive of academic diligence and persistence, and young people may even feel competitive pressure from peers to excel in their studies. Among involuntary minorities the opposite pattern has been documented.

For example, African American and Afro-Caribbean students who accept school authority are sometimes accused by peers of "acting white," obeying white orders and working for whites rather than themselves, just as in the days of slavery (Fordham and Ogbu 1987; Gibson 1991a; Ogbu 1991a, 1991b). Likewise, Chicano students use the term "wannabe" (wants to be white) to tease Mexican-descent classmates who conform too closely to teachers' expectations and demands (Matute-Bianchi 1991). Unwilling to be ridiculed or made to feel outcast, some minority youths simply turn their attentions elsewhere.

The role of the peer group in promoting or impeding success in school is a topic that merits much greater research attention. We need to know, for example, if academically successful involuntary minority students encounter the same pressures to resist school authority as those less successful, and, if so, we need to know how they deal with these pressures. Do they feel they must choose between their identity and their friendship networks, on the one hand, and academic success on the other? Recent research indicates otherwise. Navajo children who maintain strong ties to their grandparents and their traditional culture do better in school than Navajo children who have lost these ties (Deyhle, cited in LeCompte and Dworkin 1991: 74). Moreover, when formerly low-achieving African American and Mexican American students are placed in academically demanding and untracked AVID classes, they create their own student support groups and, much like the Valleyside Punjabis, practice a strategy of accommodation without assimilation. They accommodate to the school's rules for academic success but they resist pressures to assimilate culturally (Mehan, Hubbard, and Villanueva 1994).

Gender Differences

Gender differences must be considered in analyzing and understanding the school-adaptation patterns of immigrant and other minority students. Immigrant girls, especially those raised from childhood in the United States, may find themselves caught between mainstream American values, which place great emphasis on the individual's right to make independent decisions and to pursue the academic and career goals of her own choosing, and the values their parents have brought with them from their countries and communities of origin. Their parents may place great emphasis on group decision making, give little autonomy to adolescent females, and consider higher education for daughters a low priority, possibly even undesirable because it promotes independent thinking. Teachers need knowledge of immigrants students' family values and circumstances, including cultural conflicts between home and school that may bear no easy resolution.

Although teenage girls sometimes experience the pull between home and school cultures more intensely than boys, perhaps because the maintenance of family honor and traditions often rests more heavily on their shoulders, they also are less likely than their brothers to develop an oppositional relationship with the school system or to view schooling as a threat to their identity. In Valleyside, for example, Mexican girls receive better grades than Mexican boys, are more likely to be placed in college preparatory classes, and are less likely than the boys to oppose school authority (Daoud 1993). I found a similar pattern to exist among Crucian girls and boys during their junior high years (Gibson 1991a). We need to know more about how generalizable these gender differences are and about the forces that account for them.

Additive versus Subtractive Acculturation

In addition to the instrumental value of schooling—in providing the credentials and skills needed for employment—many immigrant parents welcome the school's role in helping their children master the dominant language and culture. They recognize that this is essential to their children's successful participation in the larger society. At the same time, they worry about the conformist pressures placed on their children. They want their children to be competent in the ways of the mainstream but not at the expense of their ethnic identity and culture.

Pressures to conform culturally contribute to immigrant children's difficulties in school and, in some cases, may lead students to resist teacher authority and to drop out of school. Studies of Italian immigrants in Germany today and in the United States earlier in this century provide a picture of teenage boys who deliberately disrupt the classroom as a protest against their teachers' assimilationist agendas (Malhotra 1985; Ware 1935). In Britain, Bhattra Sikhs—a low-caste and very orthodox group—perform less well than white peers and are often withdrawn from school at an early age by their parents. By restricting their children's social arena, the Bhattras have been able to maintain their orthodox traditions and distinctive identity in the new setting (Ghuman 1980).

Let me distinguish here between the terms acculturation and assimilation. *Acculturation* is a process of culture change and adaptation that occurs when individuals with different cultures come into contact. The end result need not be the rejection of old traits or their replacement. Acculturation may be an additive process or one in which old and new traits are blended (Haviland 1985). *Assimilation*, on the other hand, is the process whereby individuals of one society or ethnic group are incorporated or absorbed culturally into another. It implies replacing one's old identity with a new identity. At the individual level, the former culture is lost.

Immigrant parents generally encourage acculturation, to a point, but not assimilation. They want their offspring to be competitive in the new country, but they are often extremely uncomfortable with the idea of their children "becoming Americanized." To them, Americanization means to forget one's roots and to adopt the worst (as well as the best) that this country has to offer. Valleyside Sikhs were deeply resentful of their children being told in one way or another that Indian ways are inferior to Western ways, or at least not suitable in this country. To guard against social conformity, they discouraged their children from participating in extracurricular activities and from mixing socially outside of school with non-Punjabi friends. In part, they were fearful for their children's safety, not understanding or condoning many of the activities that the mass of American adolescents engages in today, but they were also consciously and carefully holding their children within the cultural fold.

At the same time, Sikh parents taught their children to be respectful of teachers and adult authority, and to do whatever they must to succeed in school. "Dress to please the people, but eat to please yourself" was their motto, meaning accommodate to the degree necessary in public but remain steadfast to your deepest values and identity. Their children's strategy tended toward embracing American culture far more than many of their parents liked, but they remained all the while Punjabi.

Ethnographic studies point to similar patterns among other immigrant groups. First-generation youths are often successful in school not because they assimilate but because they employ a *strategy of additive acculturation*. I build here on Wallace Lambert's (1975) concept of additive and subtractive bilingualism. In Lambert's usage, subtractive bilingualism occurs when in learning English the immigrant or language-minority child ceases to maintain his or her proficiency in the mother tongue. English has replaced the child's first language. On the other hand, when English becomes a second (or third) language in the child's repertoire, additive bilingualism occurs.

Valleyside Sikhs, like many other immigrant groups, view the acquisition of English and skills in the dominant culture as an additive process so long as their children remain firmly anchored in their Punjabi and Sikh identities. This process is often fraught with conflict, however, because schools encourage the children of immigrants, including those born in the United States, to relinquish their "foreign" ways. Pressure for what I refer to as *subtractive acculturation* underlies the "English Only" movement in this country, as well as the U.S. Department of Education's current bilingual education rules. The latter treat native language instruction as a tool to achieve competence in English rather than as an instructional strategy to nurture and maintain two languages. The federal government's early efforts to assimilate Indochinese refugees through a policy of dispersal is another example of subtractive acculturation (Kelly 1981).

At a local level, assimilationist policies are more frequently implicit than explicit. Many well-intentioned teachers promote a subtractive or *replacement model of acculturation* and, in so doing, contribute to the cultural tug-of-war experienced by immigrant youths. Some clash between cultures is inevitable, but the conflicts are exacerbated when immigrant children are told directly or indirectly that assimilation is the surest route to success. To fit in socially the children of immigrants may adopt the values, even the prejudices, of mainstream American peers and come to see their parents as too authoritarian, backward, and foreign. At a point in their lives when they most need parental and extended family support to find their way through a maze of colliding cultures, they may feel caught in a no-win situation. The pressures placed on them to rebel against their immigrant parents in order to be accepted by their American peers can have unintended and injurious consequences.

Schools have rarely encouraged minority children to maintain their home languages and cultures in any serious way. This is the case even though an educational policy of replacement acculturation, or assimilation, may undermine just those qualities that enable minority children to excel in school. Many first- and second-generation immigrant children are successful precisely because they draw strength from their home cultures and from a positive sense of their ethnic identities (Caplan, Choy, and Whitmore 1992; Cummins 1986; Gibson and Ogbu 1991; Hoffman 1988; Rumbaut 1990, this volume; Vigil and Long 1981).

Involuntary Minority Adaptations

An interesting connection can be made between research on immigrant minorities and related research on involuntary minorities. Ethnographic studies indicate that some of the involuntary minority children who experience the most difficulty in school are those who feel they must choose between success in the mainstream culture and loyalty to their ethnic group (Cummins 1981; Deyhle 1991; Fordham 1988; Fordham and Ogbu 1987; Gibson 1991a; Jordan, Tharp, and Vogt 1986; Kleinfeld 1983; Kramer 1983; Matute-Bianchi 1991; Ogbu 1987, 1991a; Petroni 1970). When children believe they are faced with a trade-off between their ethnic identity and success in school, some, perhaps many, choose their identity. Others opt for a form of subtractive acculturation, but in the process they may find themselves estranged from their families and their natal communities (see Rodriguez 1983).

The U.S. educational system has been strongly assimilationist throughout much of its history. This can be seen most clearly when we examine the plight of American Indian children who were sent away to government-run boarding schools where, far from the security and guidance of their families, they were punished for speaking their mother tongue and coerced into learning the ways of the European Americans. In some cases Indian children were even prevented from returning home during holidays because contact with their home communities was considered a deterrent to their gaining skills in the dominant (and presumably superior) culture and language. The tragic outcome of such a policy can be measured in part by the low school achievement and school persistence rates among American Indians today. Coercive acculturation strategies have led to equally disastrous educational outcomes in other Western countries (Barrington 1991; Gibson 1993b).

The Accommodating Diversity Project

The overwhelming majority of California's teachers are themselves of European ancestry, but Euro-American students now comprise less than 50 percent of the K–12 population. Students of Latino and Asian descent are rapidly becoming a majority. As the number of immigrant children, both first and second generation, continues to change the face of California schools, it is important to know what impact the new demographics are having on teachers' assumptions about acculturation and assimilation. Do teachers continue to feel, as many have in the past, that immigrant students must shed their "foreign" ways in order to fit in at school? Do they believe that assimilation is a prerequisite to achieving success in U.S. schools and in mainstream American society? Or do teachers encourage immigrant and other minority students to maintain their home languages and cultures? Do they embrace a philosophy of additive acculturation? What do teachers mean when they use the terms assimilation and Americanization? Are teachers aware that large numbers of first-generation immigrant students are achieving success in school without assimilating? Are they aware of the recent studies indicating that pressures placed on immigrant and other minority children to assimilate may have a negative impact on their sense of self, may pull them away from their families, and may in fact serve to impede their success in school? What do teachers see as their role and the role of schooling in the acculturation process?

These and related questions are the focus of field research that I and a team of University of California-Santa Cruz graduate students have been pursuing over the past year in Valleyside.[2] Preliminary analysis of teacher interviews and questionnaires provides beginning answers to these questions in this one site. Although Valleyside is distinctive for its large Asian Indian population, it is not unlike other California school districts that have experienced significant demographic change since the early 1970s. Over the past two decades the percentage of white students enrolled at Valleyside High School has declined from more than 90 percent to 59 percent. During this same period, the Asian (mainly Punjabi) enrollment has grown fivefold, from 3 percent to 16 percent, and Mexican enrollment has increased fourfold, from about 5 percent to 21 percent. Today, almost one in three of all Valleyside children (K–12) speaks a language other than English at home, and the school district ranks in the top 16 percent statewide in terms of the proportion of its students who have been identified as limited-English-proficient. The

[2]This project was supported by small grants from the Spencer Foundation, the University of California's Linguistic Minority Research Institute, UC MEXUS, and the Division of Social Sciences, University of California-Santa Cruz. The full data base for the project includes comparative interviews with a stratified sample of 48 Mexican high school students, their parents, and 30 of their teachers; questionnaires from 128 Mexican students and 107 teachers; and academic achievement data for all high school students in the class of 1995—Mexican, Punjabi, and Anglo. I wish to thank Ed Aguilar, Annette Daoud, Carly de Ortiz, Lara Handsfield, and Estella Mejía for their many contributions to data gathering and analysis. My thanks go also to the Valleyside School District for its collaboration, and in particular to the high school faculty members who have shared their ideas and insights with us in the hopes that this study will make a difference for their students.

increase in LEP students in this district in 1989–1990 was over double that for the state as a whole (data provided by the district).

While the high school's student body has changed dramatically, the composition of the high school faculty has changed very little. More than 90 percent are white. Three-quarters have been teaching at Valleyside High for more than ten years, and 44 percent for more than twenty years. In 1980–1981 about two-thirds of the faculty were male, including the top six administrators. Today, 59 percent are male, including five of the six senior administrators. As in 1981, all but a handful hold master's degrees or the equivalent. As a group, faculty members are dedicated, experienced, and hard working. They teach because they feel they can make a difference for their students, because they enjoy teaching, and because they believe they are good at what they do.

The 1980–1981 Context

My earlier research indicated that a substantial number of teachers adhered to a subtractive model of acculturation. They assumed that "American" ways work better in the United States, that it was the immigrants' responsibility to take up the new ways, and that it was their job as teachers to help immigrant students adapt as rapidly as possible. By and large, teachers equated American ways with the ways of the white majority.

Many, perhaps most, felt that it was best to treat all students the same, without regard to cultural and ethnic differences. To do otherwise, some teachers noted, would be to impose a double standard. However, "to treat all students the same" often, and quite unconsciously, carried with it the expectation that all students shared or should share core values common to the Euro-American majority—but often not common to the Punjabis and other children of color.

One teacher, who related how most Punjabi girls objected to the standard physical education uniform of short shorts, went on to explain his position: "We expect the kids to be Americanized. I tell the parents this. . . . A great portion of them want to change. That's why they're here. I tell the parents to go elsewhere, back to India, if they don't like these things." Rules were rules, he said, and the Punjabis, like all other students, simply had to accept them. It mattered little that parents admonished their adolescent daughters not to wear skimpy clothing or do anything else that would dishonor the family's good name. Although this teacher's views were extreme, many of his colleagues believed that only time could solve the problems because it would take a generation or two for the Punjabis, like other immigrant groups before them, to join the "melting pot."

In the early 1980s ethnic tensions were running high, and anti-Punjabi sentiments were pervasive within the white Valleyside community. The problems would only lessen, teachers believed, when the Punjabis made a greater effort to fit in. And to fit in socially was, for many teachers, a major aspect of having a successful high school experience. Teachers were understandably disturbed, therefore, that Punjabi parents often prohibited their teenage children, especially their daughters, from taking part in the high school's rich array of clubs, sports, and social activities.

The 1992–1993 Context

Like their counterparts elsewhere in the state, Valleyside teachers are working extremely hard to keep up with demographic changes and to meet the needs of all their students, but they are disturbed by the pace of immigration, illegal immigration in particular. One teacher explained: "I personally resent the lack of immigration control and the quantity of illegals who are using multiple benefits, with multiple identities, and this is common practice in this community, not only among Hispanics, but East Indians and perhaps other groups as well." Among high school faculty members, anti-immigration sentiments are voiced more loudly than twelve years ago. Although not all teachers believe that large numbers of immigrants are double-dipping, most agree that something must be done to stem the immigration tide. Their views in this regard are similar to those of 65 percent of all Americans (Gallup Organization 1993).

Over the past decade, the faculty has shifted its focus of concern from the Punjabis to the Mexicans. The high school's ESL and Newcomer programs, staffed by three Punjabi teachers, are better established now and can more readily respond to the needs of Punjabi students, even those arriving during their teenage years. Moreover, about half of the Punjabis at Valleyside High are now U.S. born or raised from early childhood in this country. Teachers are more comfortable today than a decade ago with the Punjabi students in their classes, and they are more accepting of the Punjabi presence in the larger community. Not so with the Mexicans, as the following teacher comment suggests:

> There are a lot of Hispanics coming into this area, a lot of Asians coming into this area. . . . Asians are goal oriented, are striving to achieve and get the best education. Unfortunately, I don't have that same attitude [about], nor do I see that same attitude reflected by the Hispanic community. . . . I don't think it is within the Hispanic family structure to value education (long-term Valleyside resident).

Many of Valleyside's Mexican students never finish tenth grade, either dropping out by this point or transferring to the district's continu-

ation high school. In the fall of 1991 there were 161 Hispanic students—
mostly of Mexican origin—attending grade nine, but only 65 in grade
twelve. The previous year only 33 Mexican students graduated from
Valleyside High. Few of the Mexican students who persist through
twelfth grade take the college preparatory courses necessary to gain
admission into the California State University or University of California
systems.

Although the overall number of Mexican students enrolled at Valleyside High has doubled since 1981, the percentage who are foreign
born has remained constant at about 30 percent. Approximately half of
the Mexican students qualify for assistance through Migrant Education
(federal support available to the children of migrants), but few of their
parents currently follow the crops. Most are settled more or less permanently in Valleyside; those who go back each winter to Mexico—and
many do—return to Valleyside as soon as the agricultural season begins.
More than a third of the students in our sample have at least one U.S.-
born parent. Most members of Valleyside's Mexican community are
struggling to make ends meet economically. Nearly a third of the
sampled students (N = 128) reported that their fathers were not "employed at the present time," and of those who had regular work, half
were either farm laborers or cannery workers. Seven or eight years of
schooling is the median for both fathers and mothers.

Preliminary Findings

Of the 110 teachers and administrators who completed our questionnaire, 86 percent either "strongly agreed" or "agreed" that "recent
immigrants should encourage their children to Americanize as rapidly
as possible." Follow-up interviews with 30 teachers confirmed this view.
As in 1981, Valleyside High faculty members continue to believe that it is
part of their responsibility as teachers to facilitate the Americanization
process. Quite a few also believe that the Mexican parents are at fault for
not doing more to encourage and even help their children make the
transition. One teacher explained:

> I think some assimilating has to take place. [The stu-
> dents] have to make changes, and I think they want to.
> They want to become a part of this society. But, on the
> other hand, I think they're torn at home. Many of them,
> their parents, speak another language. . . . I don't think
> most of the parents see them becoming [want them to
> become] Americanized. . . . The parents, for whatever
> reason, haven't become fluent in English. So they still
> speak their native tongue. . . . It would help [the
> students] out if they learned to speak English at home.

> Going home and speaking a foreign language doesn't
> reinforce what we're doing in school.

What teachers mean by "Americanize" and "assimilate" varies widely, but most equate the terms with some form of acculturation. At an abstract level most believe in additive acculturation. One teacher explained: "I think it's the responsibility of that incoming person to make major efforts to assimilate into the society . . . without losing their ethnic identity." A majority of her colleagues would concur. On a concrete level, however, the manner in which many teachers assume that this process ought to occur implies the replacement of the old language and culture, and thus a subtractive form of acculturation.

The formal study of Spanish during high school provides one example.[3] While 62 percent of the teachers agree[4] that "it's very important for Mexican students to receive encouragement from their teachers and counselors to take Spanish classes in high school," only 26 percent of Mexican students in the class of 1995 actually took a full year of Spanish during tenth grade, and only 12 percent had taken Spanish in both ninth and tenth grades. Several students reported that some school authority—a teacher, counselor, or administrator—had told them they did not "need" Spanish because they already "knew" it, with no attempt made to ascertain the student's actual ability to read, write, or speak this language. One student, a boy with a Hispanic surname who knew almost no Spanish and very much wanted to study it, reported that despite his protestations he was placed in German class in ninth grade. He had been identified as a strong student and potentially college bound. His was the exceptional case. Only a handful of Mexican students were assigned a "foreign" language on entering high school. School administrators explain variously that few Mexican students meet their placement criteria, which include high marks in eighth-grade English, teacher or counselor recommendation, and placing in the 53rd percentile or better on the English language portion of the Stanford Achievement Test taken in eighth grade.

Valleyside teachers, counselors, and administrators generally assume, moreover, that "foreign" language study is for the college bound, required for admission directly into a four-year college but unnecessary for the average student. As in most California high schools, the study of a second language is not viewed as a normal part of one's secondary education. Furthermore, and in apparent contradiction to the stated placement criteria, Valleyside educators explain that first-year Spanish is

---

[3]See Handsfield 1993 for theoretical discussion of the gap between abstract and concrete attitudes, including the relationship between concrete attitudes and school performance among Mexican students attending Valleyside High.

[4]Percentages include those who responded "strongly agree" as well as "agree." The remainder answered either "disagree" or "strongly disagree."

"too easy" for many of the Mexican-descent students. Some are placed directly, therefore, into second-year Spanish. When asked if the high school might consider a "Spanish for Spanish speakers" class or sequence of classes, one knowledgeable and well-intentioned administrator dismissed the idea because it would cause a "scheduling nightmare." An underlying assumption of this individual was that few Mexican students would actually elect such a class and that the complexities of scheduling classes for 2,200 students make it impossible to tailor the schedule to the needs of only a few.

In actuality, the potential target population is quite large; one-fourth of all Valleyside ninth graders are now of Hispanic descent. It remains an open question how many would take Spanish if strongly counseled to do so and if classes were tailored to meet students' backgrounds and preexisting Spanish language abilities. Our interviews with Mexican students and parents suggest that, with a combination of community outreach and student counseling, the support would be widespread.

Teachers' responses to other questions further illustrate the gap between the abstract value placed on bilingualism and the actual support for fluency in two languages. Both teacher interviews and teacher questionnaires indicate that at least half of the high school faculty disapproves of Mexican students speaking Spanish at school, even informally to their friends.[5] Seventy-nine percent agree that Mexican parents should encourage their children to use English as much as possible at home; 43 percent agree that monolingualism is the best avenue to an integrated society. Only 30 percent agree that Mexican-origin students should develop their Spanish language skills even if this detracts from the time they have available for studying English, and only 26 percent agree that it is appropriate for Mexican parents to insist that their children speak with them only in Spanish.

Although the teachers interviewed display a wide range of knowledge about Mexican history and culture and a continuum of attitudes about acculturation processes, their responses indicate that many, if not most, blame Mexican parents for what the teachers perceive to be an unwillingness to learn and speak English and an unwillingness to assimilate. The Mexican students' sense of identity, self-esteem, and response to schooling are clearly affected by these attitudes. Although students believe overwhelmingly in an abstract way that one can be both

---

[5]On the questionnaire, 51 percent of the teachers either agreed or strongly agreed with the statement, "Mexican students would fit in better at the high school if they didn't speak Spanish to each other." Interestingly, there were sharp age and gender differences, with 67 percent of the "older" teachers (those at Valleyside High School for over twenty years) and 65 percent of the men (regardless of age or years at Valleyside High) responding agree or strongly agree, compared to 39 percent of the women (all ages) and 26 percent of the "younger" teachers (one to ten years teaching at Valleyside High). Gender and age differences in teachers' attitudes about accommodating diversity will be explored more fully in future publications (see Gibson 1993a).

Mexican and American, one-third (31 percent) feel that at school they "sometimes have to choose between being Mexican and being American." One in seven feels Mexican-descent students have to "lose" their Mexican culture to get ahead in the United States. Although 87 percent report that their teachers encourage them to do well, 71 percent also believe that some of their teachers are prejudiced. Most feel that Mexican students are sometimes treated inequitably by teachers and administrators (Daoud 1993).

Teachers in Valleyside, no less than teachers elsewhere, want their students to be successful, and they are genuinely concerned about the comparatively low academic achievement levels of Mexican-descent students. Most see little or no relationship, however, between the Mexican students' school performance and school response patterns and teacher attitudes regarding acculturation and assimilation. The underlying problem—in the view of many, although certainly not all, teachers—is the Mexican family and traditional Mexican values. Little will change in school, teachers say, until Mexican students and their parents change their attitudes and behaviors.

The following passage from one teacher interview is illustrative of this deficit perspective:

> *Teacher*: I feel that we are increasingly getting large numbers of young Hispanic males [who] don't want to buy into the culture. It's like, "We want to be here" but "No, I'm not American. I'm Mexican." Even though they are second, third generation, they still want to hold that idea. . . . This kind of bothers me, because part of my idea is to teach the American culture, and we're not getting across to these kids. . . . The Asian kids do not feel that way, none of the other ethnic groups.
>
> *Researcher*: Why do you suppose it's occurring with this particular group?
>
> *Teacher*: I think if Mexico were where India is, we would not have that problem. I think it's this constant reindoctrination by these periodic visits. . . . The Asian kids tend to move fairly well into the system here.
>
> *Researcher*: That's really interesting, because if it were only a color barrier you'd [also] see the Asian not doing well in school. But you say they are.
>
> *Teacher*: They're very much so [doing well in school]. It's a cultural thing, I think. It's basically . . . I think if

Mexico were where India is, where you could break that length of constantly going back into the area. I applaud [these students] for trying to maintain their cultural identity, but to reject coming into our particular system is the problem I'm having as a teacher.

Researcher: Do you see anything in particular in the Mexican culture that would prevent their success in school?

Teacher: I think school, education, is a very low priority. . . . Perhaps access to education has long been denied the poor family in Mexico. And because it's never been a part of them, it has not received a great deal of importance. I think this is being carried over here. It's going to take a couple of generations to overcome that.

This particular teacher is deeply committed to teaching and is well respected by other members of the faculty. He also is clearly concerned by the pattern of low academic performance among Valleyside's Mexican-descent population, and he notes that this is the leading problem now facing the high school. He feels quite powerless, however, to impact the problem, defining it, as he does, as rooted squarely in the Mexican family and culture. His assumption that Mexican families place little value on formal education is at odds with what both students and parents report. For example, when asked how far they would like to go with their schooling, 84 percent of the Mexican students (ninth graders at the time) said they wanted to finish high school and go on to college, 61 percent aspiring to a four-year degree or better and the remainder opting for two years at a community college. Their parents also stated strongly and repeatedly their belief that education is the key to their children's future and the surest way to escape the drudgery of agricultural labor. Most wanted a college education for their children but, for the most part, had little concrete information about their children's academic progress or the path that must be followed to prepare for college.

The students' educational aspirations are largely unknown to their teachers, 78 percent of whom believe that "most Mexican students at Valleyside High do not aspire to a college degree." At the same time, a majority of the teachers recognize that they are not well informed about the cultural backgrounds of their Mexican-descent students. The large majority (79 percent) believe, moreover, that they would be more effective teachers if they were better informed.

At Valleyside High and in other schools throughout the state, teachers recognize the value of knowing as much as possible about their students' backgrounds and families, believing that this knowledge will help them be more successful in addressing students' needs. Teachers are far less conscious of the importance of knowing more about their own attitudes, beliefs, and prejudices, including their attitudes about acculturation and assimilation and how these play out in the day-to-day lives of their students.

Additive Acculturation and Educational Policy

The academic achievements of many immigrant children, including those only recently arrived, provide strong evidence that an educational policy that reinforces additive acculturation will, in the long run, prove more effective than one that presses for subtractive or coercive accultura- tion (Gibson 1988; Rumbaut, this volume; New York City Public Schools 1992).[6] We need to send a clear message to all students that cultural diversity is the bedrock of this nation and that multiculturalism is indeed the normal human experience (see Goodenough 1976). We also need to move away from a cookie-cutter concept of culture that equates each ethnic group with one culture. Members of any single ethnic group represent a range of cultures. Such a perspective, if incorporated more fully into educational policy and programs, would alleviate the tendency to stereotype students according to ethnic identities and would promote a fuller exploration of the similarities as well as the differences between students of different ethnic groups (Gibson 1976b).

Implementing a policy of additive acculturation, or multiculturalism as the normal human experience, in our schools would help resolve the conflict that at least some students now feel between acquiring new cultural competencies and maintaining their social identity. Schools have an important role to play in helping students feel they can become competent in many different cultures without forsaking their identity or being disloyal to their families and ethnic communities.

One Valleyside teacher explained this relationship as follows:

> For me, acculturation can mean to become fluent in [another] language. That does not deny my own lan- guage. In the same way, if I were working with a group

---

[6]Data prepared by the New York City Public Schools for a May 1992 workshop on "Immigrants and Public Education" reveal that, for two consecutive years, recently arrived immigrants show significantly larger gains on standardized tests in reading and math than other students, at all grade levels and for all countries surveyed (New York City Public Schools 1992). This is true despite the fact that a higher percentage of the new immigrants live below the poverty level than the longer-settled immigrants and the U.S. born (25 percent and 16 percent, respectively).

of men and I was the only female there, . . . it would be a gender kind of acculturation. I might be comfortable working with those individuals, but it wouldn't deny my woman-ness. I see acculturation as being able to work with, communicate openly with [the other group], but in no way would that deny myself. It would just add to what I already have.

As it relates to Mexican American students, . . . Spanish-speaking American-born individuals, I see acculturation being similar. In the sense that I would not want to lose myself when I joined [learned] another culture, I would hope that the students would not feel the need to, nor be forced to, lose their own identities, their language, their unique humor, their unique cultural advantages. And yet I would hope that they would be able to understand the Caucasian culture, the California culture, the beach culture as opposed to the mountain culture.[7]

Schools are excellent arenas for promoting just the kind of awareness of and proficiency in multiple cultures described by this teacher. Such awareness can lead multicultural education toward a fuller appreciation of the range of cultural competencies available to *all* students, immigrant and nonimmigrant alike. A policy of additive acculturation cannot resolve all the problems facing immigrant children in our schools today, but it is clearly a step in the direction of addressing their needs and those of their classmates as well.

References

Barrington, John M. 1991. "The New Zealand Experience: Maoris." In *Minority Status and Schooling*, edited by M.A. Gibson and J.U. Ogbu. New York: Garland.

Bhachu, Parminder K. 1985. "Parental Educational Strategies: The Case of Punjabi Sikhs in Britain." Research Paper 3. Coventry: Centre for Research in Ethnic Relations, University of Warwick.

Caplan, N., M.H. Choy, and J.K. Whitmore. 1992. "Indochinese Refugee Families and Academic Achievement," *Scientific American*, February, pp. 36–42.

Cummins, Jim. 1981. "The Role of Primary Language Development in Promoting Educational Success for Language Minority Students." In *School and Language Minority Students*. Sacramento: Office of Bilingual, Bicultural Education, California State Department of Education.

---

[7]This teacher actually used the word *assimilation*, but what she describes is in fact *additive acculturation*, as defined in this chapter. I have taken the liberty of editing the quotation to allow for consistency of terminology without, I trust, altering her meaning.

————. 1986. "Empowering Minority Students: A Framework for Intervention," *Harvard Educational Review* 56 (1): 18–36.

Daoud, Annette M. 1993. "Resistance Behavior in Adolescents: A Study of High School Mexican-Descent Students." Master's thesis, University of California, Santa Cruz.

De Ortiz, Carlotta. 1993. "At a Loss: Teachers' Perspectives on the Academic Performance of Mexican-Origin Students in a California High School." Master's thesis, University of California, Santa Cruz.

De Vos, George. 1975. "Ethnic Pluralism: Conflict and Accommodation." In *Ethnic Identity: Cultural Continuities and Change*, edited by G. De Vos and L. Romanucci-Ross. Palo Alto, Calif.: Mayfield.

Deyhle, Donna. 1991. "Empowerment and Cultural Conflict: Navajo Parents and the Schooling of Their Children," *International Journal of Qualitative Studies in Education* 4 (4): 277–97.

Eldering, Lotty. 1992. "African, Surinamese and Moroccan Pupils in the Netherlands." Paper presented at the Annual Meeting of the American Educational Research Association, San Francisco, Calif., April 20–24.

Erickson, Frederick. 1987. "Transformation and School Success: The Politics and Culture of Educational Achievement." In "Explaining the School Performance of Minority Students," theme issue edited by E. Jacob and C. Jordan. *Anthropology and Education Quarterly* 18 (4): 335–56.

Fordham, Signithia. 1988. "Racelessness as a Factor in Black Students' School Success: Pragmatic Strategy or Pyrrhic Victory?" *Harvard Educational Review* 58 (1): 54–84.

Fordham, Signithia, and J.U. Ogbu. 1987. "Black Students' School Success: Coping with the 'Burden of Acting White,'" *Urban Review* 18 (3): 176–206.

Gallup Organization. 1993. "Public Wants Fewer Immigrants," *San Francisco Chronicle*, July 23.

Ghuman, Paul A.S. 1980. "Bhattra Sikhs in Cardiff: Family and Kinship Organisation," *New Community* 8 (2): 308–16.

Gibson, Margaret A. 1976a. "Ethnicity and Schooling: A Caribbean Case Study." Ph.D. dissertation, University of Pittsburgh.

————. 1976b. "Approaches to Multicultural Education in the United States: Some Concepts and Assumptions." In "Anthropological Perspectives on Multi-Cultural Education," theme issue edited by M.A. Gibson. *Anthropology and Education Quarterly* 7 (4): 7–18.

————. 1983. "Ethnicity and Schooling: West Indian Immigrants in the United States Virgin Islands," *Ethnic Groups* 5 (3): 173–98.

————. 1988. *Accommodation without Assimilation: Sikh Immigrants in an American High School*. Ithaca, N.Y.: Cornell University Press.

————. 1991a. "Minorities and Schooling: Some Implications." In *Minority Status and Schooling*, edited by M.A. Gibson and J.U. Ogbu. New York: Garland.

————. 1991b. "Ethnicity, Gender and Social Class: The School Adaptation Patterns of West Indian Youths." In *Minority Status and Schooling*, edited by M.A. Gibson and J.U. Ogbu. New York: Garland.

————. 1992. "Variability in Immigrant Students' School Performance: The U.S. Case," *American Educational Research Association-Division G, The Social Context of Education Newsletter*, Winter 1992/93, pp. 5–7.

————. 1993a. "Accommodating Diversity: Teachers' Perspectives on Meeting the Needs of Language Minority Students." Santa Cruz: Merrill College, University of California, Santa Cruz. Manuscript.

Gibson, M.A., ed. 1993b. "Minorities and School Performance: International Comparisons." Manuscript.

Gibson, M.A., and P.K. Bhachu. 1991. "The Dynamics of Educational Decision Making." In *Minority Status and Schooling*, edited by M.A. Gibson and J.U. Ogbu. New York: Garland.

Gibson, M.A., and J.U. Ogbu, eds. 1991. *Minority Status and Schooling: A Comparative Study of Immigrant and Involuntary Minorities.* New York: Garland.

Gillborn, David. 1990. *'Race,' Ethnicity and Education: Teaching and Learning in Multi-Ethnic Schools.* London: Unwin Hyman.

Giroux, Henry. 1983. "Theories of Reproduction and Resistance in the New Sociology of Education: A Critical Analysis," *Harvard Educational Review* 53 (3): 257–93.

Goodenough, Ward. 1976. "Multiculturalism as the Normal Human Experience." In "Anthropological Perspectives on Multi-Cultural Education," theme issue edited by M.A. Gibson. *Anthropology and Education Quarterly* 7 (4): 4–7.

Handsfield, Lara J. 1993. "Abstract and Concrete Attitudes among Mexican-Descent High School Students." Master's thesis, University of California, Santa Cruz.

Haviland, William A. 1985. *Anthropology*. New York: Holt, Rinehart & Winston.

Hoffman, Diane M. 1988. "Cross-Cultural Adaptation and Learning: Iranians and Americans at School." In *School and Society*, edited by H. Trueba and C. Delgado-Gaitan. New York: Praeger.

Jordan, Cathie, Roland Tharp, and Lynn Vogt. 1986. "Differing Domains: Is Truly Bicultural Education Possible?" Working Paper. Honolulu: Kamehameha Center for Development of Early Education.

Kelly, Gail. 1981. "Contemporary American Policies and Practices in the Education of Immigrant Children." In *Educating Immigrants*, edited by J. Bhatnagar. New York: St. Martin's Press.

Kleinfeld, Judith. 1983. "First Do No Harm: A Reply to Courtney Cazden," *Anthropology and Education Quarterly* 14 (4): 282–87.

Kohl, Herbert. 1991. *I Won't Learn from You! The Role of Assent in Learning.* Thistle Series of Essays. Minneapolis, Minn.: Milkweed Editions.

Kramer, B.J. 1983. "The Dismal Record Continues: The Ute Indian Tribe and the School System," *Ethnic Groups* 5 (3): 151–71.

Lambert, Wallace E. 1975. "Culture and Language as Factors in Learning and Education." In *Education of Immigrants*, edited by A. Wolfgang. Toronto: Ontario Institute for Studies in Education.

LeCompte, Margaret D., and Anthony G. Dworkin. 1991. *Giving Up on School: Student Dropouts and Teacher Burnouts.* Newbury Park, Calif.: Corwin.

MacLeod, Jay. 1987. *Ain't No Makin' It: Leveled Aspirations in a Low-income Neighborhood.* Boulder, Colo.: Westview.

Malhotra, M.K. 1985. "Research Report: The Educational Problems of Foreign Children of Different Nationalities in West Germany," *Ethnic and Racial Studies* 8 (2): 291–99.

Matute-Bianchi, Maria E. 1991. "Situational Ethnicity and Patterns of School Performance among Immigrant and Nonimmigrant Mexican-Descent Students." In *Minority Status and Schooling,* edited by M.A. Gibson and J.U. Ogbu. New York: Garland.

Mehan, Hugh, Lea Hubbard, and Irene Villanueva. 1994. "Forming Academic Identities: Accommodation without Assimilation among Involuntary Minorities," *Anthropology and Education Quarterly* 25 (2): 91–117.

New York City Public Schools. 1992. Paper prepared by the Office of Research, Evaluation and Statistics for New York City Board of Education Workshop on "Immigrants and Public Education," May 6. Mimeo.

Ogbu, John U. 1978. *Minority Education and Caste: The American System in Cross-Cultural Perspective.* New York: Academic Press.

———. 1987. "Variability in Minority School Performance: A Problem in Search of an Explanation." In "Explaining the School Performance of Minority Students," theme issue edited by E. Jacob and C. Jordan. *Anthropology and Education Quarterly* 18 (4): 312–34.

———. 1991a. "Immigrant and Involuntary Minorities in Comparative Perspective." In *Minority Status and Schooling,* edited by M.A. Gibson and J.U. Ogbu. New York: Garland.

———. 1991b. "Low School Performance as an Adaptation." In *Minority Status and Schooling,* edited by M.A. Gibson and J.U. Ogbu. New York: Garland.

Petroni, F.A. 1970. "'Uncle Toms': White Stereotypes in the Black Movement," *Human Organization* 29 (4): 260–66.

Rodriguez, Richard. 1983. *Hunger of Memory: The Education of Richard Rodriguez — an Autobiography.* Boston, Mass.: D.R. Godine.

Roosens, Eugeen. 1992. "'Young 'Newcomers' in Belgium and California Compared." Paper presented at the Annual Meeting of the American Educational Research Association, San Francisco, Calif., April 20–24.

Rumbaut, Rubén G. 1990. *Immigrant Students in California Public Schools: A Summary of Current Knowledge.* Report No. 11. Baltimore, Md.: Center for Research on Effective Schooling for Disadvantaged Students, Johns Hopkins University.

Suárez-Orozco, Marcelo M. 1991. "Immigrant Adaptation to Schooling: A Hispanic Case." In *Minority Status and Schooling,* edited by M.A. Gibson and J.U. Ogbu. New York: Garland.

Sung, Betty Lee. 1979. "Transplanted Chinese Children." Report to the Administration for Children, Youth and Family, Department of Health, Education and Welfare, Washington, D.C.

Vigil, J., and J. Long. 1981. "Unidirectional or Nativist Acculturation—Chicano Paths to School Achievement," *Human Organization* 40 (3): 273–77.

Walker, Wendy D. 1989. "The Challenges of the Hmong Culture: A Study of Teacher, Counselor and Administrator Training in a Time of Changing Demographics." Ed.D. dissertation, Harvard University.

Ware, Caroline F. 1935. *Greenwich Village 1920–1930: A Comment on American Civilization in the Post-War Years.* Boston: Houghton Mifflin.

Willis, Paul E. 1977. *Learning to Labour: How Working Class Kids Get Working Class Jobs.* Westmead: Saxon House.

5

Korean and Russian Students in a Los Angeles High School: Exploring the Alternative Strategies of Two High-Achieving Groups

Mia Tuan

Immigrant students from diverse political, sociocultural, and economic backgrounds are changing the face of California's public schools. In 1990 the number of limited-English-proficient (LEP) students, the over-whelming majority of whom are recent immigrants, reached nearly 862,000—more than twice what it was in 1980 (Los Angeles County 1991). Over 18 percent of California's current *total* student enrollment is LEP, with all signs indicating continuing growth. Despite the sizable numbers and high visibility of immigrant students, relatively little is known about their adaptive experiences.

Traditionally, school authorities and researchers alike have held that immigrants who embraced American ways and assimilated as rapidly as possible fared the best, while those who did not ran the risk of falling into the cracks (Fass 1989; Carlson 1975; Cohen and Mohl 1979). More recently, theorists such as Ogbu (1987, 1983, 1978) have argued that school success depends primarily on historic factors that determine what "type" of minority (i.e., autonomous, voluntary, caste-like) a newcomer is; that how a group becomes labeled has largely to do with the original conditions and terms under which the group entered the host society. I argue that neither the assimilation framework nor Ogbu's typology can capture the full range of experiences and responses that

The author would like to thank Lawrence Bobo, Mehdi Bozorgmehr, John Horton, Melvin Oliver, Jiannbin Shiao, and Roger Waldinger for their comments on drafts of this chapter.

newcomer students may develop, and that both subsequently miss a large part of the immigrant adaptation picture. I also argue that, rather than passively conforming to the given structure and expectations of schools, growing numbers of newcomers are employing distinct adaptive strategies that suit their unique circumstances and goals (Gibson 1988; Rumbaut and Ima 1988; Suárez-Orozco 1987). In this process, *race*, above and beyond any other minority classification, plays a role in shaping perceptions of opportunity and ensuing adaptive strategies. Racially distinct groups confront additional concerns that racially or phenotypically indistinguishable (i.e., white European) immigrants do not face to an equivalent degree, such as fears of racial discrimination and exclusion lasting beyond the first generation.

In this chapter these issues are explored through an examination of the experiences of Korean and Russian Jewish students attending a Los Angeles public high school.[1] Why study Koreans and Russians? To start, both groups mutually diverge from the assimilationist trajectory; they associate primarily with co-ethnics, rarely participate in school functions or extracurricular activities, and are seen by many faculty as maintaining clannish rather than assimilationist attitudes. Nevertheless, school authorities consider Koreans and Russians to be high achievers and college bound. Each group, however, employs vastly different strategies in adapting to school. While the Korean students are more likely to see their way through high school, receive diplomas, and attend junior college or university, many Russians, in their rush to attend college, are leaving high school without graduating. Paradoxical as it may seem, Russians are so eager to attend college they are dropping out to do so. In one school year as many as 50 percent of the Russian student population left to enroll in local junior colleges.[2] While Koreans and Russians mutually diverge from the school's expectations, each group pursues a distinctive strategy for getting to college.

While a number of factors contribute to their divergence in strategies, the role played by race is of particular importance. Koreans, as nonwhite immigrants, must incorporate worries over persistent discrimination and exclusion into their adaptive strategies in ways that Russians, as white immigrants, need not be concerned with. In today's racially turbulent times, as recent events in Los Angeles can attest, we live in a society far from ready to transcend racial categorizing. Koreans find that they are continually reminded of their "foreignness" in both

---

[1] While all the Russian students in the sample were Jewish, the role of religion in shaping adaptive strategies was not explored.

[2] Specific ethnic/racial breakdowns of dropouts are not kept by the school, making it difficult to gauge exactly how many Russians, who are considered "Anglo" on official rosters, have left. Estimates by teachers and the ESL department suggest that around 30–50 percent out of nearly two hundred Russians attending the school in 1991–1992 dropped out.

subtle and not so subtle ways. Their strategies, then, are influenced by their concerns over racial targeting and bigotry; it affects their views about opportunities in America and is always a factor in their decisions.

Los Angeles, of course, is an extreme setting; the magnitude with which newcomers have transformed the look of local schools is staggering. Nearly one out of every two LEP students in the *entire* state attends school in Los Angeles, and more than one in four students attending a local county school is classified as LEP (California Department of Education 1990). According to the Los Angeles County Office of Education (1991: 1.6), without new limited-English-proficient pupils added to Los Angeles County's enrollments each year, there would have been a 23 percent enrollment loss in the county's schools during the 1980s; with them, there was an actual *gain* of 12 percent. What is happening in Los Angeles, however, is a harbinger for other immigrant cities and major urban centers. Up until the mid-1970s school diversity meant little more than black and white students attending the same schools. Today, diversity means that students from around the world, especially immigrants from Latin America and Asia, are attending school together. With this growing complexity comes the need for new ways of approaching, thinking about, and studying schools. This chapter is an effort to move in that direction.

Perspectives on Immigrant Adaptation

Much of the previous literature on immigrant adaptation has assumed that assimilation into American culture is an inevitable as well as desirable goal for newcomers (Gordon 1964; Mole 1981; Park 1950; Schlesinger 1992; Warner and Srole 1945). The faster the immigrant shed his or her cultural "baggage," the sooner she or he would reap the benefits of being an American. Immigrants were expected to acquire the "right" (i.e., American) values and follow prescribed patterns of incorporation as preconditions to their acceptance and success. Public schools have historically played a critical role in this process by teaching these values and rules to newcomers (Vinovskis 1990; Fass 1989; Strouse 1987; Carlson 1975). Efforts to assimilate immigrant children through school "Americanization" programs were largely prompted by nativists' fears that the lack of linguistic and cultural conformity would bring about divisiveness and disorder (Kaestle 1973; Schultz 1973). Consequently, from this point of view, signs of a newcomer unwilling to relinquish his/her cultural heritage or accept the schools' expectations of compliance were likely to lead to his/her academic failure.

Despite the current fashion of multiculturalism and its appreciation of racial and cultural diversity in schools, conformist assumptions still persist, albeit in more subtle forms (Schlesinger 1992; Sleeter and Grant

1988; Strouse 1987; Sagar and Schofield 1983; Cohen and Mohl 1979). The assimilation of immigrant students into an assumed American main-stream continues to be a desired goal:

> The impact of ethnic and racial pressures on our public
> schools is . . . troubling. The bonds of national cohesion
> are sufficiently fragile already. Public education should
> aim to strengthen those bonds, not to weaken them. If
> separatist tendencies go on unchecked, the result can
> only be the fragmentation, resegregation, and tribaliza-
> tion of American life (Schlesinger 1992: 18).

However, a growing body of literature has emerged that presents a challenge to assimilationist assumptions (Matute-Bianchi 1991; Caplan, Choy, and Whitmore 1991; Rumbaut 1990; Gibson 1988, 1987; Rumbaut and Ima 1988; Suárez-Orozco 1987). These authors provide examples where newcomers have undergone only limited cultural and/or struc-tural acculturation, yet have excelled in school. Gibson (1988, this volume) refers to this type of adaptation as "accommodation without assimilation," whereby immigrants fit themselves to the official ways of the school, adopt "desirable" American ways, but resist full assimilation by maintaining their separate cultural identities. In her study of Punjabi Sikh Indians, she discusses how Punjabi students do best when they employ a strategy of deliberate resistance to assimilation while also accommodating to the ways of the host society when they believe this to be in their best interests. As Gibson puts it, "Although proud to become Americans, most Punjabi Sikh immigrants openly and actively reject the notion that Americanization means giving up their separate identity" (1988: 24). Similarly, Rumbaut and Ima (1988) found a strong correlation between ethnic resilience and GPA in their study of Southeast Asian refugees; the stronger the sense of ethnic resilience, the higher the GPA of the students. Likewise, Suárez-Orozco (1989, 1987) argues that Cen-tral American refugee students did not equate succeeding in school with forgoing their cultural ties or merging with the majority group. Much like Gibson's Punjabis, Central Americans did best when they employed an accommodative strategy of adaptation:

> A strategy of superficial accommodation without really
> giving up core cultural values is perceived as ideal. . . .
> In these cases, the immigrants see their experiences in
> the new land as an "additive" phenomenon: not wish-
> ing to give up their own cultural code for behavior, but
> readily adapting to learn the language and to acquire
> the behaviors and symbols seen as required for success
> in the host society (Suárez-Orozco 1989: 92).

While it could be argued that the experiences of Punjabi, Southeast Asian, and Central American students fall in line with the assimilationist trajectory, I would maintain that something new is going on here. Today the context of schooling, its social and political tone, is more amenable to racial and cultural diversity than it has been in the past. In spite of assimilationist assumptions, multiculturalism has created an environment more receptive of diversity. More opportunities are available to newcomers to successfully negotiate their way through schools while maintaining a separate cultural identity. As in the above cases, the active mechanism underlying this new form of adaptation is the conscious, deliberate decision to remain rooted in the ethnic community, accompanied by the belief that success does not necessitate the loss of cultural ties. Studies such as these open the door to an alternative way of thinking about and discussing immigrant student adaptation.

Minority Typology

While not dealing directly with immigrant student adaptation, education anthropologist John Ogbu (1987, 1983, 1978; Gibson and Ogbu 1991) has proposed a theoretical model that may be extended to this issue. According to Ogbu, minorities may be classified into one of three types: autonomous, immigrant/voluntary, and caste-like or involuntary. How a group becomes categorized is largely a function of its history of subordination by the host society or lack thereof and its subsequent relations with host people.[3]

> The main factors differentiating the more successful from the less successful minorities appear to be the nature of the history, subordination, and exploitation of the minorities, and the nature of the minorities' own instrumental and expressive responses to their treatment (1978: 317).

Autonomous groups refer to self-segregating groups, such as Jews and Mormons, who are minorities in a numerical but not usually racial sense; they do not experience disproportionate, persistent problems in school and in fact tend to do quite well.[4] Immigrant/voluntary groups are people who have moved more or less voluntarily to the United States

---

[3]Ogbu acknowledges that changes in status may occur; however, the general sense seems to be that movement across the types is a rare occurrence.

[4]Since the crux of Ogbu's argument lies in comparing the experiences of voluntary and involuntary groups, autonomous groups will not be considered further.

in search of better lives.[5] Involuntary or caste-like groups, on the other hand, are people with a history of caste-like subordination in the host society; they were incorporated into the society against their will through slavery, conquest, or colonization. To this day they continue to be haunted by the legacy of their oppression as evidenced by their persistent problems adjusting to and performing in school.

The reasons why voluntary groups are able to succeed academically where involuntary groups generally fail have largely to do with key features differentiating the two groups. These differences include: (1) incorporation into the social and economic structure; (2) outlooks and reactions to the same social situation; (3) levels of trust toward the host society; (4) frames of reference; and (5) difficulty of surmounting cultural incongruities with the host society. Each of these is briefly considered below, given their analytical relevance to the present study.

Voluntary and involuntary groups occupy very different social positions within the host society. While voluntary groups are able to rise up the ranks, involuntary groups are relegated to the bottom rungs of the economic opportunity structure. Regardless of the amount of effort put in or education credentials received, members of involuntary groups find they are unable to break through the job ceilings and other exclusionary practices that impede their advancement. According to Ogbu (1978) these blockades stem from involuntary groups' historically subjugated positions within the host society, a legacy that continues to dictate their life chances and the life chances of their offspring. Over time, involuntary groups come to understand that the host society does not offer them the same opportunities provided for others.

Because voluntary groups have not experienced the generations of oppression that involuntary groups have endured, they generally consider any obstacles they may face as "temporary," thus enabling them to maintain a positive attitude toward the host society and its institutions even during difficult times. Consequently, the process of learning the ways of the host society is not considered threatening to their identity. They may even rationalize discrimination and prejudice as part and parcel of their assimilation process. In this sense, voluntary groups buy into the host society's "folk theory" of making it: through hard work and persistence they may overcome hostility and be accepted by the host society. This is not so for involuntary groups, who believe they will never be accepted; discrimination is institutionalized and a lasting part of their lives. Over the years, then, involuntary groups have adapted to their conditions by developing an oppositional stance characterized by anger, discouragement, and disillusion.

---

[5]This category includes current as well as former immigrants. For example, a third-generation Chinese American would be classified in the same immigrant/voluntary category as a recent Chinese immigrant.

Moreover, voluntary groups are characterized by "primary" cultural differences, while involuntary groups possess "secondary" ones. According to Ogbu, primary cultural differences pose fewer problems because they are not oppositional in nature to the values and cultural attributes of the host society. Rather, they are the cultural beliefs, values, and mores held by the group prior to emigration. Secondary cultural differences, in contrast, are cultural adaptations made in response to harsh treatment and conditions in the host society; they are "markers of identity to be maintained," symbols of an oppositional stance to the host society.

Voluntary and involuntary groups also utilize different frames of reference. Since involuntary groups are not newcomers, their reference or comparison point is the host society. They are well aware of the differential treatment accorded them and are resentful of this perceived injustice. For voluntary groups, in contrast, the frame of reference is their homeland. While the situation may not be ideal in the host society, the ability to compare their situation to that of peers back home who may be even worse off may help to offset growing discouragement. Ogbu also notes that voluntary groups have more options than do involuntary groups, such as the ability to return to their homeland or move to a new country if conditions in the host society become intolerable. He does acknowledge, however, that the situation may be different for political refugees and exiles who are not able to return to their homelands. Nevertheless, according to Ogbu's typology, refugees are considered voluntary/immigrant minorities.

Without a doubt, Ogbu's framework is valuable. His focus on the interaction between cultural and structural variables, the dynamics of minority-majority group relations, contexts of arrival, and a minority group's subsequent responses to treatment by the host society is an advance over the ahistorical, nondifferentiated picture presented by earlier assimilation theorists. Ogbu goes far in shedding light on the complex processes affecting minority student performance and immigrant adaptation. Nevertheless, questions remain. For example, are all voluntary groups able to overcome their difficulties? Do any experience persistent discrimination? What of voluntary groups who are racially distinct from the host society? Are their experiences similar to those of groups who are racially indistinguishable from host natives? For Ogbu the distinguishing factor lies in the group's minority classification. By placing such importance on this, however, he downplays the continuing influence that race may have in the lives of all nonwhites in the United States, above and beyond any other imposed label or minority classification. What happens over time to racially distinct voluntary groups who find they are not accepted by the host society? Do they end up adopting some of the same oppositional characteristics attributed to involuntary groups such as disenchantment with and rejection of the host society's culture?[6]

Ogbu's time frame is also ambiguous. According to Ogbu, one of the advantages possessed by voluntary groups is their ability to return to their homeland in the event of failure or persecution in the host society. By treating the experiences of newly arrived immigrants in the same manner as those who arrived generations earlier, however, Ogbu disregards the significant differences that separate their experiences. Time does not stand still for voluntary groups. While some newcomers possess the option of returning to their homeland, this is less likely for a third- or even a second-generation offspring of an immigrant or refugee. Eventually, for all voluntary groups just as for involuntary groups, the frame of reference becomes the host society. They can no sooner go back to the mythical homeland than can an involuntary group. Home is the host society, like it or not. Ogbu pays close attention to the adaptive responses involuntary groups make to repeated discriminatory treatment by the host society, yet he fails to pay the same close attention to those processes as they might apply to voluntary groups. By delineating such broad categories, Ogbu misses the finer gradations within each category and the overlap between them. While acknowledging that differences between and within groups may exist, he fails to discuss at length groups who fall between the cracks of his framework. Considering, however, that the bulk of individuals currently arriving in the United States are made up of the groups in dispute here—i.e., racial minorities—much more needs to be said about their experiences and adaptive concerns (Portes and Rumbaut 1990; First and Carrera 1988).

Examining the experiences of Korean and Russian students provides an opportunity to apply Ogbu's framework, to point out its strong points as well as its weaknesses. According to his typology, both Koreans and Russians are immigrant/voluntary minorities. Yet, as we shall see, neither group fits neatly within this category, and Koreans in fact may possess some of the characteristics that Ogbu reserves for involuntary groups.

Methodology

Fieldwork was carried out over a one-year period in a Los Angeles public school called Rose High.[7] The first phase of research involved becoming acquainted with the dynamics of the school, its students, administrators, and faculty. Field observations of various English as a Second

---

[6]See Huhr and Kim 1984 for an extended discussion of this in the case of Korean immigrants.

[7]The name of the high school and those of all faculty and students have been changed to protect their anonymity.

Language (ESL) classes and informal interviews with teachers and staff were conducted to learn more about the school and how it has changed since its "ethnicization."

The second phase consisted of formally interviewing students and teachers. Thirty in-depth, structured interviews were conducted in English with sixteen Korean and fourteen Russian students ranging from grades ten to twelve, and from sixteen to nineteen years of age. Topics included their experiences in adapting to an American school, relations with established residents and other immigrants, perceptions of opportunity, and educational aspirations. Interviews were obtained through snowball sampling and faculty referrals and were contingent upon a student's willingness to be interviewed. Most interviewed students were currently enrolled in ESL or were recent graduates of the program. Of the students still in ESL, only those in advanced ESL classes were interviewed, given language barriers. However, the varying language ability of the students required that I rephrase questions at times or elaborate on my meaning. Since my sample was limited to those students with adequate fluency in English, the responses of more recent arrivals from both populations were excluded.

Over twenty interviews were conducted with teachers, principals, ESL staff, counselors, and community workers to develop a fuller picture of the students and the factors influencing their experiences. Several unsuccessful attempts were also made to interview Russian students who had left Rose before graduating, but they did not wish to be singled out for their experiences or stated that they did not have the time to be interviewed.

The fact that the researcher is an Asian-American woman undoubtedly affected the students' responses. It is likely that the Korean respondents felt more comfortable in discussing their feelings about racism and other sensitive matters, while the Russians may have felt more inhibited in discussing their opinions about Korean students, since members of both groups assumed I was Korean.

Koreans and Russians at Rose High

> We still like to think of ourselves as an academically oriented school, but it's harder now that the school is so much more complicated. It used to be predominantly middle class and everyone was very similar. Now we have students who are not part of the average profile (fifteen-year veteran teacher).

Rose High School has an ethnic minority population of over 70 percent. As recently as fifteen years ago, Rose catered to a predominantly white, middle-class, Jewish population and was reportedly the flagship of the district. Today, it is a designated PHBAO school (Predominantly Hispanic, Black, Asian, and Other) with a student population comprised of approximately 34 percent Latino, 29 percent Anglo, 18 percent African American, and 20 percent Asian (Filipinos and Pacific Islanders included). Racial and ethnic diversity are matters of fact at Rose, as a glance through its recent yearbooks can attest. Approximately 1,800 regular students attend school here, of whom nearly *one-third* are currently in ESL or are awaiting reclassification into the regular population. This figure does *not* include those students who are graduates of the ESL program now mainstreamed into regular classes; if they were included, the number would be much higher. When the current ESL director came to the school in 1982, approximately one hundred ESL students were enrolled. Since that time, she has witnessed the program swell to its current population of over six hundred students. Over thirty-four foreign languages are spoken by Rose students, the most common being Spanish, Russian, and Korean. Accordingly, these three correspond to the largest subpopulations of the ESL community, with Latinos (Mexican, Central and South American) representing 50 percent, Koreans 17 percent, and Russians 19 percent. Approximately two hundred (ESL and regular population) Korean and two hundred (ESL only) Russian students attend the school.

Interviews with Rose teachers revealed that Korean and Russian students have very different reputations among faculty and administrators. Koreans are perceived as quiet, well behaved, and compliant, while Russian students are considered arrogant, loud, and aggressive. The latter also have extensive problems with cheating and "ditching," i.e., skipping classes or not coming to school. According to teachers, Russians have an "I can't be bothered with coming to school" attitude.[8]

> Some of my Russian kids are really obnoxious. They think the work I give them is "baby work" . . . that it's too easy. They act like I'm insulting them by expecting them to do the work, but they don't understand that I have reasons for giving them each lesson. . . . They can still learn from the exercise.

Despite their opposed images, both groups are highly motivated to attend college, and both see education as being the key to their success in the United States. Where they differ is in their estimations of the usefulness of high school in helping them achieve their goals. As mentioned earlier, the Koreans are more likely to see their way through

---

[8]This is not to imply that Korean students do not have any disciplinary problems at Rose. Rather, they are involved in far fewer incidents than are Russian students.

Rose, receive diplomas, and enroll in college or university, while the Russians are more likely to bypass high school.

In the eyes of faculty and staff, then, neither group completely conforms to the school's expected norms for adaptation. It is clear from their comments that faculty envision a "better" way of adapting to school, more closely resembling the strategy adopted by the Koreans, since it better fits the traditional view of appropriate school behaviors. However, even the Koreans are viewed with reservation since their "clannish" tendencies are interpreted as signs of unwillingness to assimilate. The Russians' tactics are viewed with even more reservation, as placing them at risk of not graduating. Nevertheless, Korean and Russian students are going on to college, and in that sense both groups are adapting successfully.[9]

How have the two groups come to adopt their respective strategies? Why do Koreans and Russians view high school differently? These questions will be taken up in the remainder of this chapter through an exploration of the students' social and material conditions before migrating (socioeconomic origins, parents' social class and occupation, home country educational system), their subsequent conditions in the United States (immigration status, parents' mode of incorporation into the U.S. economy, ethnic networks), and the role that race does or does not play in shaping their strategies.

"America Is Where Study Is Better": Reasons for Emigrating to the United States

The majority of Korean students specifically cited the improvement of their educational opportunities as paramount in their families' decision to migrate. Three students even came to Los Angeles by themselves, while their families remained in Korea, in order to take advantage of educational opportunities in the United States.

> My parents, they decide for me to come to America. . . . America is where study is better. Here it's brand new, more creative, more opportunity to study. They care about other people's opinions. If you fail in Korean school, very bad.

Two other Koreans live with their mothers in the United States while their fathers live/work in Korea. Like the students who are here by themselves, they cited improved educational opportunities as the main

---

[9]Quantitative data were unavailable to confirm this statement. The claim is based on the opinions of teachers, administrators, and academic counselors who feel both the Korean and Russian populations are going on to college at above-average rates, as well as on the author's own fieldwork and notes.

reason for their parents' decision to divide the family. The Russians, on the other hand, gave reasons for emigrating ranging from "more freedom" and a "higher standard of living" to "more opportunities for the entire family." While the improvement of their educational opportunities was a factor, the Russians felt it was a part of rather than the primary motive in their families' decisions. In sum, educational factors played a greater role in the migratory decisions of Korean compared to Russian families, which may have great bearing on the way Korean students view their U.S. education and the pressure they feel to do well in school.

Another difference emerges between Koreans and Russians when we examine the mode of economic incorporation experienced by parents. Both Korean and Russian parents are highly educated, and the majority were skilled professionals in their homelands. Unlike Korean parents, however, Russian parents are more likely to be found in similar rather than unrelated fields of work in the United States. Some Russian parents are even waiting for jobs commensurate with their professional skills and expertise rather than taking just "any" job. According to their children, the Russian parents do not appear to question their eventual participation in the American labor market.

A different picture emerges for the Korean parents. Whereas in Korea many fathers held professional jobs, in the United States they are working in the Korean ethnic economy as shopkeepers or workers in small ethnic businesses, reflective of a general trend found among Korean immigrants in Los Angeles (Light and Bonacich 1988). Only two Korean fathers are employed in positions similar to those they held in Korea; both, however, service the Korean community.[10] The rest are in fields unrelated to their previous occupations. The following is a typical response when students are asked why their fathers were not employed in similar occupations: "No American company will hire [him] . . . his English no good."

Differences in the ways the two groups of parents are incorporated into the local economy may in turn influence how they encourage their children to view their American education. Korean parents made personal sacrifices specifically to expand their children's educational opportunities, knowing they would be "giving up" the social and possibly economic status derived from their occupations. In comparison, Russian parents, while also sacrificing, emigrated with the belief that they would be able to continue in their chosen occupations, albeit at lower social status. These differences have largely to do with the two groups' respective immigration statuses in the United States and the resources they command as a result.

Russians are considered refugees and are eligible for Refugee Cash Assistance and resettlement services such as job training programs,

---

[10]One father is a pastor; the other works in construction.

social and educational services (English language classes), health benefits, and permanent resident status (Gold 1992; Gold and Tuan 1993;
Office of Refugee Resettlement 1990).[11] Access to these benefits enables
them to spend at least some time searching for "good" jobs and
acquiring necessary language skills. Koreans, as voluntary immigrants,
are not eligible for similar government support and thus have to concern
themselves more immediately with the exigencies of earning a living.
The presence of a strong Korean community and numerous information
networks greatly aids them in their social and economic integration.
Socially, these buffer them from the difficulties of relocation by providing a stable and culturally familiar environment. Economically, they
provide vital information regarding job opportunities, work conditions,
wages, and sources of investment capital (Light and Bonacich 1988).
Moreover, unlike Russians, the Koreans are able to maintain economic
ties with the Pacific Rim. As mentioned earlier, two Korean students are
living in the United States with their mothers while their fathers maintain their business ties in Korea. Russians, in contrast, must sever their
relationship to the former Soviet Union. "Refugees lack the ability to
return home, the possibility of bringing large sums of money with them
and the potential to maintain economic links with the home country"
(Gold 1985: 211). At least initially, they must rely on cash assistance
provided by the U.S. government, Jewish relocation agencies, and kin
who sponsor them.

Previous research also points to the different attitudes that migrants
may have to the host country, depending on their immigration status.
"Soviet Jews, especially, arrive expecting to better themselves and are
unwilling to put up with what they regard as second-class treatment"
(Morgan and Colsen 1987: 8). According to Gold (1992), refugees who
previously have experienced authority as corrupt and/or oppressive are
more likely to be skeptical of authority now. They are likely to be
suspicious of government and to have a strategy of "survivor-ism." Gold
refers to this as a "culture of savvy," whereby unconventional means are
used to obtain scarce goods or, in the case of the Russians at Rose,
passing grades. This may partially account for why Russians have such a
reputation for excessive cheating. In contrast, voluntary migrants, such
as Koreans, may be more accepting of their current circumstances
because they can compare them to those of peers in the homeland.
Moreover, they have the option to return to their home country, while the
Russians do not. The fact that refugees cannot return, however, means
that their experiences diverge from more traditional immigrant/volun-
tary groups.

---

[11] Fieldwork for this study was conducted in 1991. Due to the massive changes that have
occurred in the former Soviet Union since the end of the Cold War, immigration laws have
been in flux. While still possible, it is now more difficult for Russians to acquire refugee
status.

Dual Frames of Reference: Schooling in South Korea and Russia

The role that education plays in South Korea is of paramount importance to its citizens. Education is seen not only as the key to financial security but as a measure of personal worth and family honor (Lee 1991; Sah-Myung 1983). Parents have high expectations and put pressure on their children to excel. University admission is based almost solely on test results, and competition is fierce (Sah-Myung 1983). Moreover, junior colleges are looked upon as being inferior in Korea, a belief that carries over to the United States. According to a counselor from a local Korean youth center, "In Korea it is shameful and embarrassing for children to attend junior college. If their children attend junior college, they [the parents] are considered no good."

Schooling in the former Soviet Union is also more rigorous and demanding. Students learn more material within a shorter period of time compared to their American counterparts, with compulsory education extending over a ten- as opposed to a twelve-year system.[12] Consequently, curriculum and age at exposure to subject material are structured differently than in the United States. Russian students typically study biology and geography in form 5 (equivalent to the fifth grade in the United States), physics in form 6, and trigonometry and chemistry in form 7 (Kashin 1988). Moreover, due to the unpredictable timing of their emigration from the former Soviet Union, students may arrive in the United States at any point during the school year.

Differences in the educational systems of Korea and Russia compared to the United States and contexts of arrival may lead the two groups of students to look upon their current educational situations quite differently. There is more structural congruity between the Korean and American educational systems since the Korean system was influenced by the American model (Light and Bonacich 1988); both employ twelve-year compulsory systems and rely (albeit to different degrees) on entrance examinations for college admission. Age-grade discrepancies between the Russian and American systems, on the other hand, result in structural incongruity. Moreover, the former Soviet Union relies on alternative forms of higher education such as vocational and technical schools and other specialized training programs to a higher degree than does the United States (Kashin 1988). These disparities, or lack thereof, need to be kept in mind when trying to understand the different attitudes that Korean and Russian students have toward their current educational experiences and these students' subsequent actions.

---

[12]Since the fieldwork was conducted for this study, compulsory education in the former Soviet Union has been raised to eleven years.

"I'm Wasting My Time"

Compared to South Korea and especially the former Soviet Union, the United States has a more permissive, less demanding educational system, a point both groups of students agree upon. Nonetheless, the two groups respond differently to these incongruities, with Russians more frequently expressing dissatisfaction. Koreans view American schools with a sense of relief. Attending school here is seen as a respectable alternative in the event or fear of failure in Korean schools. Russian students, in contrast, resent having to remain in school for what they perceive as an extra two years. Vlad's frustrations over "wasting time" echo those of other Russians:

> The things I learn here in World History are 99.9 percent things I learned five to six years ago. I'm wasting my time, but I'm taking it easy. . . . I just don't care about it. What can I do?

Koreans, while acknowledging that Korean schools teach more, emphasize their appreciation for a less stressful environment as well as comparative ease of schoolwork:

> In Korea, you study very hard, 7:30 a.m. to 11 p.m., you study at school, with lunch and dinner. You learn more in Korea, but here it is more interesting. Teachers are very "strong" in Korea. . . . They hit with stick. Plus, it's very difficult to continue the studies.

Prior to migrating, both the Koreans and Russians knew little about American schools. In general, both groups had high expectations and assumed American schools would be superior due to the way the United States is portrayed in their media. They now realize that their expectations were too high. Russians, in particular, feel let down:

> Before I think, okay, I'm coming to America to study, and not just to spend my time. . . . It's not Russia anymore, I should be studying more. . . . [But] after one year I understand Russia is better in school. I'm not mean all Russia, but school better. I was interested in studying, but here program for me is a little bit easy. At Rose, program is like, you know in Russia [equivalent to] grade 5 or 6, you know, so I know everything. I mean English difficult but work is easy.

For many Russians the incongruity between the two systems seems inordinate. These are the students who speak of leaving Rose early. No one is aware how the trend began, but thanks to the speed and efficiency of ethnic networks, all the Russians know of co-ethnics who have dropped out of Rose and are attending local junior colleges:

> I know about eighteen friends [who left] all in the last year. Most of them were seventeen to eighteen [years old]. I have some friends that left Rose to go to Santa Monica College.

The incongruities also lead to "ditching" since the Russians feel they are wasting their time by having to relearn material:

> I think the main problem is just a higher level of knowledge. You don't want to go to the next period if you know what they're going to do there. And if it's just boring, people do not want to come.

A different picture emerges for the Koreans. Upon being asked whether they had ever considered dropping out, the majority of Koreans expressed great surprise at the question. Sunny's response is typical: "Me? No, I never think of it without school. . . . School is part of my life." This may be due to the greater similarity between the Korean and American educational systems, as well as the added parental pressure to excel in American schools. In sum, Koreans are more willing to accept the conditions at hand, harbor fewer resentments, and feel less of a need to act on them.

"But for English I Can't Go to University": Educational Aspirations and Revised Expectations

Both Korean and Russian students have professional aspirations, and *all* fully expect to attend college. Their expectations regarding which college and of what prestige level, however, have gone through reassessment, as Svetlana's quote expresses:

> I want university. I would like to go to UCLA or USC. . . . I want to be a lawyer. But I don't know. . . . I look at SAT and they want ten words, ten synonyms for one word, I didn't know what it is.

While both groups unanimously agree that American schools are easier, their limited proficiency in English prevents them from demonstrating their ability:

> I really want to go to university. I want to be doctor . . . but I think university should do something for immi-

grant people. Maybe I know more, but for English I
can't go to university.

In response, both groups have had to lower their aspirations; their
resolutions, however, differ. While at first expecting to attend a prestigious local university, such as UCLA or USC, most Russians now
expect to attend a local junior college and transfer to a university at a
later date. The majority of Koreans, on the other hand, still hope to enter
university directly from high school, and apparently many are succeeding in doing so.[13] It seems likely that Korean students feel that remaining in high school is helping them achieve their goals. Moreover, Korean
students are aware that their current situation is still considerably better
than that of their peers in Korea.

For Russians, on the other hand, skipping high school and going
directly to junior college seems an appropriate and practical path since
most are resigned to doing so anyway. "At least I get college credit" was a
common sentiment expressed when students explained the benefits of
junior college. Given their understanding of the American educational
system, Russian students are taking matters into their own hands and
pursuing what they see as the fast track to a college education. In the
process of deciding whether or not to stay in school, however, the
Russians' inability to become engaged in schoolwork leads to "ditching"
and to faculty perceptions of them as "arrogant." The Russians' "can't be
bothered" attitude, however, is actually reflective of frustration over an
inability to demonstrate their competence and knowledge.

"For What Should I Stay?"

Because program not interesting, people doesn't like
school. They just ditch school. For what should they be
going to school if not interested? I have friend, he ditch
every day. Sometime like he not be at school for one
week, two week, and he say "I don't care, so maybe I not
have [good grade]. . . . It's okay for me. I just want to
graduate this school and go to college. I don't like this
school, I don't want to come." Because he's eighteen, he
has diploma, they [the junior college] have to let him in.
Now he study every day because he's interested. But in
our school he wasn't.

While the young man in the example above did decide to remain in
school and graduate (albeit at the minimal level of attendance and

---

[13]Data were unavailable to confirm this statement. According to academic counselors,
more Koreans than Russians were going directly into university at the time of fieldwork.

performance), many Russians choose not to stay. In assessing their situations, Russians weigh the benefits of leaving early versus staying in high school and obtaining their diplomas. Those Russians who are inclined to remain still feel they have time "to spare" and can find some additional benefit to remaining in high school, such as improving their English skills; those who do not are the ones who leave.[14] For them, Rose is a holding cell; real education begins in college:

> College is more bigger than school, is first reason [why people leave Rose]. In school they think we're little children, but in a college they don't. We're not children, so if I'm in college they treat me more as adult. Second reason is our school is more special than other school in Los Angeles because too much immigrants here. So if I'm going to college I'm not really immigrant. I'm just American people; I just talk to them. In college, there's many groups and if you speak just Russian it's not good because they didn't understand, so it's better for my English (Erina, eighteen-year-old senior).

The first concern Erina raises of being treated "like a child" is typical of most Russians. Their sense of feeling more mature has much to do with their impatience and belief in the need to get on with their lives. Because students typically graduate at the age of sixteen in the former Soviet Union, Russian students who are seventeen or older feel especially out of place. To make matters worse, official records are difficult to acquire from the former Soviet Union, leaving students unable to prove their completion of coursework. Rose administrators subsequently place them in their age-appropriate grades. The second concern Erina raises, regarding Rose's substantial immigrant population, is revealing in that she does not wish to be recognized as an immigrant. She believes she will more easily merge with native students in a college environment. Because she is racially white, Erina may indeed "blend in," an ability she hopes to utilize. Koreans, in contrast, are unable to slip unobtrusively into American society without being recognized as somehow different from other "American people." They are very aware of their racial differences, a fact that has great bearing on their adaptive strategies. The role that race plays in shaping the two groups' respective strategies is a topic to which we now turn.

---

[14]Of course, Russian students I spoke with are still attending Rose. Several unsuccessful attempts were made to interview Russian students who left early. Unfortunately, their views are not reflected in this chapter. However, roughly half of the Russians I did speak with were considering leaving Rose at the time of interview.

"They Are Not from America . . . They Are from Korea": Fears of Racism and Exclusion

Being racially identifiable has important ramifications for Korean students in the United States. While Russian students may feel distinct and removed from the regular student population, they are racially indistinguishable from native "whites." As Erina mentioned earlier, she possesses the ability to pass for a native: "I'm just American people." Gold (1985: 111) similarly points out that "Soviet Jews see themselves, racially, as part of the white American community. . . . Soviet Jews appreciate Russian language and Soviet order, but feel less attachment to their past way of life."

Koreans, in contrast, will always be racially identifiable, resulting in a permanent sense of attachment to their racial and cultural roots. Waters (1990) discusses this issue in her study of ethnicity among latter-generation white Americans. Whereas for white Americans, celebrating or even identifying with their ethnic heritage is a matter of choice, nonwhite Americans' lives are strongly influenced by their race or national origin. In effect, there is no element of choice: "The social and political consequences of being Asian or Hispanic or black are not symbolic for the most part, or voluntary. They are real and often hurtful" (Waters 1990: 156). In a sense, then, Asians and other nonwhite groups are permanent immigrants, forever foreigners, always reminded of their status as "other." This fact affects Korean adaptation in a number of ways.

First, Korean students are keenly aware of their racial differences, and virtually all of them reported incidences of racial slurs and run-ins with fellow students and teachers:

> I had trouble with black people. . . . I hate them, you know. Just for example, my friend is girl and one day black people stand in front of her seat. She said "excuse me." She wanted to pass by and they said something else, "fuck you," something like bad word and they wanted to hit her. . . . I hate them, you know.

As a result, the Koreans purposely maintain low profiles so as not to incite any additional racism or tension. Unlike the Russians, they are less likely to make demands or cause trouble for fear of drawing attention to themselves. Second, while they all accept the assumption that schooling is the vehicle for social and economic mobility, the Koreans feel the need to safeguard themselves in the event of racial exclusion. While they all prefer to work in the mainstream economy, the majority of Korean students look to the ethnic economy as something to fall back on in the event of exclusion from the U.S. labor market: "I try to work in American company, but if not, [then] Korean." That is, if racial discrimination were to block them from advancing in their chosen fields, they would return to the ethnic economy to find work. Their belief in the need for protection from social and economic exclusion also carries over to their future child-rearing practices. Virtually all the Koreans spoke of the necessity for their future children to learn Korean, not only for cultural but for pragmatic reasons:

> I will teach Korean. They need to learn. They are not from America. They are from Korea but born in America. They can't be American and they are not Korean, so I think they don't have true identity. They need to learn the Korean, everything, culture. . . . When they have . . . job, they need Korean because [if] they got job in America and Americans doesn't like, so they don't speak Korean, they work in Korean store, [but] if they don't speak Korean, how can they work? They need Korean.

Especially since the Los Angeles Rebellion in summer 1992, when they were the targets of looting and violence, Koreans have increasingly become disillusioned with their future prospects in the United States. More than ever, they feel the need to look out for themselves since their faith in state and federal government has been shaken. Korean students' adaptive strategies, then, are influenced by their perceptions of racial hostility and possible exclusion, concerns that Russians do not face. It affects their views about opportunities in the United States and is always a factor in their decisions, educational or otherwise.

Conclusion/Implications

There are many aspects of Ogbu's framework that have proved useful in examining the adaptive experiences of Korean and Russian students at Rose High, particularly his discussion of dual reference frames. Nevertheless, neither group fits neatly within the parameters of his classification schema. Contrary to Ogbu's claim that immigrant/voluntary groups are inured to the psychological costs of discrimination, the Koreans' experiences suggest that concerns over racial exclusion and targeting may well be perceived as a lasting threat. Fears of discrimination, then, do not confine themselves to the realm of involuntary minorities. As their comments suggest, Korean students do not necessarily believe that hard work and diligence will lead to their or their future children's acceptance by the host society, nor are they shielded from the effects of rejection. Instead they feel the need to safeguard themselves in the event of lasting racial exclusion. In short, nonwhite voluntary groups may end up adopting some of the same characteristics attributed to involuntary groups, such as disenchantment with and rejection of the host society. For now, however, the Koreans' resultant strategies are "additive" rather than "oppositional" and have not led to counterproductive outcomes. Their response to exclusionary treatment has not hardened to the same degree as traditional caste-like groups such as African Americans because the Koreans have not had to endure generations of oppression or the same intensity of discrimination. The possibility is always there, however, especially if events such as the Los Angeles Rebellion and its frustrating aftermath come to dominate their view of life and of the opportunities available in the United States.

While Ogbu acknowledges variability within and between groups, he spends little time elaborating on groups whose experiences fall between the categories he proposes. In this study I have argued that this is a notable shortcoming in his theoretical model and one that needs to be addressed. Unlike earlier waves of immigrants, the majority of whom were European, the bulk of today's newcomers are nonwhite (Rumbaut 1990; Olsen 1988; First and Carrera 1988), making the need to specify and nuance their experiences in his framework all the more pressing. Furthermore, I would argue for a separate treatment of the refugee experience. Ogbu acknowledges that refugees do not have the option of returning to their homeland; nevertheless, he continues to treat them as a voluntary group, with all the advantages associated with that status. Their unique contexts of arrival, subsequent conditions, resources, and ensuing outlooks are so distinct from more traditional immigrant/ voluntary groups that an independent discussion is warranted.

Despite these weakness, the general value of Ogbu's theory is worth underscoring. My criticisms lie not with the overall contours of the framework but with its inadequate discussion of the role played by race. Greater emphasis on the salience of race as an involuntary label carrying social, political, and economic consequences in its own right is needed if Ogbu's framework is to sufficiently account for the experiences of nonwhite immigrant groups.

In this chapter I have attempted to show that immigrant students are not passive participants in the processes of socialization and adaptation. Rather, they actively interpret the meaning of school assimilation and employ strategies that are suited to their particular circumstances and goals. They are not free to choose and act as they will, however; they must work within the constraints established by the social and material conditions framing their experiences. For Koreans, this includes confronting the problems associated with being nonwhite in a society seemingly unable to move beyond racial categories. Russians, as white immigrants, are moving in a different direction. Like their parents, they feel optimistic about their future work opportunities and do not appear to question their eventual participation in the mainstream labor market. They have, however, had to revise their immediate educational goals. While initially expecting to attend prestigious universities, they have come to accept that their limited proficiency in English makes this goal extremely difficult to achieve. Older Russians especially believe they arrived at too late an age to fit into the American educational system. With this realization comes impatience and a belief that they are wasting their time in high school; what they consider to be important is a college credential. Consequently, Russians take matters into their own hands and attempt to make the educational system work for them. Their ability to innovate to the degree they have, however, is tied to the fact that they are not overly concerned with having to incorporate possible racial exclusion into their adaptive strategies.

Immigrant students have embraced the ideal of American schools as the gatekeepers to social and economic security, but not unreservedly. Their belief in the validity of schooling is not unresponsive to objective conditions: "Prejudices and hostility against them teach immigrant students that such intolerance is part of the social fabric of America. And they learn to participate" (Olsen 1988: 37). Policy makers should pay close attention to the dynamics of racial exclusion lest they wish to be faced with upcoming generations of disillusioned students who may join ranks with involuntarily incorporated groups. High dropout rates, truancy, suspensions, poor academic performance, indifference, and other myriad problems plaguing involuntary groups may in time come to characterize nonwhite voluntary groups as well if their experiences with exclusion and injustice become pervasive.

Lastly, schools have been places where immigrant students join American society, but not necessarily on the terms school authorities would prefer. As the Russian and Korean cases illustrate, immigrants may adapt to schools in a number of ways. While their strategies may seem unusual or counterproductive to school authorities, it is important to recognize that, given their understanding of the American educational system, immigrant students are taking what they feel is an appropriate path to achieve their goals. This needs to be kept in mind as we try to understand why different immigrant groups behave as they do.

References

California Department of Education. 1990. *Language Census Report for California Public Schools, 1990*. Sacramento: California Department of Education.
Caplan, Nathan, Marcella Choy, and John Whitmore. 1991. *Children of the Boat People: A Study of Educational Success*. Ann Arbor: University of Michigan Press.

Carlson, Robert. 1975. *The Quest for Conformity: Americanization through Education*. New York: John Wiley and Sons.

Cohen, Ronald, and Raymond Mohl. 1979. *The Paradox of Progressive Education: The Gary Plan and Urban Schooling*. New York: Kennileat.

Fass, Paula. 1989. *Outside In: Minorities and the Transformation of American Education*. New York: Oxford University Press.

First, Joan McCarty, and John Wilshire Carrera. 1988. *New Voices: Immigrant Students in U.S. Public Schools*. Boston: NCAS.

Gibson, Margaret A. 1987. "Punjabi Immigrants in an American High School." In *Interpretive Ethnography of Education at Home and Abroad*, edited by George D. Spindler and Louise S. Spindler. Hillsdale: L. Erlbaum Associates.

———. 1988. *Accommodation without Assimilation: Sikh Immigrants in an American High School*. Ithaca: Cornell University Press.

Gibson, Margaret A., and John Ogbu, eds. 1991. *Minority Status and Schooling: A Comparative Study of Immigrant and Involuntary Minorities*. New York: Garland.

Gold, Steven. 1985. *Refugee Communities: Soviet Jews and Vietnamese in the San Francisco Bay Area*. Ann Arbor, Mich.: Dissertation Information Service.

———. 1992. *Refugee Communities: A Comparative Field Study*. Newbury Park, Calif.: Sage.

Gold, Steven, and Mia Tuan. 1993. "Jews from the Former U.S.S.R. in the United States." New Faces of Liberty Series, Zellerbach Family Fund. San Francisco: Many Cultures Publishing.

Gordon, Milton. 1964. *Assimilation in American Life*. New York: Oxford University Press.

Huhr, Won Moo, and Kwang Chung Kim. 1984. "Adhesive Sociocultural Adaptation of Korean Immigrants in the U.S.: An Alternative Strategy of Minority Adaptation," *International Migration Review* 18:188–216.

Kaestle, Carl. 1973. *The Evolution of an Urban School System: New York City, 1750–1850*. Cambridge, Mass.: Harvard University Press.

Kashin, M. 1988. "The Soviet Union." In *Encyclopedia of Comparative Education and National Systems of Education*, edited by T.N. Postlethwaite. Oxford and New York: Pergamon.

Lee, Yongsook. 1991. "Koreans in Japan and the U.S." In *Minority Status and Schooling: A Comparative Study of Immigrant and Involuntary Minorities*, edited by Margaret Gibson and John Ogbu. New York: Garland.

Light, Ivan, and Edna Bonacich. 1988. *Immigrant Entrepreneurs: Koreans in Los Angeles, 1965–1982*. Berkeley: University of California Press.

Los Angeles County Office of Education. 1991. *The Condition of Public Education in Los Angeles County, 1990–1991, Annual Statistical Review*. Los Angeles: Los Angeles County Office of Education.

Matute-Bianchi, Maria E. 1991. "Situational Ethnicity and Patterns of School Performance among Immigrant and Nonimmigrant Mexican-Descent Students." In *Minority Status and Schooling: A Comparative Study of Immigrant and Involuntary Minorities*, edited by Margaret Gibson and John Ogbu. New York: Garland.

Mole, R. 1981. "Cultural Assimilation versus Cultural Pluralism," *Educational Forum*, March, pp. 323–32.

Morgan, Scott, and Elizabeth Colsen, eds. 1987. *People in Upheaval*. New York: Center for Migration Studies.

Office of Refugee Resettlement. 1990. "Report to the Congress." January 31.

Ogbu, John. 1978. *Minority Education and Caste: The American System in Cross-Cultural Perspective.* San Diego, Calif.: Academic Press.

———. 1983. "Minority Status and Schooling," *Comparative Education Review* 27:168–90.

———. 1987. "Variability in Minority School Performance: A Problem in Search of an Explanation," *Anthropology and Education Quarterly* 18:312–34.

Olsen, Laurie. 1988. *Crossing the Schoolhouse Border: Immigrant Students and the California Public Schools.* San Francisco: California Tomorrow.

Park, Robert. 1950. *Race and Culture.* Glencoe: Free Press.

Portes, Alejandro, and Rubén G. Rumbaut. 1990. *Immigrant America: A Portrait.* Berkeley: University of California Press.

Rumbaut, Rubén G. 1990. *Immigrant Students in California's Public Schools: A Summary of Current Knowledge.* CDS Report No. 11. Baltimore: Johns Hopkins University.

Rumbaut, Rubén G., and Kenji Ima. 1988. *The Adaptation of Southeast Asian Refugee Youth: A Comparative Study.* Washington, D.C.: U.S. Office of Refugee Resettlement.

Sagar, H. Andrew, and Janet Schofield. 1983. "Integrating the Desegregated School: Problems and Possibilities." In *Motivation and Achievement: A Research Annual,* edited by M. Maehr and D. Bartz. Greenwich: JAI Press.

Sah-Myung, Hong. 1983. "The Republic of South Korea." In *Schooling in East Asia,* edited by R.M. Thomas and T.N. Postlethwaite. Oxford: Pergamon.

Schlesinger, Arthur. 1992. *The Disuniting of America.* New York: Norton.

Schultz, Stanley. 1973. *The Culture Factory: Boston Public Schools: 1789–1860.* New York: Oxford University Press.

Sleeter, Christine, and Carl Grant. 1988 . *Making Choices for Multicultural Education: Five Approaches to Race, Class and Gender.* Columbus, Oh.: Merrill.

Strouse, Joan. 1987. "Continuing Themes in Assimilation," *Equity and Excellence* 23:105–13.

Suárez-Orozco, Marcelo M. 1987. "Toward a Psycho-Social Understanding of Hispanic Adaptation to American Schooling." In *Success or Failure? Learning and the Language Minority Student,* edited by Henry Trueba. Cambridge, Mass.: Newbury House.

———. 1989. *Central American Refugees and U.S. High Schools: A Psychosocial Study of Motivation and Achievement.* Stanford, Calif.: Stanford University Press.

Vinovskis, Maris. 1990. "Immigrants and Schooling in the United States." Paper prepared for the "Conference on Immigration in France and United States in Comparative Perspective."

Warner, Lloyd, and Leo Srole. 1945. *The Social Systems of American Ethnic Groups.* New Haven, Conn.: Yale University Press.

Waters, Mary. 1990. *Ethnic Options: Choosing Identities in America.* Berkeley: University of California Press.

6

The Psychological Dimension in Understanding Immigrant Students

Amado M. Padilla and David Durán

Introduction

The academic difficulties that some groups of immigrant students experience in American schools are well documented. However, with few exceptions little importance has been given to the psychological difficulties that these children and adolescents experience following immigration and during attendance at school. This chapter addresses the psychological costs of immigration and how they affect immigrant students. By psychological costs we mean the difficulties that some immigrant students have in adjusting emotionally to their new surroundings. These costs influence how students perceive their abilities, how they view their family and home, and how they establish social relationships in the school and community at large. Our central thesis is that the mental health of immigrant students should receive the same level of attention as that which has been given to educational interventions such as English language programs (e.g., bilingual education, English as a Second Language [ESL], etc.), newcomer centers, and multicultural pre-service and in-service teacher training programs.

A review of the literature on immigrant students and mental health status reveals that only a few studies have examined the psychological impacts of immigration on children and adolescents. The little literature that is available is inconsistent. For example, in a review of some of the literature on immigrant children that included Ugandan Asian families in Canada, West Indian and Spanish immigrants in England, and Latinos in the United States, Rakoff pointed to both positive and negative consequences associated with immigration during childhood and early adolescence. On the one hand, Rakoff observed that:

> The children of immigrant families need to adapt to the
> changed behavior, and (often) status of their parents,
> while they accommodate to the demands of the host
> society. Frequently they adapt more completely than
> their parents and they may find themselves in the
> paradoxical position of being more accomplished in the
> new society: they may become parents of their parents
> (1981: 144).

Many individuals familiar with immigrant families have corroborated Rakoff's observation about young children serving as translators
for their parents or other adult family members. However, Rakoff does
not point out that this role reversal between parents and children may in
fact be the source of new conflict and stress for children and parents.
Some commentators have noted that the role reversal places considerable
stress on the child translator who is empowered because of his or her
bilingual ability but who is still dependent on the parents.

In the apparent multiple conflicts that this role reversal creates,
Rakoff goes on to state:

> [The children] are frequently excessively cathected by
> the parents, and the burden of expectations and nurtur-
> ance may on occasion be pathogenic. As a consequence
> separation is often more stressful and threatening than
> usual: At its extreme it can be perceived as disloyalty
> and abandonment. If adaptation does not occur be-
> cause of the family or society and the host society
> remains alien, it may generate diminished academic
> achievement, anxiety, and/or delinquency (pp. 144–45).

Clearly the negative consequences of immigration on children have
to do with the psychological difficulty of separation between children
and adults and with the level of adaptation that each generation makes
to the host culture. If there are sustained difficulties in separation and/or
adaptation to the host culture, then the negative effects are noted in poor
school performance and in behavioral problems. However, Rakoff cau-
tions us by pointing out that:

> In spite of these burdens and difficulties the majority of
> children of immigrants do adapt and display no more
> pathology than comparable indigenous children (p.
> 145).

Rakoff cited no epidemiological evidence to support this conclusion.
In fact, little epidemiological research involving native and foreign-born

children and adolescents and their mental health status has been conducted, so Rakoff's conclusion about "no more pathology" in immigrant children remains speculative. Remaining optimistic, Rakoff concluded her review with the following thought:

> Indeed it would be remiss, in a paper of this kind, not to mention the positive aspects of the immigrant experience: the increased family closeness; the clear articulation of life goals; the aspiration (and frequently optimism) that may generate energy and creativity, which becomes the stuff of family legend in later generations (p. 145).

Clearly there is a kernel of truth in Rakoff's positive outlook. The difficulty is that we have little good quantitative information about how many immigrant children are affected negatively by the disruption of moving to a new country or how the life circumstances of families are improved following immigration. An implication here is that some suffering toughens the individual and that this shapes character and possibly produces the resiliency needed to overcome the odds and succeed in the new country. While this makes for a great narrative, we do not know how many immigrants fail for every "success" simply because they lack a modicum of support at a critical point to help them through the stresses of adaptation.

School-based Psychological Services

The delivery of psychological services to immigrant children involves balancing theoretical concerns with practical needs. These children may have special needs because of the difficulties of adjusting to a new culture, a new language, and a new way of life. Youthful migrants sometimes leave behind the security of a home and friends and enter a strange and sometimes hostile environment. Other young immigrants feel relief when leaving a stressful or violent community; but rather than finding comfort in their new surroundings, they may be confronted by new stressors that perpetuate their psychological difficulties. There is little research on the mental health symptomology of immigrant children (an exception is Masser 1992). War in Central America and Southeast Asia has undoubtedly had a tremendous psychological impact on the children immigrating from these areas (Cerhan 1990; Le 1983; Masser 1992). Exposure to such events can affect a child's psychological well-being for many years. The trauma of war is compounded by the problems of immigration and adjustment to a new culture, and linguistic and socioeconomic barriers make the process even more difficult.

Another potential area of conflict for many immigrant children has to do with the fact that they must adapt to an English-speaking environment much more quickly than their parents (Yao 1985). These findings contrast with work done on immigrants in Europe, in which researchers claim that family dysfunction has a greater impact on children than does the act of migration itself (Steinhausen et al. 1990).

The psychological risks inherent in unstable and conflict-ridden environments may be intensified for children who cross national borders. Several disorders arise from this difficult transition. Immigrants suffer from a variety of stress-related illnesses and ailments, including depression and other psychosomatic and physical illnesses (Ima and Hohm 1991). One psychological disorder associated with the trauma of being a victim of and witness to war is posttraumatic stress disorder (PTSD). In working with children, McNally (1991) indicates that PTSD is most likely to arise following a sudden, unpredictable, life-threatening event (especially of human design) involving exposure to grotesque death, personal injury, or injury to loved ones. Studies have shown that PTSD occurs in immigrant children and adolescents from Central America and Southeast Asia (Cerhan 1990; Le 1983; Lyons 1987; McNally 1991). The Hmong have a particularly difficult time adjusting to life in the United States (Cerhan 1990). In addition, research has suggested that because of language difficulties, immigrants are more likely to develop socioemotional problems and less likely to be provided with the resources to work on these problems (Henggeler and Tavormina 1978; Olsen 1988).

One major issue facing mental health professionals is delivery of services. People from certain cultures tend to avoid using social services or mental health services. In one study, Hall (1988) reported that Central American immigrants do not seek help from the public health and social service systems in the United States. According to Yao (1985) this underutilization reflects the fact that immigrant students are not accustomed to seeking counseling or professional help for two major reasons: (1) the unavailability of professional counseling in their native countries, and (2) a reluctance to admit a need for assistance in handling their problems. Thus, while immigrant children and their families are exposed to psychological stressors that make them vulnerable to social, emotional, and academic problems, they also tend to have limited support systems (Esquivel and Keitel 1990).

Importantly, the need for more, rather than fewer, psychological services among minority children than among majority students is well documented (Tomlinson et al. 1977). The challenge to policy makers is to develop programs that meet the special needs of these children. The challenge to mental health professionals is to devise ways to deliver services that are culturally appropriate to the needs of these children.

Olsen (1988) has done the field of immigrant education a service by articulating the mental health needs of immigrant and refugee children in California schools. In *Crossing the Schoolhouse Border*, Olsen identified a number of factors that contribute to the possible school-related difficulties of California's immigrant and refugee children. According to Olsen, some of the important factors are: age at the time the young person relocated to the United States; whether the child had received any formal instruction prior to enrolling in a U.S. school; physical and psychological hardships associated with the immigration journey; whether the relocation was voluntary or involuntary; and the family's legal status once in the United States. In addition, Olsen recognized the importance of war-related traumas on normal child and adolescent development and how these may depress school performance. Olsen concluded:

> Many immigrant children, particularly those from Central American and Southeast Asian countries, have suffered trauma from war and political violence; for most, this is the reason for immigration. Many have lost close relatives or friends—and have themselves been threatened and exposed to excessive violence, people dying and starving, war atrocities and destruction. Along with psychological and physical hardships, these disruptions bring major gaps in schooling and academic development to children whose present and future plans are unsettled and insecure (1988: 22).

Olsen goes on to note that these conditions put these children at high risk for school problems, failure, and early school departure. Despite the richness of Olsen's observations regarding immigrant students, her work is primarily qualitative and does not tell us about the extent of the problem or how it is manifested psychologically. Further, as noted above, there is little empirical research that documents the type of problems that newcomers encounter as they adapt to school and community in this country.

Similar problems appear in studies of immigrant students in other cultural contexts. For example, Douville (1985) examined the academic underachievement of Maghreb immigrants attending French schools. In many respects his report of underachievement resembles much of what has been written about immigrant children in U.S. schools. Douville attributed the Maghreb children's disproportionate rate of scholastic failure to the ethnocentrism of French schools, the clashing of two seemingly incompatible cultures, family circumstances (e.g., parental illiteracy even in the home language, frequent changes of workplace and residence), and the difficulty of learning French. However, in a study of

251 immigrant-status children in Canada, Munroe-Blum and colleagues (Munroe-Blum et al. 1989) found no evidence of greater psychological or school-related difficulties for immigrant students when compared to native-born control students. This was true even though the immigrant students were:

> 3.7 times as likely to live in overcrowded conditions, 3.1 times as likely to live in subsidized housing, 2.9 times as likely to come from larger families, 2.5 times as likely to be living on low income, 2.4 times as likely to have a mother with eighth grade education or less, and 1.5 times as likely to experience some family dysfunction (p. 515).

These findings are important for their failure to uncover any major differences between immigrant and native-born students, especially considering the relative deprivation that the immigrant students were experiencing.

Nevertheless, we will argue that a sizable proportion of immigrant students are indeed affected negatively by immigration-related experiences. The difficulty with substantiating this claim to date has to do with the insensitivity of current instruments for assessing acculturative stress with youthful immigrant populations.

Assessing Acculturative Stress in Immigrant Students

Turning to earlier work carried out by Padilla and colleagues, we will discuss the findings from three studies that indicate the direction Padilla has followed in developing instruments to measure immigrant-specific psychological stressors experienced by young immigrant students in the United States. This work relies heavily on a stress-illness-coping model advanced by Lazarus and Folkman (1984) and Pearlin and Schooler (1978). However, these studies depart from this framework in one explicit assumption: we assumed that immigrants experience many of the same stressors as nonimmigrants, but in addition they experience stressors due to their immigrant status *and* minority position in the United States. This immigrant stress model was first described by Padilla (1986) in work with foreign-born university students.

Figure 6.1 depicts the model for psychological stress, with general stressors indicated in the lower portion of the figure and immigrant-related stressors shown above. However, to understand the stressors created by relocation to a new country, Padilla and his colleagues found it necessary to develop new assessment instruments since the available life event stress instruments did not assess the types of stressors

Figure 6.1

MODEL OF ACCULTURATIVE STRESS

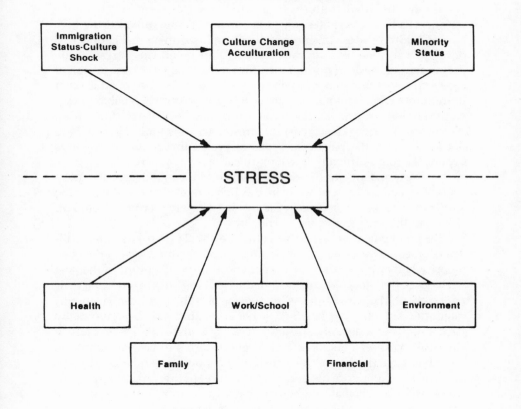

experienced by immigrants. The first study describes work with one such instrument developed specifically for studying immigrant adolescents.

Study 1: Stressful Life Events in an Adolescent Population

We have already summarized some of the impressionistic reports that suggest that higher levels of psychological distress in immigrants may be related to the trauma of relocation, such as conflicts in cultural attitudes and beliefs, language difficulties, and lowered socioeconomic conditions. In the first study to measure such distress in a scientific manner, Padilla, Cervantes, and Maldonado (1988) employed the Hispanic Children's Stress Inventory (HCSI), an instrument that Padilla had developed to identify culturally specific and potentially stressful life events among Mexican immigrant adolescents. The HCSI was designed to tap stressors that may be specific to the life experience of adolescent immigrants who are not proficient in English or knowledgeable of U.S. cultural patterns, and whose family unit may be disrupted. Such an instrument is critical since current stress measures for adolescents are not sensitive to the particular types of events that many immigrants experience (e.g., difficulty in communicating in English).

The respondents for this study were all Mexican immigrant adolescents enrolled in high schools in the Los Angeles area. Most of the students were recent arrivals in California. All were recruited from ESL classes in their respective high schools.

Respondents were asked to complete the 24-item Hispanic Children's Stress Inventory. The instrument first required respondents to report whether or not they had experienced a specific event in the past twelve months. Respondents next had to indicate on a Likert scale their appraisal of the stressfulness of the event. The appraisal response categories ranged from 1 to 5 (1 = not at all stressful; 2 = minimally stressful; 3 = moderately stressful; 4 = very stressful; 5 = extremely stressful). Respondents rated each event in terms of how stressful the event had been (in the case of occurrence) or how stressful it would be if they were to experience the event in the future. In this fashion appraised stress could be calculated whether or not the respondent had actually experienced the event during the past twelve months.

In addition to the HCSI, all respondents completed the Piers-Harris Self-Concept Scale. This is an eighty-item self-report inventory that assesses self-concept in children and adolescents (Piers 1984).

A score on the HCSI was obtained by summing each respondent's ratings on the twenty-four items. In this way a total score of 24 indicated no stress, while a score of 120 was the maximum achievable stress rating. The mean HCSI score for all respondents was 67.84. Scores on the HCSI were found to correlate significantly and negatively ($r = -.23$, $p < .001$) with the total Piers-Harris score, as well as with five of the six cluster subscales (see table 6.1). Since low scores on the Piers-Harris are reflective of lowered self-esteem or a tendency toward personal problems or difficulties in each of the six specific domains, the results suggest that as HCSI scores increase (greater perceived psychosocial stress), difficulties in overall self-esteem also tend to increase. Of particular interest is the highly significant correlation ($r = -.25$, $p < .001$) between the total HCSI score and the Anxiety subscale of the Piers-Harris. The Anxiety subscale is a cluster of 14 items described as reflecting general emotional disturbances *and* dysphoric mood. However, we can also see from table 6.1 that the higher the psychosocial stress experienced by our immigrant respondents, the lower were their self-rated intelligence, assessment of physical attractiveness, and feelings of popularity and happiness. The picture that emerges from these data is that immigrant students have very low self-images in general and low appraisals of their intellectual, physical, or social attributes.

TABLE 6.1
CORRELATION BETWEEN HCSI AND PIERS-HARRIS
SELF-ESTEEM SUBSCALES

Piers-Harris Subscales	
Behavior	−.0056
Intelligence	−.1147*
Anxiety	−.2503***
Physical attractiveness	−.1286*
Popularity	−.1784**
Happiness	−.1384*
Total self-esteem	−.2261***

*$p < .05$; **$p < .01$; ***$p < .001$.

The next step in examining the results of the HCSI was to determine whether there was a difference between male and female respondents in appraisals of stressfulness of the items. Figures 6.2 and 6.3 present the mean appraisal scores for males and females on a selected number of items. T-tests were used to detect possible gender differences on each item. Female adolescents were found to differ significantly in their appraisals on ten items, in all cases appraising the items as more stressful than did the males. For the entire sample, the mean total HCSI score was $\overline{X} = 67.84$. The mean total score for males was $\overline{X} = 64.80$; mean total score for females was $\overline{X} = 71.27$. The gender difference was significant ($p < .01$). It was also necessary to determine whether adolescents appraised items differently depending on whether or not they had

Figure 6.2

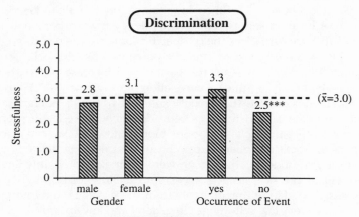

Discrimination

($\bar{x}$=3.0)

When other kids (not Latinos) talk about you.

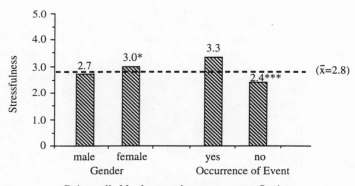

($\bar{x}$=2.8)

Being called bad names because you are Latino.

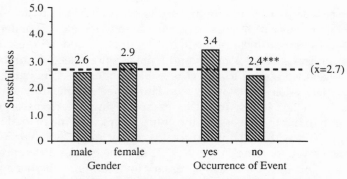

($\bar{x}$=2.7)

Being called names because you were not born in U.S.

Figure 6.3

Language

at school environment

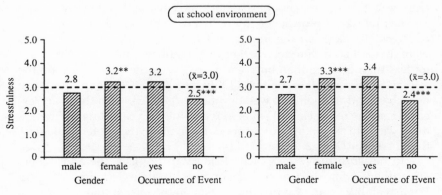

Not understanding teacher when she explains something in English.

When kids make fun of the way you speak English.

at home environment

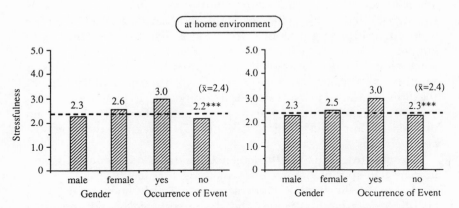

Pressure to speak only Spanish at home.

Being teased at home for not speaking Spanish well.

experienced a given event in the past year. The percent of subjects indicating that they had or had not experienced the event, along with mean appraisal scores for each item, demonstrates that appraisal ratings were significantly higher on all items for adolescents who indicated that they had recently experienced the event (see figures 6.2 and 6.3).

Because the respondents in this study were all immigrants to the United States, we also sought to determine whether length of residence and self-ratings of proficiency in English were related to the perception of stress. To ascertain the impact of length of residency, respondents were divided according to whether they had been in the United States for less than or more than one year; t-tests were then computed on the appraisal ratings of each item. Only one item ("moving from one neighborhood to another") was significant ($p < .05$), with those adolescents residing in the United States longer than one year rating the item as more stressful ($\overline{X} = 3.4$) than respondents living in the United States less than one year ($\overline{X} = 2.9$).

To measure the impact of proficiency in English, the adolescents were divided into two groups: poor English ability group and good English ability group. Computing t-tests on the stressfulness appraisal ratings between the two groups revealed significant differences on only four items. The four items that were rated as more stressful by the poor English ability group were: "making new friends at school," "when you speak in one language and your friends answer in another," "parents getting sick and going to the hospital," and "having a family member arrested." Surprisingly, only one of these items relates directly to language. The item "not understanding teacher when she explains something in English" was rated as more stressful ($\overline{X} = 3.3$) by the poor English ability group than by the good English speakers ($\overline{X} = 3.0$), but the difference failed to reach statistical significance. In addition, the item "when kids make fun of the way you speak English" showed no difference in appraisal ratings (3.4 versus 3.5) between the two language ability groups.

Results from this study demonstrate the need for investigating immigration-specific life events, something that has been largely neglected to date in childhood/adolescent research. In line with thinking about Mexican cultural values and the importance placed on family unity, we found that a significant number of the most stressful items in the HCSI revolve around family concerns, and more specifically the disruption of family unity. With the exception of the item "living in a neighborhood where there is crime," the six items rated most stressful by our sample involved disruptions to family unity. This contrasts with findings among majority-group adolescents, who report more personalized events as constituting the highest levels of reported stress (Coddington 1972; Yeaworth et al. 1980).

In addition to items related to family disruption, language difficulties also generate high levels of stress as reported by our sample (e.g.,
"not understanding teacher when she explains something in English,"
"when kids make fun of the way you speak English"). When analyzing
the data on the basis of self-ratings of English proficiency alone, items
that asked about contact with the majority group—such as managing
parental sickness and hospitalization and contact with legal/court officials—were viewed as significantly more stressful by adolescents who
have little proficiency in English.

In summary, Study 1 demonstrated that immigrants do experience
stress associated with their status as immigrants and that this stress
correlates with heightened anxiety and lowered feelings of self-worth,
including self-appraisals of intelligence and physical attractiveness.
However, this study left open the question of such students' academic
performance in school. Sylvia Alatorre Alva explored this question in
Study 2 (see Alva 1991). Her research focused on the factors that
contribute to academic resiliency among low-income Mexican American
students. Although Alva collected data on immigrant Mexican students
as well as later-generation Mexican American students, only the data
relevant to the immigrant students will be presented in this discussion.

Study 2: Academic Resilience and Immigrant Students

The respondents in Alva's study were drawn from a cohort of tenth-
grade students from a single high school in Southern California. Respondents had to be of Mexican heritage, currently enrolled in the tenth
grade, residents of the United States since at least the seventh grade, and
not currently enrolled in any type of special education, enrichment/
gifted, or ESL program.

A total of 384 Mexican American students (163 males and 221
females) participated in the study. They were recruited from a course
required for all tenth-grade students at the school; their modal age was
sixteen years. Only students who met all of Alva's selection criteria were
chosen as respondents. These subjects were asked to respond to a paper-
and-pencil survey which required approximately forty to fifty minutes
to complete. In order to cross-check the relationship between psychological variables such as self-esteem, life event stress, and social support,
Alva obtained her respondents' grades and standardized test scores
from school records.

The questionnaire that the students completed included the following inventories: the intellectual and school status subscale (17 items)
taken from the Piers-Harris Self-Concept Inventory, which measures
academic self-esteem; the Clifford Academic Achievement Accountability Scale (Clifford and Cleary 1972), which assesses the degree to

which the respondents accepted personal responsibility for their academic performance; and an environmental resources instrument specifically designed to measure the educational support that adolescents received from parents, teachers, and friends. On this latter scale the respondents were asked to evaluate separately the educational attitudes and values of their parents, teachers, and friends. Among the items in this scale are the following: "They [parents, teachers, friends] believe in the importance of getting a good education," "They encourage me to study hard," and "They value education highly."

Students' subjective appraisals of educational experiences were also measured using three scales, each of which tapped a different dimension of the school's climate: respect and care, school involvement, and college preparation. The respect and care dimension included items such as: "The teachers care about me," "Teachers treat me with respect," and "The teachers are fair." School involvement contained items such as: "I participate in school activities," "The school's organizations and clubs are interesting and fun," and "I feel pride in my school." The school's college preparatory climate was measured using items such as: "Someday I will be a college graduate," "I feel encouraged to attend college," and "I am taught subjects that prepare me for college."

Students were also asked to complete a modified version of the Hispanic Children's Stress Inventory. As modified, the scale measured the degree of stressfulness of life events or situations in three domains: family concerns, intergroup relations, and conflicts involving language issues.

The following academic outcomes were obtained from each respondent's records: (1) a composite score of the respondent's reading, language, and math skills, based on the results of the Comprehensive Tests of Basic Skills (CTBS) taken during tenth grade; and (2) a composite index of grades received during two semesters of the tenth-grade year, excluding physical education classes.

In order to examine a possible difference in academic performance between vulnerable and invulnerable students as defined by English language ability and a respondent's psychological profile, only immigrant students who scored below the median on English language exposure and usage were included in a discriminant analysis. Twenty-nine academically vulnerable and seventeen academically invulnerable students were identified. The stepwise discriminant analysis of CTBS scores for the two groups of students resulted in one underlying structure (chi-square $= 42.57$, $p < .01$), with a canonical correlation of .62. Five predictor variables significantly differentiated between the two groups of immigrant students. The school climate/college preparation subscale was the most powerful discriminator, followed by family concerns, involvement at school, stress due to poor English language ability, and support from teachers. A classification matrix revealed that the five predictor variables included in the discriminant function correctly classified 82.6 percent of the cases, with 89.7 percent of the academically vulnerable group and 70.6 percent of the academically invulnerable group correctly classified according to CTBS scores. A similar analysis carried out on grade point average, however, did not result in a significant discriminant analysis.

The results of Alva's study support the premise that a constellation of protective resources buffers and protects at-risk immigrant students from the detrimental effects of sociocultural life stress events and conditions that place them at risk for academic failure. However, it is not clear why the relative amount of English exposure and usage is important for CTBS performance and not for high school grades. One explanation is that performance on standardized tests like CTBS requires a higher level of language proficiency. A comparison of the results of the stepwise discriminant analysis for high and low groups with respect to high school grades and CTBS performance suggests that high school performance is less dependent on the mediation of language than is standardized test performance. As Cummins (1979) points out, the linguistic competence of most bilinguals is based on several proficiency thresholds. Although these thresholds have not been defined in absolute terms, the notion of thresholds serves to underscore the importance of the contextual milieu in determining language proficiency. Even though all students in this study were beyond the threshold requiring ESL instruction, the attainment of a second, higher level of linguistic competence appears to be necessary for successful performance on the CTBS and other standardized tests. In contrast, the linguistic demands of the classroom setting require a lower threshold of linguistic competence in English.

The results of the discriminant analysis for high school grades suggest that the comparison groups were most dissimilar in their environmental resources and appraisals. On environmental support, the academically invulnerable students reported higher levels of educational support from their teachers and friends. In contrast, the failure of parental support to predict high school grades was surprising. The literature consistently suggests that educational support from parents is strongly associated with achievement. However, the failure to find a relationship between parental sources of educational support and high school grades is attributed to the very high scores on the parental support measure. The median score on the parental support subscale was 49 out of a possible total score of 50. This indicates that all parents were supportive of their children's educational pursuits and that the major factor in whether immigrant students succeeded in school was the academic climate created by teachers.

In terms of subjective appraisals, academically invulnerable (or resilient) students were more likely to: (1) feel encouraged and prepared to attend college, (2) enjoy coming to school and being involved in high school activities, (3) experience fewer conflicts and difficulties in their intergroup relations with other students, and (4) experience fewer family conflicts and difficulties.

The primacy of the school's college preparatory climate in differentiating academically invulnerable and vulnerable students underscores the importance of maintaining a strong college preparatory climate. The results suggest that such a climate plays a critical role in encouraging students to succeed in high school. Overall, a student's appraisal of the school's college preparatory climate was the single best discriminator of academically resilient students and academically vulnerable students.

Finishing high school and gaining admission to college depend on successfully completing a fixed number of required courses and performing well on standardized tests (e.g., the SAT). Study 2 clearly shows that by the tenth grade, students make important decisions that affect their educational future based largely on their appraised likelihood of attending college. Mexican immigrant high school students who believed that they would someday graduate from college and who felt encouraged and prepared to attend college were most likely to have internalized an academically resilient self-image.

In conclusion, these results identify the need for early and continued contact between counselors and students, serving to motivate and encourage students to attend college. Studies have shown, however, that counselors typically do not assist high school students with their college plans until their junior or senior year. In an analysis based on the High School and Beyond longitudinal study, Lee and Ekstrom (1987) report that 50.4 percent of the high school sophomores reported no contact with a guidance counselor when making decisions about their school program. In a time when the college admission rate of Hispanic high school students is considerably lower than that of non-Hispanic whites (Olivas 1986), there is no doubt that greater attention needs to be focused on strengthening the link between high school and college for immigrant students. In sum, immigrant students need early and positive contact with counselors, teachers, and school administrators aimed at motivating and encouraging them to attend college.

Study 3: Immigrant Students and Posttraumatic Stress Disorder

Study 3 extended the conceptualization of immigration-related stress to a sample of young adult immigrants from Mexico and Central America. The informants for this study were attending day classes at an adult school, where they were enrolled in ESL classes. The objectives of the study were to determine the psychometric properties of a Hispanic

Stress Inventory and to assess the relationship between immigration-related stress and various psychological difficulties. The factors that differentiate this study from other mental health studies conducted with immigrant populations are the use of the Hispanic Stress Inventory, developed specifically for research with Latino immigrants, and the educational background of the informants. Unlike the typical immigrant from Latin America, who possesses an average of six to eight years of formal schooling, the respondents in this study had completed at least twelve years of schooling. Many were studying English at the adult school with the hope that they would enroll in a community college or state university once they had gained sufficient English proficiency.

The findings from this study are based on a sample of 305 Latino immigrants (Mexican = 138; Central American = 120; other Latin American = 47), including 177 males and 128 females. Their mean age was 24.3 years, and they had an average of thirteen years of formal schooling. The majority were single (78.4 percent) and unemployed (60 percent) at the time of the study. Their average length of residence in the United States was 2.2 years.

The respondents were given a questionnaire which contained 133 psychosocial life event stress items and were instructed to indicate for each whether they had experienced the situation in the past three months. If the person responded affirmatively to a particular item, he or she was then asked to rate the degree of stressfulness of that event on the five-point Likert scale.

In addition, all respondents completed the following psychological scales: Center for Epidemiological Studies Depression Scale, or CES-D (Radloff 1977); the Depression, Anxiety, and Somatization subscales of the Symptoms Checklist-90-Revised, or SCL-90-R (Derogatis 1977); the Rosenberg Self-Esteem Inventory (Rosenberg 1965); and the Campbell Personal Competence Inventory (Campbell et al. 1960). These measures have all been used previously with immigrant populations (see, e.g., Padilla, Cervantes, Maldonado, and García 1988). Estimates of internal consistency were computed for each of the symptom-related criterion measures. Coefficient alphas of 0.85, 0.91, and 0.90 were found for the Depression, Anxiety, and Somatization subscales of the SCL-90-R, respectively. An alpha coefficient of .87 was obtained for the CES-D.

The 133 psychosocial stress items were factor analyzed using an oblique factor rotation (for details regarding the analysis, see Cervantes et al. 1991). A five-factor solution was obtained for the immigrant respondents. An item on a factor was retained if it had a loading of .30 or greater and was not found to load on more than one factor. Using all retained items, another oblique factor analysis was done and a final and refined five-factor solution was obtained.

The five factors or subscales were then labeled according to the salient features of the items within each factor. The subscales on this new

Hispanic Stress Inventory (Immigrant Version) were: Occupational/ Economic Stress; Parental Stress; Marital Stress; Immigration Stress; and Family/Culture Stress. These five subscales were found to be highly reliable by both the method of internal consistency and test-retest (see Cervantes et al. 1991 for a summary of these reliability coefficients).

The two subscales of greatest interest for the present discussion are the Immigration Stress and Family/Culture Stress subscales of this new instrument. The items included in these two subscales are shown in table 6.2. When the HSI subscale scores were subsequently correlated with the mental health criterion measures, important findings emerged (see table 6.3). The findings indicate that greater immigration-related stress was positively related to depression (both scales) and somatization. Further, the stressors associated with family and culture conflicts and the mental health indicators were even more revealing. From table 6.3 we see that Family/Culture stress correlated positively with depression (both scales), anxiety, and somatization, and negatively with self-esteem.

These findings are very important because they reveal the difficulties that immigrants encounter as they begin the process of acculturating in a new country. Clearly the immigration process is very stressful even for these young, comparatively well-educated adults. One might expect that the adjustment process for the respondents of this study would be less difficult than for the younger immigrant students who participated in Studies 1 and 2 because of their greater educational attainment, better preparation prior to immigration, and ability to more effectively access social and educational services to ease their adaptation once in the United States. Despite these potential advantages, the findings demonstrate that young adult immigrant students also suffer the psychological costs of immigration, as seen in their less-than-positive mental health profile.

The psychological costs related to immigration are even more striking when examined from the perspective of posttraumatic stress disorder (PTSD). Until recently, the study of PTSD has focused on the psychological aftershock experienced by victims of natural and personal disasters. However, studies have documented that many political refugees suffer from PTSD because of their exposure to violence (Boehnlein et al. 1985). Such studies suggest that political refugees, despite differences in country of origin, education level, and socioeconomic status, share two characteristics. First, refugees are not voluntary immigrants. They have been forced to leave their respective home countries and thus are both physically and psychologically displaced. Second, refugees have experienced varying kinds and degrees of psychological trauma due to prolonged exposure to violence and war. Messer and Rasmussen (1986) have even suggested that the greater the refugee's premigration trauma, the more difficult the process of adaptation to the host country.

TABLE 6.2
HISPANIC STRESS INVENTORY, IMMIGRANT VERSION

Immigration Stress Scale

Since I don't know English, hard interacting with others.
I felt pressured to learn English.
Since I'm Latino, difficult to find work I want.
Thought I'd be deported if went to social/government agency.
Due to poor English, people treated me badly.
Due to poor English, hard dealing with daily situations.
I feared consequences of deportation.
I avoided immigration officials.
Due to poor English, have had difficulties in school.
I had difficulty finding legal services.
I felt guilty leaving family/friends in home country.
Legal status limited contact with family or friends.
Felt never regain status/respect I had in home country.
Felt unaccepted by others due to my Latino culture.
I've been questioned about my legal status.
Haven't forgotten war deaths of friends/family.
Haven't forgotten last few months in my home country.

Family and Culture Scale

There have been conflicts among family members.
I had serious arguments with family members.
There's been physical violence among family members.
Felt family members are losing their religion.
Personal goals conflicted with family goals.
Some family members have become too individualistic.
Family considered divorce for marital problems.
Due to different customs, had arguments with family.
Due to lack of family unity, felt lonely and isolated.
I noticed religion less important to me than before.
Being too close to family interfered with own goals.
Felt family relations less important for those close to me.
I've been around too much violence.

Preoccupation with past traumatic events such as significant losses and exposure to extreme violence, as well as the migration experience itself, may impede the acculturation process.

In order to determine whether our respondents suffered from PTSD, an eleven-item scale was devised by assembling items from different scales included in the questionnaire battery used to develop the Hispanic Stress Inventory. The scale was based on the Diagnostic Standard Manual-III (DSM-III) criteria for PTSD.

The items that were used to assess PTSD included persistent re-experiencing of war-related deaths and events that took place during the last few months in the home country; constriction of interests, including lowered libido; feelings of detachment and loneliness; generalized

TABLE 6.3
THE HISPANIC STRESS INVENTORY

PEARSON CORRELATIONS OF HISPANIC STRESS INVENTORY SUBSCALES
WITH CRITERION MEASURES

SYMPTOMATOLOGY SCALES
SCL-90-R

Immigrant version (n = 305)				
Immigration	.27*	.26*	.17	.20*
Family/Culture	.45*	.36*	.31*	.30*

Note: CES-D = Center for Epidemiological Studies Depression Scale (L.S. Radloff, "The CES-D Scale: A Self Report Depression Scale for Research in the General Population," *Applied Psychological Measurement* 1 [1977]: 385–401); SCL-90-R = Symptom Checklist-90 Revised (L.R. Derogatis, *SCL-90 [Revised] Version Manual-1* [Baltimore, Md.: Johns Hopkins University School of Medicine, 1977]).

*$p < .05$.

pessimism and hopelessness about the future; sleep disturbances; difficulty in concentrating; survivor's guilt; and avoidance of activities that recall the trauma or that might result in deportation to the home country.

Presence or absence on each item was obtained for all Central American and Mexico-origin immigrants described above. Further, the Central Americans were divided into two groups depending on whether their reason for immigrating to the United States was war related or was linked to some other factor such as opportunities for economic improvement, education, etc. Forty-four respondents indicated that war conditions in their country had motivated their relocation to the United States; seventy-six informants gave other reasons for their relocation. Table 6.4 presents the percent of immigrants who admitted to each symptom associated with PTSD.

From table 6.4 we can see that a higher percentage of Central American war immigrants reported symptoms across eight of the eleven criteria, compared with the other two groups of immigrants. Equally interesting, the Central American group who migrated for reasons other than war were more likely to report symptoms than were the Mexican immigrants.

Of particular interest was the similarity of reporting among the three groups of immigrants with regard to symptoms of loneliness and isolation, concentration difficulties, lowered interest levels, and feelings of hopelessness about the future. This specific symptom picture appears to capture the psychological impact of the migration process itself. In fact, this group of symptoms resembles the DSM-III-R criteria for a depressive episode.

Respondents who experienced at least one symptom of persistent re-experiencing of the event, one symptom of numbing of responsive-

TABLE 6.4
SYMPTOMS OF PTSD REPORTED BY CENTRAL AMERICAN IMMIGRANTS,
BY CAUSE FOR MIGRATING, AND BY MEXICAN IMMIGRANTS
(PERCENT OF SUBJECTS)[1]

| PTSD symptoms[2] | Central Americans | | Mexicans |
	War	Other Reasons	
Persistent re-experiencing of traumatic event			
Unable to forget war-related deaths of family members or friends	55	32	12
Unable to forget last few months in home country	61	47	41
Numbing of responsiveness to outside world			
No interest in usual activities	66	61	59
Feelings of loneliness and isolation	68	79	73
Loss of sexual interest or pleasure	46	32	29
Feelings of hopelessness about the future	66	57	55
Related symptoms			
Restless sleep	68	54	50
Guilt about leaving family	46	40	30
Trouble concentrating	68	76	66
Avoidance of activities, such as consulting social service agencies, that might result in deportation	46	20	21

[1]Central American immigrants who migrated because of war = 44; those migrating for other reasons = 76. N of Mexican immigrants = 138.

[2]All subjects had experienced migration, the first of the eleven items on the PTSD scale.

ness, and two related symptoms (see table 6.4) were considered to meet the DSM-III criteria for PTSD. The subsample of Central Americans who reported migrating because of war or political unrest were found to have the highest rate of PTSD (52 percent), followed by the Central Americans who migrated for other reasons (49 percent), and Mexican immigrants (25 percent). The difference among the groups was highly significant ($\overline{X}$ = 16.90, df = 2, $p < .001$).

Conclusions from Studies 1–3

The purpose for including a brief discussion of these three studies was to demonstrate quantitatively the magnitude of psychosocial stress due to immigration-related experiences among different young populations and, further, the relationship between stressful life events and lowered self-esteem, increased depression, and heightened anxiety. Researchers and educational practitioners have pointed generally to the adjustment difficulties encountered by immigrant students, but very few studies have been carried out to estimate the magnitude of the problem in any fashion other than qualitatively through interviews. In our discussion of Studies 1 and 3, we demonstrated that new and culturally appropriate instruments are necessary if we are to completely understand the life event stressors and the sequelae of posttraumatic stress disorder. Study 2 shows that not all immigrant youths are affected in the same way by their immigration status. In fact, some immigrant adolescents appear to be resilient or invulnerable to the stressors associated with immigration. These invulnerables, as Alva refers to them, appear to be doing quite well academically. Importantly, these invulnerables report that they have a social support network consisting of parents, friends, and teachers who buffer life event stressors. These students also report more positive school experiences with teachers and administrators and indicate that these individuals care about them and about their academic attainment. The vulnerable students do *not* have support networks, and they report few positive experiences with teachers and school administrators. Our experience with schools suggests to us that "vulnerable" students are much more common than resilient students. We will now turn our attention in the remainder of this chapter to the shortage of psychological services in our schools to meet the challenges posed by the many "vulnerable" immigrant students.

Meeting Immigrant Students' Psychological Needs

In order to determine how California schools are meeting the psychological needs of immigrant students, we interviewed school administrators, school psychologists, and special immigrant program personnel. In addition, we visited a number of schools in order to observe special programs for immigrant students.

Based on our interviews it is clear that California has no centralized structure for delivering psychological services in the schools. This lack of services is not unique to California; it is repeated throughout the country (Burke, Hawthorne, and Brantley 1983). In California the provision of psychological services to students is determined by each of the state's more than 1,100 school districts. While the California State Department of Education maintains a list of competencies for the certification of school psychologists, how these competencies are acquired varies somewhat among universities that offer graduate programs in school psychology. Overall, such programs are few in number although many universities offer graduate courses to meet the state-mandated competencies; the vast majority of state-certified school psychologists have master's degrees.

Because of the importance of providing services to immigrant students in their home language, we sought information about the coordination of bilingual competency and school psychology certification requirements. Our inquiry revealed that there is no bilingual school psychologist certification, although classroom teachers can be certified for bilingual competency. Some districts such as the Los Angeles Unified School District do identify bilingual school psychologists. This has come about as a result of the demand for psychological services staff with bilingual skills in the district and the collective bargaining effort that these individuals have made to have their skills recognized. The percentage of bilingual psychologists in Los Angeles mirrors the level found in other districts surveyed, with 15 percent of school psychologists statewide recognized as bilingual but only about 7 percent of all school academic counselors identified as bilingual. This is lamentable because in fall 1992 California recorded over one million limited-English-proficient students. Approximately 50 percent of the total K–12 student population in California come from minority home backgrounds; yet little attention has been given to developing a cadre of bilingual school psychologists to meet the needs of immigrant students.

Another important aspect is that psychological services vary from district to district. Districts may be served by school psychologists, school counselors, guidance counselors, academic advisers, and/or guidance learning directors, etc., depending on how each particular district designs its program. In many districts the school psychologist must devote primary attention to special education assessments and placements. This would support research that states, "Results of the current survey suggest that for many students in secondary schools, psychological services are not available" (Carroll, Harris, and Bretzing 1979).

In recent years the trend has been toward increased academic guidance in matters of course schedules and college applications and a lesser focus on personal counseling. According to J.A. Platow, executive director of the California Association of School Psychologists, personal counselors have nearly disappeared in the state. According to Platow, "as the demand for learning disability diagnosis consumes nearly all the school psychologist's time, there has never been a time when school psychologists provided all psychological services." Further, Platow acknowledges that in cases involving potential counseling services, the role of the school psychologist is simply to provide referrals to outside agencies; in affluent areas these referrals are to private therapists, and in less affluent areas to county mental health or nonprofit service agencies. In addition, because of the large number of students referred to outside therapists or agencies, the school psychologist does not have the resources to effectively monitor assistance provided to these students. Platow stated that schools were being asked to shoulder too large a responsibility for societal problems. The responsibility of providing social services should not be forced on the schools; the responsibility should be shared by the whole community. In addition to teaching academics, schools are being given more responsibilities at the same time that their staffs and funding are being reduced (personal communication, May 1993).

Platow's observation stands in contrast to research that suggests services would best be delivered by an interagency approach that uses the school as the base for student contact (Esquivel and Keitel 1990; Hall 1988; Olsen 1988). His position is also in contrast with the goal of California Senate Bill 620, the Healthy Start Initiative, introduced in 1991, which has as one of its main objectives collaboration between different social service providers.

Data collection on psychological services also varies from district to district. In some counties the county department of education provides school psychologists to the smaller school districts and keeps track of the contacts made by them. However, in larger districts these contacts may be kept by the district or by the individual schools. According to M. Christopherson, a former member of the executive board of the California Association of School Psychologists, some contacts may not be recorded at all because of the large number of contacts with psychological services staff and the burden of filling out reports (personal communication, March 1993). Thus it is difficult even under the best of circumstances to get good estimates of the services provided to students in schools.

Psychological services for immigrant students are even more difficult to track for two reasons. The first involves the limited number of school psychologists and related staff with bilingual skills. In a survey of several northern California school districts identified as having large numbers of immigrant students, only eight of the forty-nine psychological services staff members were identified as bilingual by their respective districts. The second reason has to do with identifying the psychological needs of immigrant students, since none of the districts surveyed had a process for compiling the number of immigrant students seen by psychological services staffs.

Because of the variability in the psychological services provided by each school district, the ratio of psychological services staff to students varied tremendously. The ratio of school psychologists to students ranged from 1:1000 to 1:3500. These ratios attest to the scarcity of services that school districts can provide to students. To confirm the research findings on the shortage of psychological services for elementary school-age children, we contacted elementary school districts in northern California and found, not surprisingly, that most offered little or no psychological services beyond intelligence testing as part of the district's individual education plans (Carroll, Harris, and Bretzing 1979). Because of the regulations governing state and federal programs dealing with migrant and immigrant children, several schools surveyed are mandated to follow the progress of limited-English-proficient and non-English-proficient students. This includes educational services provided to these students and careful attention to attendance. However, the psychological needs of immigrant children are often beyond the focus of the schools.

Some school districts are implementing school-based health centers to address concerns of the students. These centers are based on California Senate Bill 620, the Healthy Start Initiative, which specifically focuses on providing social and health-related services to children and families. One such service extends to mental health care and includes primary prevention, assessments, crisis intervention, referrals, and training for teachers in the detection of mental health problems. The bill also provides for the coordination of services for students. One school in our survey that had a Healthy Start program offered a variety of coordinated services to its non-English-speaking student population. They had one Spanish-speaking and one Vietnamese-speaking therapist as part of their team approach to providing psychological services. In addition, several community-based agencies were providing support groups in English, Spanish, Vietnamese, Cambodian, and Laotian. Unfortunately, this school is an exception, and often the children most in need of psychological services are furthest from receiving them.

Making Schools Responsive to Immigrant Students

Educational approaches such as newcomer centers and bilingual programs that help children acquire a new language and adjust to education in the United States have been the focus of attention when defining services for immigrant children. However, before learning can begin, a child must be emotionally and psychologically ready to learn. Schools are under enormous pressure to provide social services to students and their families regardless of immigration status. In fact, most of the social services that school officials have discussed recently have little to do with immigrant students but rather concentrate on the larger student population. The school is a logical center for coordination because of its role in the lives of children and its position in the community.

Political and economic factors worldwide are causing many individuals to leave their home countries and migrate to other nations. For immigrant students, the traumas endured prior to immigration can have enormous and long-term effects on their social-emotional and cognitive development. Unfortunately, economic conditions in this country are such that essential health and social services are increasingly unavailable to these students, not to mention for those students coming from countries that are not experiencing social upheaval but who nevertheless must deal with the problems of adjusting to a new language, a new culture, and a new society. Although psychological services have never been an important component of school life, these services now have been reduced further, and the few psychologists who still function in schools devote most of their time to intellectual assessments for special education placements.

The psychological needs of immigrant children vary so greatly that addressing this issue area involves looking at several aspects of the problem. It is important to develop programs that provide at least minimal service to these children and their families. However, because of economic concerns some of these recommendations may not be easily put into action. The following recommendations draw on a variety of sources, including our research, interviews with school personnel, and the relevant literature on immigrant students.

• Epidemiological research is critically needed on the psychological well-being of immigrant children and adolescents. Information is essential on the number of children affected by psychological problems such as PTSD, anxiety disorders, and somatization due to psychological stress. Only with good estimates of the number of students affected by psychological distress can educators and providers of health and social services know what services are most urgently needed.

• A school reporting system that can identify the contacts that nurses, counselors, and psychologists have with immigrant students needs to be put into place. This would include reason for contact and type of referral provided. In addition, information is needed regarding follow-up care to determine how the student is progressing, both for the purpose of evaluating the intervention and for planning prevention programs.

• Support services should be provided for the entire family and in the home language.

• Schools need to be linked with the services of traditional support agencies such as churches, local ethnic community centers, and grassroots organizations. Involving individuals known to the parents can be effective in getting children and families into programs that provide counseling and related self-help skills.

• For effective service provision, services for immigrant children must be coordinated so that parents and school personnel do not have to travel long distances for psychological or health services. Proximity of services is critical because immigrant families are frequently the least able to commute long distances to receive services.

- It is important to reduce the amount of paperwork involved in implementing programs that provide services to students in schools. The most frequent complaint from individuals working within schools was the amount of paperwork required to document services provided to students. Valuable time was often spent on this task and not with children in need of services. Record keeping is essential, but more efficient means of collecting and documenting services is necessary.

- Schools and service providers should enhance efforts to incorporate paraprofessionals from the school community who have the skills to provide support services for immigrant students and families in their native languages. The schools in our survey that did have support groups for students had individuals from the respective ethnic groups working with the school to assist immigrant students.

- There is a need for psychological training teams to provide staff development in-service training for teachers and other school staff on detecting psychological distress, teaching stress management and reduction techniques, and referring students to trained professionals. This in-service training should be available to anyone at a school who comes into contact with students inside or outside of the classroom.

- Emergency psychological teams should be established to provide services to children in their native languages. A concern of many school personnel was not knowing where to turn in cases of emergency because of the lack of familiarity with bilingual and bicultural service providers.

- Schools need to better coordinate with county mental health agencies and community-based organizations that provide psychological services to children and adolescents. Many immigrant students referred for psychological services by school psychologists are placed on long waiting lists at county mental health programs or community-based providers and frequently fail to receive services of any type. Through enhanced communication and coordination, students' progress could be monitored more easily, and communication among schools, parents, and service providers would translate into more responsive care of students having adjustment difficulties at school.

In conclusion, we offer these recommendations for improving the psychological services offered by schools that serve immigrant students. Although there are no good estimates of the number of immigrant students who might be at risk of psychological distress, our review of the research literature and the results of our own studies clearly suggest that many students may require personal counseling and other forms of psychological services rarely provided by schools. Educators may continue to deny that immigrant students are at great risk for psychological distress which interferes with effective learning, or they can approach immigrant students with the more comprehensive educational and social services that currently exist in the handful of schools that see the issue of immigration in a broader and more complex social context. We believe that the long-run costs to society will be less if educators attend to the whole student rather than only to those parts of the student for which we currently have programs.

References

Alva, S.A. 1991. "Academic Invulnerability among Mexican American Students: The Importance of Protective Resources and Appraisals," *Hispanic Journal of Behavioral Sciences* 13.

Boehnlein, J.K., D.J. Kinzie, R. Ben, et al. 1985. "One-year Follow Up Study of Posttraumatic Stress Disorder among Survivors of Cambodian Concentration Camps," *American Journal of Psychiatry* 142:956–59.

Burke, J.P., C.E. Hawthorne, and J.C. Brantley. 1983. "School-psychologist Providers: A National Survey of State Departments of Education," *Psychology in the Schools* 20:191–96.

Campbell, A., P.E. Converse, W.E. Miller, and D.E. Stokes. 1960. *The American Voter*. New York: Wiley.

Carroll, J.L., J.D. Harris, and B.H. Bretzing. 1979. "A Survey of Psychologists Serving Secondary Schools," *Professional Psychology*, October, pp. 766–70.

Cerhan, J.U. 1990. "The Hmong in the United States: An Overview of Mental Health Professionals," *Journal of Counseling and Development* 69:88–92.

Cervantes, R.C., A.M. Padilla, and N. Salgado de Snyder. 1991. "The Hispanic Stress Inventory: A Culturally Relevant Approach to Psychosocial Assessment," *Psychological Assessment: A Journal of Consulting and Clinical Psychology* 3:438–47.

Clifford, M.M., and T. Cleary. 1972. "The Relationship between Children's Academic Performance and Achievement Accountability," *Child Development* 43:647–55.

Coddington, R.D. 1972. "The Significance of Life Events as Etiological Factors in the Disease of Children: A Survey of Professional Workers," *Journal of Psychosomatic Research* 16:7–18.

Cummins, J. 1979. "Linguistic Interdependence and the Educational Development of Bilingual Children," *Review of Educational Research* 49:222–51.

Derogatis, L.R. 1977. *SCL-90 (Revised) Version Manual-I*. Baltimore, Md.: Johns Hopkins University School of Medicine.

Douville, O. 1985. "School Adaptation Process of Maghreb Children in France," *Cahiers d'Anthropologie et Biometrie Humaine* 3 (3–4):23–45.

Esquivel, G.B., and M.A. Keitel. 1990. "Counseling Immigrant Children in the Schools," *Elementary School Guidance and Counseling* 24:213–21.

Hall, L.K. 1988. "Providing Culturally Relevant Mental Health Services for Central American Immigrants," *Hospital and Community Psychiatry* 39:1139–44.

Henggeler, S.W., and J.B. Tavormina. 1978. "The Children of Mexican-American Migrant Workers: A Population at Risk?" *Journal of Abnormal Child Psychology* 6:97–106.

Ima, K., and C.F. Hohm. 1991. "Child Maltreatment among Asian and Pacific Islander Refugees and Immigrants," *Journal of Interpersonal Violence* 6:267–85.

Lazarus, R.S., and S. Folkman. 1984. *Stress, Appraisal, and Coping.* New York: Springer.

Le, D.D. 1983. "Mental Health and Vietnamese Children." In *The Psychosocial Development of Minority Group Children*, edited by G.J. Powell. New York: Brunner/Mazel.

Lee, V.E., and R.B. Ekstrom. 1987. "Student Access to Guidance Counseling in High School," *American Educational Research Journal* 24 (2):287-310.

Lyons, J.A. 1987. "Posttraumatic Stress Disorder in Children and Adolescents: A Review of the Literature," *Developmental and Behavioral Pediatrics* 8:349–56.

Masser, D.S. 1992. "Psychosocial Functioning of Central American Refugee Children," *Child Welfare* 71:439–56.

McNally, R.J. 1991. "Assessment of Posttraumatic Stress Disorder in Children," *Psychological Assessment: A Journal of Consulting and Clinical Psychology* 3:531–37.

Messer, M.M., and N.H. Rasmussen. 1986. "Southeast Asian Children in America: The Impact of Change," *Pediatrics* 78:323–29.

Munroe-Blum, H., M.H. Boyle, D.R. Offord, and N. Kates. 1989. "Immigrant Children: Psychiatric Disorders, School Performance, and Service Utilization," *American Journal of Orthopsychiatry* 59 (4):510–19.

Olsen, L. 1988. *Crossing the Schoolhouse Border: Immigrant Students and the California Public Schools.* San Francisco: California Tomorrow.

Olivas, M.A., ed. 1986. *Latino College Students.* New York: Teacher's College Press.

Padilla, A.M. 1986. "Acculturation and Stress among Immigrants and Later Generation Individuals." In *The Quality of Urban Life: Social, Psychological, and Physical Conditions*, edited by D. Frick. Berlin: Walter de Gruyter.

Padilla, A.M., R. Cervantes, and M. Maldonado. 1988. "Psychosocial Stress in Mexican Immigrant Adolescents." Manuscript.

Padilla, A.M., R.C. Cervantes, M. Maldonado, and R. García. 1988. "Coping Responses to Psychosocial Stressors among Immigrants from Mexico and Central America," *Journal of Community Psychology* 16:418–27.

Pearlin, L.I., and C. Schooler. 1978. "The Structure of Coping," *Journal of Health and Social Behavior* 19:2–21.

Piers, E.V. 1984. *Piers-Harris Children's Self-Concept Scale: Revised Manual 1984.* Los Angeles: Western Psychological Services.

Radloff, L.S. 1977. "The CES-D Scale: A Self Report Depression Scale for Research in the General Population," *Applied Psychological Measurement* 1:385–401.

Rakoff, V. 1981. "Children of Immigrants." In *Strangers in the World*, edited by E. Eitinger and D. Schwartz. Bern: Hans Huber Publishers.

Rosenberg, M. 1965. *Society and the Adolescent Self-Image*. Princeton, N.J.: Princeton University Press.

Steinhausen, H.C., E. Edinsel, J.M. Fegert, D. Gobel, E. Reister, and A. Rentz. 1990. "Child Psychiatric Disorders and Family Dysfunction in Migrant Workers' and Military Families," *European Archives of Psychiatry and Neurological Sciences* 239:257–62.

Tomlinson, J.R., N. Acker, A. Canter, and S. Lindborg. 1977. "Minority Status, Sex, and School Psychological Services," *Psychology in the Schools* 14:456–60.

Yao, E.L. 1985. "Adjustment Needs of Asian Immigrant Children," *Elementary School Guidance and Counseling* 19:222–27.

Yeaworth, R., J. York, M. Hussey, M. Ingu, and T. Gordman. 1980. "The Development of an Adolescent Life Change Event Scale," *Adolescence* 15:93–97.

7

The Cultural Patterning of Achievement Motivation: A Comparison of Mexican, Mexican Immigrant, Mexican American, and Non-Latino White American Students

Marcelo M. Suárez-Orozco and Carola E. Suárez-Orozco

This chapter examines some important themes in the cultural psychology of Mexican, Mexican immigrant, Mexican American, and non-Latino white American students. We explore central aspects of the immigrant experience among first- and second-generation individuals and families. We refer to some very interesting findings by our colleagues who work with Mexican immigrants, Mexican Americans (the largest Latino group in the United States), as well as to our research findings among Mexican students in Mexico, Mexican immigrant students, Mexican American students, and a control sample of non-Latino whites. We consider how certain enduring psychocultural features in the Latino experience may be of importance to understanding—and ameliorating—the educational condition of these subgroups.

It is impossible to discuss the Latino condition as if it were a monolithic phenomenon. Mexican Americans, Cuban Americans, mainland Puerto Ricans, and immigrants from Central and South America are distinct populations although they share a number of unifying characteristics. These include various degrees of familiarity with the Spanish language and such cultural traits as the importance of the

This essay was completed while the authors were in residence at the Center for Advanced Study in the Behavioral Sciences, Stanford (1992–1993). Marcelo M. Suárez-Orozco is grateful for financial support provided by the Spencer Foundation and the John D. and Catherine T. MacArthur Foundation.

extended family ("familism"), an emphasis on spiritual and interpersonal relationships, respect for authority, and an emphasis on the "here and now" rather than the future-time orientation valued by the dominant American culture.

It is important to emphasize that Latinos in the United States are a demographically and socioculturally diverse population. Latinos come from many different countries and different socioeconomic, educational, and professional backgrounds. Many have been in the United States for several generations. In the case of immigrants, we find special problems relating to whether they entered the United States as "documented" or "undocumented" migrants (see Leo Chávez 1992), whether they came voluntarily or involuntarily (many recent arrivals from Central America migrated to escape political persecution; see M. Suárez-Orozco 1989), whether they are seasonal migrants who plan to return home or migrants with plans to stay in the United States more or less permanently, and whether they came to the United States as a family unit or as individuals. All of these factors greatly impact opportunities and the migration experience. If we were to search for a common denominator in the experiences of Latino immigrants, it is that most are coming (or came) from relatively impoverished "developing" countries, and typically from the lower socioeconomic strata, into a more affluent, industrialized society.

The Immigrant Paradox: Instrumental Gains and Affective Losses

It is well recognized that immigrants often come as pioneers with a dream of making a better life for themselves and their children. Their objectives are relatively clear: to get a job, earn money, learn a new language, educate their children, and improve their lot in life. The obvious difficulties that most immigrants face include language inadequacies, a general unfamiliarity with the customs and expectations of the new country (what anthropologists refer to as "cultural discontinuities"), limited economic opportunities, poor housing, discrimination, and what psychologists term the "stresses of acculturation" (Rogler, Cortés, and Malgady 1991: 585–97).

Although from the perspective of the host country the immigrants' living circumstances may seem "poor" and "disadvantaged," in many cases immigrants see their lot as having improved from what it was in their country of origin (M. Suárez-Orozco 1989). As a result, immigrants may fail to internalize the negative attitudes that the host country holds toward them, maintaining their country of origin as a point of reference. Hence immigrants commonly view and experience their current situation not in term of the ideals and expectations of the majority society but rather in terms of the ideals of the "old culture."

This is part of an interesting immigrant orientation that we have termed "the immigrant's dual frame of reference" (M. Suárez-Orozco and C. Suárez-Orozco 1993). That is, immigrants are constantly comparing and contrasting their current lot in the host society against their previous experiences and expectations in their respective country of origin. During the earliest phases of immigration, the new arrivals may come to idealize the host country as a land of unlimited opportunities. Many new arrivals may at the same time concentrate on the negative aspects of life in the land left behind. After the initial excitement and idealization, there may be a period of letdown accompanied by a realization of the hardships that immigrants face in the host society.

It is important to note that first-generation immigrants may increase not only their own standard of living but also (and perhaps more importantly) the standard of living of family members left behind. Latino immigrants almost universally assist their relatives in the home country with regular and substantial remittances from the United States (see Gamio 1971).

We would also like to explore the psychological toll that individuals pay when they migrate to another country and how this affects immigrant children in schools. Although immigration may bring about an improvement in economic conditions, migration also ruptures the "immigrant's supportive interpersonal bonds" (Rogler, Malgady, and Rodríguez 1989: 25), well recognized to be crucial for psychological well-being. Psychologically, migration may represent a cumulative trauma; it often results in multiple losses whose effects are not always immediately apparent (Grinberg and Grinberg 1989).

Rogler, Cortés, and Malgady summarized their recent overview of the literature on acculturation and mental health status among Hispanics in the United States as follows:

> Migration is likely to disrupt attachments to supportive networks in the society of origin and to impose on the migrant the difficult task of incorporation into the primary groups of the host society. The migrant is also faced with problems of economic survival and social mobility in an unfamiliar socioeconomic system. These uprooting experiences are accompanied by problems of acculturation into a new cultural system, of acquiring the language, the behavioral norms and values characteristic of the host society (1991: 585).

In those individuals who possess sufficient psychological resources to withstand the trauma and who have adequate available social support, the migration experience can result in personal enrichment and psychological growth. For many, however, the losses result in an exacerbation of psychological traits and problems. Rogler, Cortés, and Malgady report that those immigrants "with fewest psychological resources for coping with the new environment reported the worst stress outcomes" (1991: 593).

Grinberg and Grinberg (1989) outline three typical patterns of psychological problems that may occur after migration. These include problems with "persecutory anxiety" (whereby the host environment is experienced as hostile and persecutory in nature), "depressive anxiety" (when the individual is preoccupied with his or her losses due to migration), and "disorienting anxiety" (which results from disorientation about the "old" and the "new" ways of being, time, and space).

Persecutory anxieties may be manifested in the form of irrational fears of aspects of life in the host society. During the first days of the 1991 Persian Gulf War, a rumor spread rapidly among Mexican migrants in Southern California that all "undocumented" persons captured by the Border Patrol would be sent to fight in the front lines! The (undocumented) immigrants' well-grounded fear of persecution by the Border Patrol metamorphosed into an irrational fear of being sent to war. Immigrants may also feel disappointment after realizing that their initial idealization of life in the new land was erroneous and that life in the new country may well be very difficult.

A sense of "depressive anxiety" is characterized by migrants' excessive preoccupation with psychological losses. A young Latino immigrant speaks of the tremendous sense of loss he feels in the new land:

> Here I have no family, I have no home. If I had my family and a home here I would be more optimistic. Now I feel tired. I am sure that if I had a home here, my mother would be waiting for me with my food ready. Now I come back home, and I have to make my own food. I get up in the morning to go to school, and I am all by myself. I make my own coffee, iron my clothes, do everything alone. I come back from work at night and I am all alone. I feel very low. I sit in bed all alone, and I lose morale. I think about my future and about being all alone. This depresses me a lot; I feel desperate (Grinberg and Grinberg 1989).

The sense of anxious "disorientation" that Grinberg and Grinberg found among new immigrants is related to what anthropologists have termed the sense of "culture shock" one typically experiences entering a radically different way of life. The children of Mexican immigrants may become the repositories of the parents' anxieties, ambitions, dreams, and conflicts (Trueba et al. 1993; Trueba 1989; Delgado-Gaitán and Trueba 1991). They are frequently vested with responsibilities (such as translating and sibling care) beyond what is normal for their stage of psychological development. Due to a lack of linguistic skills, Latino immigrant parents are often unable to help their children in school-related tasks. This may bring about further anxieties and a sense of inadequacy in the parents. At the same time, and perhaps related to the last point, Latino immigrant parents typically over-restrict the activities of their children and attempt to minimize the host country's influence.

The losses and disruptions of migration and the poisons of discrimination may undermine immigrant children's self-confidence and development (Padilla, Alvarez, and Lindholm 1986). Feelings of inadequacy and inferiority may reduce a child's faith in his or her ability to succeed in the new setting (Grinberg and Grinberg 1989). A psychological choice for young adults seems to emerge: either "dropping out" or overcompensating by overachieving.

The Second Generation: "Multiple Marginalities" and Ethnic Identity

The children of immigrants born in the new land (the second generation) do not share their parents' dual frame of reference. Not being immigrants themselves, they cannot frame their current experiences in terms of the old country's ideals, standards, and expectations. They are less likely to send remittances to relatives in the old country. Rather than seeing themselves as better off vis-à-vis the old country (as their parents did), the second generation often views their situation as one of deprivation and marginality vis-à-vis the majority culture's (American) "dream" (Horowitz 1983). Thus the second generation often faces the same discrimination and economic difficulties as their parents but without the perceived benefits.

Rogler, Cortés, and Malgady explore the psychosocial consequences of an important generational discontinuity between Mexico-born parents and their California-born children that relates to the immigrants' dual frame of reference. They write:

> The selectivity of the migration stream from Mexico to California tends to create a psychologically robust first-generation immigrant population who feels less deprived because migration has increased their standard of living; in contrast, the Mexican Americans born in the United States feel more deprivation because of their much higher but unrealized aspirations (1991: 589).

Ongoing discrimination and ethnic tension have an erosive effect particularly in the more vulnerable *children* of immigrants.

De Vos (1980) and Ogbu (Ogbu 1978; Gibson and Ogbu 1991) have argued that the specific problems facing immigrants and minority groups in general must be seen in the context of the distinct psychosocial experiences of each group as it enters a majority dominant society. Ogbu (1978) describes what he terms "involuntary minorities." These are minorities that have been initially incorporated into a dominant society against their will (such as African Americans through slavery, or American Indians and the original Mexican Americans through conquest). In addition to their original subordination, these groups have been subjected to a "job ceiling." Ogbu maintains that many of the involuntary minorities were traditionally channeled into the least desirable jobs in the opportunity structure and could not rise above these menial positions regardless of talent, motivation, or effort.

We would add that in addition to "instrumental exploitation" for economic purposes (for example, to maintain a pool of low-skilled, low-paid workers to do undesirable but necessary jobs), these minorities are also used for "psychological exploitation." That is, they may also be the target of psychological abuse such as stereotyping as "innately inferior," "lazier," and therefore less deserving of sharing in the dominant society's "dream." Economic exploitation and psychological exploitation are, in a sense, two sides of a coin: psychological exploitation and disparagement help the dominant society rationalize its economic treatment of these groups.

In some cases the children of immigrants raised in a context of ethnic disparagement may "identify" with an oppressing dominant group and attempt to join them, leaving their own ethnic group behind (see Rodriguez 1983). In other cases they may creatively navigate antagonistic cultural and ethnic borders, creating their own syntheses of traditions and acting as cultural translators and facilitators between groups. In yet other cases the children may resolutely reject the society that rejects them and turn to others sharing their predicament—their peers. From this last situation typically emerge countercultural groups or gangs that reject the dominant society and affirm their own ethnic identity.

Poor achievement in school tends to be a serious problem among Latinos (Pathey-Chávez 1993; M. Suárez-Orozco and C. Suárez-Orozco 1993; C. Suárez-Orozco and M. Suárez-Orozco n.d.; Trueba 1989). The reasons for this are complex. Vigil (1988a and 1988b) attributes this to the fact that many Latino immigrant parents have not had much education themselves and yet have attained a modest degree of prosperity (relative to whence they came). Hence some parents may be sending the following message to their children, "We made it without a formal education; so can you." Latino families facing economic hardships may encourage youths to seek early employment. There are also cultural expectations regarding marriage and child bearing which may divert some youths from investing in formal education.

A problem with this line of argument, as Trueba and his associates have eloquently demonstrated, is that Latino parents typically say they *want* their children to have the formal education they themselves could not have (Trueba et al. 1993; Trueba 1989; Delgado-Gaitán and Trueba 1991). Ogbu (1978) has approached the problem of poor Latino performance in school from a different but related perspective. According to Ogbu there is a perception among some Latinos, particularly Mexican Americans and mainland Puerto Ricans, that high school graduates are not much more successful financially than those who dropped out of school to work. Hence these Latino youths may not invest in school because they do not see that they will get any additional rewards in the posteducational job market.

School personnel are often indifferent, or even hostile, to the linguistic and other cultural needs, as well as the special circumstances, of immigrant Latino families (Pathey-Chávez 1993; M. Suárez-Orozco 1989). This indifference, coupled with the economic pressures of providing for a large family, may lead to Latinos' ambivalent attitudes toward school and the value of education. Consequently, a high dropout rate from school continues to be a severe problem in the Latino community (Horowitz 1983; Pathey-Chávez 1993; M. Suárez-Orozco 1989; Vigil 1988a, 1988b).

Grinberg and Grinberg (1989) and Vigil (1988a) maintain that a critical issue facing the children of immigrants is that of developing a sense of "identity." According to Erikson (1964), evolving a sense of identity is the critical task in development during adolescence. In order to develop "ego-identity" (a healthy sense of who one is), there must be a certain amount of complementarity between the individual's sense of self and the social milieu. If there exists too much cultural dissonance and role confusion, there may be difficulties in developing a strong sense of identity.

Children of Latino immigrants may suffer from what Vigil terms "multiple marginalities," which in some cases compromise the development of a sense of identity. Vigil and others have noted that children in these contexts are likely to experience intense culture conflict on both an individual and group level. For many second-generation Latino youths:

> Language inconsistency at home and school, a perceived gap in the status of their parents and the quality of their environment and those of the larger society, and the dangers and attractions of *barrio* streets create an ambiguity in their ethnic identity. Parents and older siblings are often unable to effectively guide youngsters in ways to reconcile the contrasting cultural

worlds, and this results in an uneven adoption of
acculturative strategies (Vigil 1988a: 41).

In some cases, youths attempt to resolve identity issues by embracing total assimilation and a wholesale identification with mainstream
American values. In other cases, a new ethnic identity is forged,
incorporating both Latino and dominant American culture (in which
cases bilingual fluency is often achieved). Yet in other cases the adaptation is not smooth, and a "subculture of cultural transitionals" develops
(Vigil 1988a: 39). These "transitional" youths are sometimes called *cholos*.
Within the same family each child may adopt his/her own way individually, resulting in various siblings occupying very different sectors of the
spectrum—from *cholo* to "anglicized," and from bilingual to "Spanglish"
speaking, to English-only speaking (Vigil 1988a).

It is precisely such identity issues that propel many second-generation Latino youths to join gangs. In fact, Vigil (1988a, 1988b) contends
that gangs are largely a second-generation immigrant phenomenon. In
his perceptive studies, Vigil traces the historical pattern of gang formation in urban areas beginning with the large-scale Mexican immigration
to the United States before the turn of this century. He accounts for
several key factors in the development of Latino gangs: low socioeconomic status, urban poverty, and limited economic mobility; ethnic
minority status and discrimination; lack of training, education, and
constructive opportunities; and a breakdown in the social institutions of
school and family.

Vigil also points out major causal factors in "a first- and second-
generation conflict within each ethnic group, which creates loyalty
discord and identity confusions; and a noted predisposition among
youths to gravitate toward street peers for sources of social associations
and personal fulfillment" (Vigil 1988a: 4). All of these factors hold
particularly true for many second-generation Latino youths. In addition,
we must note that "*cholo* gangs" have been a long-lasting, rather than
transitory, phenomenon due to a unique situation of continuous migration from Mexico which brings in reinforcements of the traditional
culture, and new cycles of "marginality," on an ongoing basis.

Gangs provide a "mechanism of adaptation for many youths who
need a source of identification and human support." The gang provides a
"reforging of Mexican and American patterns . . . creating a culture [and
language] of mixed and blended elements" (Vigil 1988a: 6–7). Vigil
maintains that "although *cholos* are Americanized, either by accident or
design, they refuse or are unable to be totally assimilated" (1988a: 7).
They retain certain Mexican customs, sometimes in caricature form, and
a strong sense of peer (gang) group as family, daring/bravado male
patterns of *machismo*, and an ambivalent attitude toward authority
(Horowitz 1983; Vigil 1988a, 1988b).

At the same time, youths in gangs may not feel "Mexican," and in some cases they may experience considerable antipathy toward Mexican visitors (Dayley 1991) and disparage "wetbacks" (first-generation undocumented immigrants) (Vigil 1988a). Often there is a perception of "limited good" and competition over scarce resources (such as jobs, education, housing, and so forth) with the newer arrivals. Psychologically, the second generation may view the new arrivals as embodying aspects of themselves that the second generation may wish to disclaim.

Both Vigil (1988a) and Horowitz (1983) have found that the individuals who are most heavily involved in gangs come from the most troubled families: with absent parents and with a history of alcohol or drug addiction and child neglect and/or abuse. Vigil (1988a) estimates that 70 to 80 percent of the heavily involved gang members come from such family situations. For those individuals, in the absence of more appropriate role models, gang membership becomes incorporated into their sense of identity. Gangs offer their members a sense of belonging, solidarity, and support. Although many second-generation youths may look toward gangs for cues about dress, language, and attitude, most remain on the periphery and eventually outgrow the gang mystique after passing through adolescence. Nevertheless, the gang ethos provides a sense of identity and cohesion for marginal youths during a turbulent stage of development.

Second-generation Hispanics who have the opportunity and choose to join mainstream American culture face very different day-to-day experiences but may continue to suffer from a marginal status:

> Individuals who choose to measure their competency in terms of the wider society rather than in terms of local identity risk a loss of emotional support from peers and kin. Trusting and close relationships must be developed with new people and on different terms. The movement away from the traditional sources of support and the traditional basis of social relationships can create feelings of acute loneliness. Little within the Chicano community prepares them for the competitive, individualistic Anglo world of social relationships in which they must face lack of acceptance and some degree of discrimination. They become caught between two worlds (Horowitz 1983: 200–01).

Some of those who choose to leave their ethnic group behind may even refuse to speak Spanish and reject bilingual education (see Rodriguez 1992, 1983; Linda Chávez 1991). The issue of language and identity deserves some further comment. Certainly it is true that by using "non-mainstream" English (such as Spanglish, Black English,

lower-class English) one is at a disadvantage, as evaluations are constantly being made about oneself based on language usage. However,
we would question whether it is indeed necessary to give up one's native
language, one's affective language (along with all the resulting accompanying losses), in order to "make it." In ideal circumstances, it should
not be an either/or situation.

Language has both a symbolic and an affective value. To see
language as a mere instrumental tool for communication is to miss its
deep affective roots. To give up Spanish to acquire English represents a
symbolic act of ethnic renunciation: it is giving up the mother tongue for
the instrumental tongue of the dominant group. It is in such contexts,
when learning the language of a dominant group is symbolically equated with giving up one's own ethnic identity, that language acquisition
becomes a problem. The Dutch can speak English very effectively at no
emotional cost. In contrast, the Flemish-speaking people in Belgium
have faced historical difficulties in learning French—the language of the
once dominant and oppressive Walloons. An understanding of affective
aspects of language also helps to explain why minority ethnic rights
movements often pick up language as a symbolic banner of belonging
vis-à-vis dominant groups (e.g., the Basques in Spain, the push for
bilingual education in the United States, the insistence that Black
English be given equal value to standard English, and so forth).

Empirical Findings

Our most recent study investigated how concerns regarding achievement and family orientation differ between Mexican, Mexican immigrant, Mexican American second-generation, and white non-Latino
American (the majority American culture) youth. Hence our study
attempts to address both differences between cultures (Mexican and
American) *and* generational discontinuities associated with the immigration process (nonimmigrants, first-generation immigrants, and children
of immigrants). Past research had suggested that it was likely that there
would be significant differences between groups on the dimensions
under consideration.

It must be emphasized at the outset that cross-cultural research is
fraught with methodological limitations. The challenge involves both the
difficulties of static-group comparisons (and hence of having group
equivalence) and finding "culture free" or culturally equivalent measures. Regarding the concern about group equivalence, in our research
we attempted to make the groups as representative and equivalent as
possible on what were thought to be key dimensions. In contending
with the second concern of using culturally equivalent measures, this
study used a variety of techniques to elicit the information needed to

answer the research questions. These techniques included structured ethnographic interviews, objective measures, and projective measures. A particular effort was made to strengthen the psychometric properties of the Thematic Apperception Test (TAT), as it has been both highly proclaimed and severely criticized as a tool for cross-cultural research.[1]

One hundred and eighty-eight students were evenly distributed between the groups. There was no significant difference between groups in terms of gender distribution. Participants were restricted to adolescents between the ages of thirteen and eighteen. The phase of the research dealing with Mexican students was conducted in Guanajuato, Mexico, in 1990–1991. Research with the other three groups—Mexican

---

[1] The Thematic Apperception Test is a "projective" test used by many anthropologists and psychologists. It consists of a series of pictures that are presented sequentially to the informant. The informant is told to make up a story, from the imagination, with a past, a present, and a future based on what he or she sees in the pictures. The informant is asked what the characters in the pictures are doing, what they think and feel, what happened before, and how the story ends. The TAT rests on the logic that informants, when presented with vague stimuli such as these pictures, will reveal their interpersonal attitudes and ongoing concerns. The narratives they create will, to a certain extent, reflect their own wishes, fears, hopes, and worries. When given to specific populations, the test can be used to postulate normative patterns for the group as a whole.

Some scholars in psychological anthropology have argued that the TAT may complement participant observation and ethnographic interviewing to systematically elicit certain key normative concerns or the interpersonal "atmospheric condition" of a group (De Vos 1973). When properly used, after achieving trust and rapport and having gained some ethnographic depth in which to embed the TAT results, the test may facilitate investigation of shared, affect-laden preoccupations that may not be immediately visible or easily approached through other research means. Thus the TAT allows informants to explore certain emotional issues in a relatively unthreatening manner.

Though widely used in cross-cultural research (see, for example, M. Suárez-Orozco 1989; McClelland et al. 1953; De Vos 1973) the TAT is not without its critics. Lindzey (1961) considered a number of cross-cultural studies that had been conducted using projective instruments. He found that many of the studies were seriously flawed methodologically. One of Lindzey's principal concerns was that the TAT had been used rather sloppily by individuals (mostly anthropologists) who had not been trained in systematic administration and who loosely interpreted the stories without using a standardized scoring system. Another of Lindzey's concerns had to do with the small sample sizes of many of the studies from which cross-cultural generalizations were then made. Lindzey also criticized the fact that many cross-cultural studies using the TAT lacked explicit hypotheses. And he expressed concern that the use of the TAT in a nonclinical ethnographic context could impose a language of pathology upon subjects.

We emphasize that our interest in the TAT is not in its clinical, psychodiagnostic use. For purposes of this work, we are not concerned with individual idiosyncrasies and psychopathology. Rather, we are concerned with how the TAT reflects shared, patterned thematic clusters when administered to a specific population. Further, we carefully designed the study to avoid the shortcomings outlined by critics of cross-cultural TAT research. (For a detailed discussion of the methodology of this project, see C. Suárez-Orozco 1993.) In terms of standardizing data analysis with the TAT as advocated by De Vos (1973) and his colleagues (De Vos and Suárez-Orozco 1990), we set explicit criteria for coding and analyzing narrative materials within a culturally specific framework which can be checked by others. It is essential that any projective data be used only in the context of other data, careful interviewing, and ethnographic observation. The researcher must be intimate enough with the culture and language to embed the projective materials within the context of a larger data framework.

immigrant, Mexican American, and non-Latino white American students—was conducted in Southern California in 1992–1993.

The groups were significantly different from one another on the dimension of socioeconomic status. Mexican immigrant and Mexican American students were of significantly lower socioeconomic status than either the Mexican or the American students. This is not surprising given that the measure of socioeconomic status used for this study (the Hollingshead [1975] four-factor scale) takes into consideration both a rating of the parents' occupation and years of education. The limited English-speaking abilities of the parents of many of the immigrant students tended to relegate them to positions in the laboring and service sectors. Furthermore, many of the parents of the Mexican immigrant and Mexican American students had very limited education; the educational levels of the American and Mexican students were, on the whole, higher. This finding indicates that the sample is representative of the groups under examination in the respective societies as a whole. Although an attempt could have been made to make the groups more equivalent in socioeconomic status, the resulting sample would not have been representative of the majority of Mexican immigrants to the United States.

Let us now consider each of the research questions and how they were answered using the quantitative methods employed in this study. Our findings confirm the general observation that Mexico-origin populations tend to be more family oriented than are other populations (see Becerra 1988; Karrer 1987; Vernon and Roberts 1985; Falicov 1982; Sabogal et al. 1987; Keefe, Padilla, and Carlos 1979; Murillo 1971; Montiel 1970; Hayner 1954). Further, our findings indicate that members of immigrant families become increasingly dependent on one another in the context of resettling in a foreign land (immigrants received higher scores on Sabogal et al.'s [1987] Familism scale than did Mexicans in Mexico, second-generation Mexican Americans, and the non-Hispanic white students).

There may be several factors to account for this important finding. The community networks of support that are important in daily life prior to migration (e.g., relying on neighbors, friends, and extended family to resolve everyday problems) are typically not available to newly arrived migrants in a foreign land. It would appear that migrant families turn inward as a result of this social fact. Additionally, it can be suggested that members of migrant families compensate for the individual losses accompanying migration by intensifying their affective ties with accompanying relatives (Grinberg and Grinberg 1989). Lastly, "culture shock"—the general sense of disorientation to a novel and culturally distinct setting—may also lead migrants to what is most familiar to them (i.e., members of their own family).

It is worth noting that the second-generation students fall in between the Mexican and Mexican immigrant subsamples, on the one hand, and the white non-Latino American group, on the other, in the degree of concern with familism as measured by this scale. This means that the concerns of second-generation Mexican American students are similar in many respects to those of both Mexicans and non-Latino white Americans. As could be anticipated, these students are bicultural, sharing concerns of two cultures along with their own unique configuration.

White non-Latino American students demonstrated significantly less perceived obligation to provide emotional or material support to the family than did students from any of the Latino groups. The immigrant group demonstrated the greatest concern about this dimension, followed closely by the Mexican American group. This finding again confirms the observations regarding the cultural patterning of family interdependence in Mexico-origin populations discussed above.

In the results of the TAT stories, as with the objective Familism scale (Sabogal et al. 1987), Mexico-origin individuals reveal a greater willingness than do non-Latino white Americans to provide material and emotional support to family members. A most interesting finding is that the Mexican immigrant and second-generation Mexican American youths revealed the highest concern with a sense of obligation to the family (e.g., more than white non-Latino Americans or Mexicans). Several observations could be made to account for this pattern. The Mexican immigrant and second-generation youths share an important characteristic: both have immigrant parents. The process of migration typically entails great emotional and material sacrifices on the part of the parents. It has been noted that immigrants rationalize the material sacrifices and affective losses by anticipating a better future in the new land; this future is, of course, the children. Children of immigrant parents may perceive the hardships endured by their parents as a sacrifice made so that they could have a better future. Beyond the normative difference between the Anglo and Mexican sense of obligation vis-à-vis family members, there might also be an immigrant aspect to the sense of obligation to repay parents for the sacrifices they made.

As noted earlier, the children of immigrants in some respects become "cultural translators" for their parents. These children generally speak the language of the host culture and may have a better understanding of the cultural process in the new setting than do their parents. Immigrant parents often turn to their children to help them in ways that they would not in their country of origin. Children help to translate, to open bank accounts, to intervene in emergencies, and to deal with the non-Spanish-speaking world in general. The children, aware of their parents' lack of relative competence in cultural matters, may come to feel a special sense of responsibility toward them.

The issue of whether family conflict would increase within the Mexican American second generation, as clinical observations had indicated, was also assessed. The fact that the Mexican American group did not score higher on either the objective (Beavers, Hampson, and Hulgus 1985) or TAT family conflict subscales disconfirmed this hypothesis. It should be noted that this hypothesis was developed after reviewing the clinical literature (e.g., Falicov 1982; Sluzki 1979; Vega 1990) that discusses the "cultural dissonance" and the "culture gap" that may arise between immigrant parents and their children. The sample used for this study consisted of "normals" (adolescents in high school not involved in individual or family therapy), while the clinical literature is based on patient cases seen by the clinicians. Clearly these samples are not comparable. One important finding of this study is that the so-called cultural gap does not necessarily lead to increased parent and child conflict in nonclinical adolescent children of immigrants.

Our study also considered the issue of peer influences. It was predicted, based on our reading of the relevant literature, that the Mexican American second generation and the white non-Latino American youths would express greater concerns with turning toward peers as behavioral and attitudinal referents than would either the Mexican or Mexican immigrant youths. The analysis of these data revealed that the white non-Latino American youths demonstrated the highest overall concerns with turning toward their peers for opinions regarding behaviors and attitudes. Contrary to prediction, however, the Mexican American group was very close to the Mexican and Mexican immigrant groups on this dimension.

This brings us to question the notion that adolescence is normatively a time of peer orientation and a pushing away of the family. While this may be true of white non-Latino American adolescents, it may not be true across cultures and nationalities. In his classic study of American culture, Gorer emphasized the American tradition of "the moral rejection of authority" (1963: 53) which began historically and has been perpetuated in the social and political structure of American society. Gorer discussed at length how the parent is rejected as a guide and model and how peers take on a central role in affirming self-esteem "with a feeling of far greater psychological urgency than is usual in other countries" (p. 108). In contrast, it is apparent that the family retains a key role for Mexico-origin adolescents, and peers may not necessarily achieve the same powerful degree of influence that they do for white non-Latino adolescents.

Our study also addressed questions about achievement orientation. The literature had suggested that achievement motivation may be based on different dynamics for different cultural groups (M. Suárez-Orozco 1989). This study explored this issue using the Thematic Apperception Test (as done previously by De Vos [1973]; McClelland [1961]; M. Suárez-

Orozco [1989], and others). Did the achievement motivations of white non-Latino American and Mexican youths differ from one another? Did concerns with achievement shift in relation to immigration and in the second generation? Would second-generation immigrants demonstrate achievement concerns like their parents, or would they be closer on this dimension to white non-Latino American youths? Or, alternatively, would second-generation youths significantly turn away from concerns with achievement?

It was hypothesized that both Mexican and Mexican immigrant youths would express more concern with compensatory achievement (i.e., achievement as a means to compensate for relative deprivation and poverty) than either second-generation Mexican American or white non-Latino American youths. The fact that the differences between the groups on the TAT Compensatory Achievement subscale did not reach statistical significance indicates that this hypothesis was not confirmed. However, the supplemental qualitative analysis indicated that Mexican youths voiced greater concerns with poverty than did any of the other subgroups.

Prior research with Central American adolescents (M. Suárez-Orozco 1989) had led to the hypothesis that Latinos in general, and Mexicans in particular, would construct TAT narratives in which achievement motivation would be within a framework of social obligations and mutual interdependence (i.e., achieving to help others or with the help of others). It was assumed that Mexican and Mexican immigrant youths would express more concern with affiliative achievement than would white non-Latino American youths and Mexican American youths.

However, the Mexican and Mexican immigrant youths did not in fact demonstrate higher TAT Affiliative Achievement subscale scores. Hence this hypothesis was not confirmed. After scoring the data, however, it became clear that overall affiliative concerns were differentially voiced between the groups. It was deduced that this scale was somewhat confounded as it incorporated two separate concepts (affiliation and achievement), both of which had to occur in a specific manner in order to be scored. As will be described in greater detail in the next section, there were in fact significant differences between the groups in affiliative concerns.

It was postulated that Mexican American youths would express more concerns regarding avoiding challenging tasks than would each of the other three groups. The fact that the Mexican American youths demonstrated statistically lower scores on the TAT Avoiding/Engaging Tasks subscale than did any other group confirms this hypothesis. Therefore, second-generation Mexican American youths related more narratives in which the protagonist is depicted as avoiding or giving up on the task at hand. This finding can be interpreted as follows: whereas the immigrant generation typically demonstrates high expectations and an optimism that they can achieve status mobility through schooling, the second generation may develop a less enthusiastic faith in the educational system.

Our finding is consistent with the observations of such researchers as Ogbu (1978), Matute-Bianchi (1991), and Pathey-Chávez (1993). According to these researchers, second- and third-generation Mexican American youths may respond to ongoing patterns of discrimination and cultural alienation in schools by giving up on education. As Pathey-Chávez poignantly puts it:

> Latino adolescents are highly motivated, but their expectations of success are colored by experiences of hostility and discrimination from the society at large. They question whether school is working in their interest. . . . They find it difficult to cooperate in the educational enterprise. Many of them simply leave it altogether (1993: 56).

Interestingly, the Independent Achievement scale reached significance, but in a direction that was unexpected. Analysis of this scale revealed that the Mexican subjects demonstrated significantly greater concerns with achievement in a self-initiated manner than did the Mexican American and non-Latino white American subjects. There was no significant difference on the Independent Achievement scale between Mexican and Mexican immigrant subjects.

The finding that non-Hispanic white Americans revealed less concern with self-initiated achievement than did the Mexican youths is in keeping with neither cultural stereotypes nor expectations based on the literature. Carter and Segura, for example, reviewed a number of studies that assessed teachers' views regarding "Mexican American cultural values and orientations" (1979: 83). Traits that were frequently imputed by educators to Mexican American students included fatalism, present-time orientation, low level of aspiration, and noncompetitiveness.[2] Additionally, McClelland's (1961) pioneering studies had established that self-initiated achievement motivation was the predominant achievement pattern among his non-Hispanic white subjects.

In our research, both the Independent Achievement *a priori* scale and the Internally Motivated supplemental scale demonstrated that achievement motivation was more self-initiated in the sample of Mexican youths than in that of the white non-Hispanic American youths. This last finding is particularly important when we take into consideration Ogbu's (1987) contention that "in general American social scientists . . .

---

[2] "Noncompetitive" can be read as meaning non-achievement oriented. Note the classic definition of achievement orientation given by McClelland et al. (1953: 161): "competition with a standard of excellence."

tend to assume explicitly or implicitly that the main cause of school failure lies in the background of the children." By "background" Ogbu is referring to genetic, linguistic, cultural, psychological, and social characteristics. The "cultural deprivation" model articulated by Bloom, Davis, and Hess asserted that school failures can be attributed to "experiences in the home which do not transmit the cultural patterns necessary for the types of learning characteristic of the schools and larger society" (1965: 4). In the case of Latino—and, more specifically, Mexico-origin—populations, some observers have argued that cultural background is somehow responsible for the relatively high levels of school failure and dropout. For example, Heller argued that Mexican American socialization emphasizes such values as "family ties" and "living in the present," all the while "neglecting the values that are conducive to [mobility], achievement, independence and deferred gratification" (1966: 34–35).

The findings of our study do not support these contentions. Our findings suggest that the Mexican cultural background does indeed emphasize self-initiated achievement and values the notion that hard work is critical for success, although it stresses interdependence, familism, and obtaining help from others more than does the cultural background of non-Hispanic Americans (see also Trueba et al. 1993; Trueba 1989; Delgado-Gaitán and Trueba 1991). We must conclude that a shift seems to occur in the psychosocial patterning of achievement motivation of Mexico-origin populations after moving into minority status in the United States. The narratives told by the Mexican students reveal that a pattern of self-initiated achievement orientation is fostered within the Mexican psychocultural background. Likewise, the immigrant subsample also reveals more concern with self-initiated achievement motivation than either the second-generation Mexican American or the non-Hispanic white subsample.

These findings suggest that problems in the motivational dynamics and schooling experiences of Mexico-origin second-generation youths cannot be attributed to cultural background per se. Other factors such as the stresses of minority status, discrimination, alienating schools, economic hardships, and pressures to work may all contribute to the elevated school dropout rate in this population. Further studies will be required to examine carefully the nature of this generational discontinuity.

Playing the Violin in Four Cultures

A large body of data was gathered for this project. An analysis of the entire data base goes far beyond the specific considerations and scope of this paper. It is, however, particularly instructive to delve into the most significant themes emerging from Card 1 of the Thematic Apperception Test. This card depicts a latency-age boy, pensively gazing at a violin on a table before him. This card tends to pull for the themes under consideration—achievement orientation and parent-child relations (Henry 1956). The comparative materials on Card 1 illustrate in rich and subtle detail many of the issues we have already discussed.

All of the stories on Card 1 were grouped by subsample (i.e., white non-Hispanic American, Mexican, Mexican immigrant, and Mexican American), and all of the responses for each group were read separately. In reading through the TAT responses to Card 1, it became evident that different themes seemed to predominate for each group. A list of recurring themes was compiled. All of the stories for Card 1 were then placed together randomly. The stories were read, analyzed, and discussed by two raters who were blind to the group membership of the storyteller. Each story was rated for the presence or absence of each of the themes under consideration. The incidence of each theme was tallied for each group. Chi-square analyses were then conducted to check for significant differences between groups. A number of findings resulted from this analysis (see table 7.1). Only the most significant of these will be discussed.

White Non-Hispanics

The predominant theme that emerges in analyzing the white non-Hispanic adolescents' responses to Card 1 of the TAT is that of frustration (in fully 50 percent of these narratives, contrasting with only 2 percent of the Mexican sample). In the majority of these narratives, frustration seems to be the outcome of either the difficulties and challenges of the task (learning to play the violin) or the pressures of the parental figure imposing the task on the unwilling child. Adolescents in this subgroup related narratives of pressuring parents far more frequently (in 36 percent of the cases) than did Mexican and Mexican immigrant youths (8 and 10 percent, respectively). The narratives told by the white non-Hispanic adolescents reflected concerns with independence and gave some indication that for these youths adolescence is a period of significant turmoil, which is particularly revealed by tensions with parental figures. Themes of individuation and independence are prominent within this group. Themes of turning to others for help occur very rarely in this group (4 percent). Here are some representative stories told by non-Hispanic white American adolescents:

> His parents want him to take violin lessons and they
> sent him to his room to practice until he got good. He
> doesn't like the violin and is sitting there looking at it,
> thinking that maybe he should play it to get out of his

room. But he really doesn't want to. He stares at it. He has played it and doesn't like it. Eventually his parents come up and see that he hasn't played it at all. They make him play it anyway. He feels frustrated that he can't do what he wants, but he has to do what his parents say, no matter how stupid it seems (female, age 16).

There is a boy, and for his birthday he is given a violin. His parents expect him to learn to play it but he becomes frustrated and never plays it. His mom has a party and expects him to play it there. He sits at his desk and stares at it. The day before the party, he tells his Mom the truth. She understands and forgives him. He asks if he can play a different instrument and she says that she will be just as proud. In the picture he is confused and mad that he can't play it. He feels like a disappointment to his parents (male, age 13).

This boy is sad because his parents want him to play the violin. He wants to be something else. He is sitting there and is looking at the violin and is trying to think what to say to his parents. He throws his violin and breaks it. His parents get mad and so he tells them he wants to play baseball. He is sad and angry and feels forced into something. He gets mad and they finally realize that it is his life and they encourage him to do what he wants (male, age 16).

Mexicans

In the Mexican sample, the most significant feature of the stories told by the students is a concern with self-motivated achievement orientation (54 percent versus 14 percent of American students). Themes of frustration and of the task having been imposed by others rarely occurred. Concerns with adequacy (28 percent) were frequently voiced, as was the notion that hard work was required for success (34 percent versus 10 percent of the American students). These adolescents told the most stories in which inherent pleasure derived from the activity. They also told many more stories in which the protagonist engaged in daydreaming and imagination than did any of the other groups (32 percent versus 4 percent of Americans and 2 percent of Mexican Americans). Another interesting occurrence in the Mexican stories is the number of narratives in which the parental dramatis personae are depicted as nurturing, warm, and supportive. This contrasts with the white non-Hispanic subsample, in which the parental figures were typically depicted as pressuring. A related concern in the

TABLE 7.1
RESPONSES TO TAT CARD 1

Theme	White Non-Hispanic		Mexican		Immigrant		Mexican American		Chi-square Probability
	N	%	N	%	N	%	N	%	
Parental pressure to perform	18	36	0	0	3	6	15	30	.001***
Internally motivated	7	14	27	54	16	32	9	18	.001***
Succumbing to pressure	7	14	3	6	2	4	4	8	.274
Avoiding pressure	8	16	1	2	5	10	8	16	.114
Hard work	5	10	17	34	5	10	8	16	.005**
Instant gratification	3	6	2	4	2	4	1	2	.789
Success as a result of efforts of self	5	10	15	30	10	20	5	10	.026*
Success as a result of efforts of others	3	6	3	6	5	10	3	6	.813
Success as a result of efforts of self and others	7	14	4	8	5	10	4	8	.707
Achievement motivated for self	0	0	2	4	0	0	0	0	.007**
Achievement motivated for others	1	2	4	8	5	10	4	8	.429
Achievement motivated—self and others	0	0	2	4	0	0	0	0	.707
Concerns with adequacy	8	16	14	28	17	34	9	18	.013**
Concerns with failure	2	4	1	2	1	2	14	28	.001**

TABLE 7.1 (CONTINUED)
RESPONSES TO TAT CARD 1

Theme	White Non-Hispanic		Mexican		Immigrant		Mexican American		Chi-square Probability
	N	%	N	%	N	%	N	%	
Boredom	3	6	1	2	1	2	7	14	.134
Frustration—resolved	17	34	0	0	3	6	3	6	.001***
Frustration—unresolved	8	16	1	2	1	2	4	8	.016
Broken violin—purposeful	5	10	0	0	0	0	1	2	.008**
Broken violin—accidental	4	8	0	0	7	14	4	8	.063
Mad	7	14	0	0	3	6	10	20	.004**
Sad	16	32	8	16	33	66	17	34	.001***
Searching out help	2	4	6	12	13	26	6	12	.012**
Pleasure	3	6	9	18	8	16	3	6	.115
Financial deprivation	2	4	6	12	3	6	3	6	.451
Daydreaming/imagining	2	4	16	32	5	10	1	2	.001***
What do I want to do?	6	12	0	0	0	0	1	2	.002**
Parenting style—pressuring	18	36	4	8	5	10	5	10	.001***
Parenting style—nurturing	5	10	8	16	4	8	4	8	.541
Parenting style—punitive	2	4	1	2	1	2	3	6	.644

* $p > .05$
** $p > .01$
*** $p > .001$

Mexican subsample is actively seeking help from a competent person to aid the protagonist in accomplishing the difficult task at hand. Rather than fighting off intrusive parents, Mexican students tell stories in which the protagonist is searching for an adult figure to help him with his task. Representative stories follow:

> This is a young boy who is concentrating on the violin. He's thinking that he's not going to be able to learn the notes of the melody that he wants to learn to play. But with time he keeps trying and he eventually learns to play the melody. It comes out really well because of all his efforts, and when he gets it perfect he calls his friends to show them what he has learned. They listen to him and they tell him how beautiful the music is. They tell him his success is due to all his hard work (female, age 14).

> There was a boy who wanted to learn to play the violin but he did not know how. He is sitting there thinking and contemplating about the future. He's thinking about whether he will be able to learn to play and become a great violinist. Just now he is imagining that he is in a concert hall giving a concert. After thinking about it, he tells himself that he needs to put a lot of effort and enthusiasm into learning so that he will be able to achieve his dreams in the future (male, age 14).

> This boy is looking at his violin that he inherited from his father. He doesn't have anyone to help him learn to play the violin. He is very sad and he realizes that he doesn't know how to play the violin. His mother is going to help him find someone to help him learn to play. His family doesn't have any money to get anyone to help. She manages anyway, and when he gets to be older he has learned how to play. He learns to play very well. He learned when he was fifteen years old and he began working, and with the money that he earned he took more and more lessons in order to become a better musician (male, age 14).

Mexican Immigrants

Within the Mexican immigrant subsample, the most frequently voiced theme is that of a sense of sadness or of "feeling bad" attributed to the protagonist (fully 66 percent of this sample, double the white non-Hispanic sample and Mexican American sample and four times the Mexican sample). This theme of sadness found in stories told by the Mexican immigrants is highly consistent with previous findings of depression resulting from immigration losses (see Padilla and Durán, this volume; Brenner 1990; Grinberg and Grinberg 1989).

As with the Mexican subsample, the immigrant youths articulated a preoccupation with self-motivated achievement orientation along with concerns with adequacy. However, rather than achieving the important large-scale successes recounted in the stories of the Mexican students, the narratives told by the immigrant adolescents reveal a smaller scale of success. Rather than playing in orchestras all over the world or being widely applauded (as in many of the narratives of the Mexican students), the protagonist of the immigrant stories, when he succeeds, merely learns how to play. Hence, the expected successes seem to be significantly scaled back. A greater number of the Mexican immigrant youths mentioned seeking help from others (26 percent versus 12 percent of Mexican and Mexican American youths and 4 percent of American youths) than did any of the other subsamples. Here are some representative stories illustrating these themes:

> He is sad because he is not able to play the violin and he doesn't know who he can ask to help him. He is trying to figure out how he might be able to play it. His mom is sad also because she asked him if he could play and he said no. She decided that he needed to get someone to help him. She finds someone to help him and teach him how to play and he learns how to play and he feels really happy about it (female, age 13).

> He is looking at it, trying to use it—what parts it has. He feels worried and preoccupied because he is still unable to use it well. He will find out how to play this. He doesn't have help. He does it alone. He feels sad and thinks that he needs someone who can help him, show him how to use it. He will be happy when he knows how to use it (male, age 17).

> This is a boy who liked to play the violin but he didn't know how. He is sad but he takes classes on how to learn. After a time he learns to play and he is happy (female, age 14).

Second-generation Mexican Americans

In the case of the second-generation Mexican Americans, we encountered some characteristics that are also present in other subsamples. For example, like the themes emerging in the white non-Hispanic sample, an important feature of the narratives articulated by the second generation is that of parental figures (including teachers and other authority figures in society) depicted as pressuring the protagonist to perform the task (in 30 percent of the stories). Likewise, the percentage of stories in which the predominant theme is self-motivated achievement orientation is comparable to the American subsample (14 and 16 percent, respectively). In many of these stories, the self-motivated orientation leads to success in an atmosphere of social interdependence (e.g., success is due to the inspiration of the grandfather, is achieved by a parent teaching him or by the parents providing emotional support). In these stories, hard work is involved but success is socially mediated; help or inspiration from others is crucial.

A very striking theme found in the second-generation narratives is a concern with failure. In 28 percent of the Mexican American stories, there is reference to a concern with threatened failure to achieve the task at hand. This contrasts with 2 percent among the Mexican and immigrant groups and 4 percent among the white non-Latino Americans. Whereas concerns with adequacy are voiced in many of the stories told by the Mexican and Mexican immigrant subsamples, there is a strong sense of hope and optimism for the future (i.e., the initial inadequacy is overcome and success is finally achieved through hard work). In a number of the stories told by the second generation, however, a disturbing preoccupation with failure and a sense of hopelessness emerge. In many such stories, the future looks bleak. The following are some representative stories.

> The child was very interested in playing the violin in the beginning. Now he doesn't know what to do without any help. Now he is going through stages where he puts too much effort and nothing is happening. So he is feeling depressed. He loses his interest in music and now has a mental block in himself. He can't solve other problems. He gives up all interest in music and has a mental block. He loses confidence in solving problems (male, age 18).

> He probably went to try out for a music class and he didn't make it. So he is sad. He looks sad because he didn't make it. He goes home and tells his Mom what happened—that he didn't get to make it (female, age 18).

> There was this little boy who wanted to play the violin. He had the violin but no money to take classes. He got a

job and worked and worked for days. Finally he got money but he couldn't find where to go to take classes. He looked and looked and found some place to go and learn. He took classes but couldn't learn how to play it. One day he was playing in the park with some friends and he kicked a ball and broke a window. He went to his parents and told them and asked them to pay for the window. They said "no." He either would have to work or sell his violin, they told him. He went to his room and sat down and stared at it and thought about it. He decided to sell it. He feels sad because he was starting to learn to play it and he had to let it go (female, age 14).

In some of these stories told by second-generation youths, the protagonist attempts to engage with the task; he tries to play the violin but eventually quits, realizing that he is not competent. In others, the protagonist cannot learn without help or simply tries but is unable to play adequately and is disheartened. In yet other narratives, the concern with failure is more specifically related to obstacles in the environment that prevent the protagonist from taking on the challenge. In these stories, the boy is trying to learn the violin but must give it up due to factors outside of his control. In some cases, though, the protagonist struggles with the threat of failure and eventually finds a solution by asking for help from others.

It is particularly poignant to note the discontinuities in the narratives told by the Mexicans in Mexico, the Mexican immigrants, and the second-generation Mexican Americans. Whereas Mexicans and immigrant students revealed a faith that success was possible through hard work, many of the second-generation youths told stories in which failure was a significant preoccupation. The energy and faith in "making it" that are characteristic of the Mexican and immigrant students seem to have significantly diminished by the second generation.

These findings may be related to the vicissitudes in the path from immigration to minority status. Immigrants typically endure their affective losses by concentrating on the material gains to be made by exploiting new opportunities in a host country. Members of the second generation, on the other hand, may not measure their current state in terms of their former life in Mexico. Rather, they use as their standard the ideals and expectations of the majority society (M. Suárez-Orozco and C. Suárez-Orozco 1993). Using this standard, many Mexican Americans may fall short of their aspirations. Racism, disparagement, and lack of equal opportunity may compromise the faith of at-risk youths in their ability to succeed. This may well be related to the disturbingly elevated school dropout rates among second- and third-generation Mexican

American youths (Bean et al. 1994; Chapa 1988; Kantrowitz and Rosaldo 1991).

Conclusion

A premise of this project, stated at the outset, was that Latinos are far from a homogeneous group. This study focused on the specific experiences of Mexican immigrants and Mexican Americans (and compared them to non-Latino whites and to Mexicans in Mexico). Differences in the characteristics of each subgroup were found. Perhaps the most significant finding of this study is the important discontinuity in the psychosocial profile of Mexican immigrants and second-generation Mexican Americans.

Educators working with immigrants would be wise to take into account the psychosocial consequences of the affective ruptures involved in immigration. Of particular relevance is the normative preoccupation with losses and the mourning endured in the context of immigration. Not only are immigrant youths preoccupied with their own losses, but the stresses and losses of their immigrant parents affect their psychological availability to help their children navigate the dual challenges of adolescence and the adjustment to a new cultural context. As parents' psychological resources are absorbed by their own losses, culture shock, and the need to earn a living in the new country, it is to be expected that they may have less time and energy to devote to the adolescent.

In terms of familial conflict, educators may benefit by paying attention not only to how conflicts may be age-specific (related to the adolescent phase of development in the United States) but also how they may be the product of specific acculturation stresses and discontinuities separating immigrant parents from their children. In working with the second generation (as with immigrant adolescents), it is important to take into account their (immigrant) parents' relative unavailability (due to their own losses and economic pressures), which may lead the youths to turn elsewhere for satisfaction of their affective needs. Many minority youths residing in conflict-ridden inner cities turn to peer groups for the instrumental and affective supports that help them endure their difficult surroundings (Vigil 1988a, 1988b).

The most obvious characteristic of the second-generation Mexican Americans is their participation in two distinct psychocultural universes. Not surprisingly, they operate in two cultural realms and are preoccupied with issues concerning adolescents in each of the two cultures. Issues facing the second generation are in some respects very different from the issues facing the immigrant generation. A significant proportion of second-generation youths revealed in their narratives a disturbing preoccupation about an inability to "make it." A compromised sense of self-esteem seems to be a corollary of the second generation's minority status (see Padilla and Durán, this volume; Carter and Segura 1979). Clinically, the second-generation youths reveal less concern with sadness, but issues of frustration and self-esteem appear to be significant. Providing successful role models may be an especially effective intervention in conveying hope to second-generation youths who seem concerned with failure.

In essence, second-generation children must navigate between Latino familism and the American cultural ideal of independence and making it in one's own way. Educators working with second-generation youths should locate psychological problems and conflicts in the context of the stresses facing immigrant families and their minority status youths. Given that familism is an enduring trait for the Mexican and Mexican American youths, educators should try, whenever possible, to involve the family in their interventions.

The school, perhaps more than any other social institution, is an arena in which many of the problems facing Hispanics—both first and second generation—are played out. Educators working with Latino immigrant children are often surprised to see how vigorously the new arrivals pursue their dream of a better tomorrow through education. These same educators seem puzzled to see how, contrary to common expectations rooted in a simplistic notion of "assimilation," many second- and third-generation children of Latino descent grow disaffected with the school system. Educators watch as large numbers of these youths fail to thrive in school environments, turning to gangs or "dropping out."

Educators working with Latino youths should understand that there are class, gender, and generational factors that shape experience and expectations differently across groups. They should consider the burdens (affective losses, psychological disorientation, cultural discontinuities, etc.) that immigrant children carry. Sensitive educators may emerge as "cultural brokers" bridging some of the generational discontinuities between immigrant children and their parents and between immigrants and the dominant culture.

With respect to newly arrived immigrant children, educators are placed in a strategically important position to capitalize on their dynamic of positivism, hope, and desire to succeed. Understanding motivation is at the heart of pedagogy. Yet the assumptions that have guided pedagogical practice and curriculum strategies to date are based on an understanding of motivation relevant largely to white, middle-class students from the dominant culture. As we discussed above, the cultural paradigm of individualism that defines and patterns motivation among members of the dominant culture does not apply to Latino students. Latino students, we have argued, typically achieve in the context of family and peer obligation, not in the context of individualistic self-advancement.

It is clear that the Latino immigrant experience is a rich and diverse tapestry. Gender, country of origin, socioeconomic status, legal status, level of "acculturation," generational differences, and psychological resources must all be taken into account when considering the Latino experience. Only when such issues are considered can we begin to understand, and be of service to, the various Latino groups in the United States.

References

Bean, Frank D., Jorge Chapa, R. Berg, and Kathryn Sowards. 1994. "Educational and Sociodemographic Incorporation among Hispanic Immigrants to the United States." In *Immigration and Ethnicity: The Integration of America's Newest Arrivals*, edited by Barry Edmonston and Jeffrey S. Passel. Washington, D.C.: Urban Institute Press.

Beavers, W. Robert, Robert B. Hampson, and Y.F. Hulgus. 1985. "Commentary: The Beavers System Approach to Family Assessment," *Family Process* 24:398–405.

Becerra, Regina M. 1988. "The Mexican American Family." In *Ethnic Families in America: Patterns and Variations*, edited by Charles H. Mindel, Robert W. Habenstein, and Roosevelt Wright. 3d ed. New York: Elsevier.

Bloom, Benjamin S., Allison Davis, and Robert Hess. 1965. *Compensatory Education for Cultural Deprivation*. New York: Holt, Rinehart, and Winston.

Brenner, E. 1990. "Losses, Acculturation and Depression in Mexican Immigrants." Ph.D. dissertation, California School of Professional Psychology.

Carter, Thomas P., and Roberto D. Segura. 1979. *Mexican Americans in School: A Decade of Change*. New York: College Entrance Examination Board.

Chapa, Jorge. 1988. "The Question of Mexican American Assimilation: Socioeconomic Parity or Underclass Formation?" *Public Affairs Comment*. Austin: Lyndon B. Johnson School of Public Affairs, University of Texas at Austin.

Chávez, Leo R. 1992. *Shadowed Lives: Undocumented Immigrants in American Society*. Fort Worth, Tex.: Harcourt, Brace, Jovanovich.

Chávez, Linda. 1991. *Out of the Barrio: Toward a New Politics of Hispanic Assimilation*. New York: Basic Books.

Dayley, J. 1991. "One Big Happy Family," *Reader* (San Diego) 20 (17): 5–8.

Delgado-Gaitán, Concha, and Henry Trueba. 1991. *Crossing Cultural Borders: Education for Immigrant Families in America*. London: Falmer.

De Vos, George A. 1973. *Socialization for Achievement*. Berkeley: University of California Press.

———. 1980. "Ethnic Adaptation and Minority Status," *Journal of Cross-Cultural Psychology* 11 (1): 101–25.

De Vos, George A., and Marcelo Suárez-Orozco. 1990. *Status Inequality: The Self in Culture*. Newbury Park, Calif.: Sage.

Erikson, E. 1964. *Childhood and Society*. New York: W.W. Norton.

Falicov, Celia J. 1982. "Mexican Families." In *Ethnicity and Family Therapy*, edited by Monica McGoldrick, John K. Pearce, and Joseph Giordano. New York: Guilford.

Gamio, Manuel. 1971. *Mexican Immigration to the United States: A Study of Human Migration and Adjustment*. New York: Dover.

Gibson, Margaret A., and John U. Ogbu, eds. 1991. *Minority Status and Schooling: A Comparative Study of Immigrant and Involuntary Minorities*. New York: Garland.

Gorer, Geoffrey. 1963. *The American People: A Study in National Character*. Rev. ed. New York: W.W. Norton.

Grinberg, Leon, and Rebecca Grinberg. 1989. *Psychoanalytic Perspectives on Migration and Exile*. New Haven, Conn.: Yale University Press.

Hayner, Norman S. 1954. "The Family in Mexico," *Marriage and Family Living* 11:369–73.

Heller, Celia. 1966. *Mexican-American Youth: The Forgotten Youth at the Crossroads*. New York: Random House.

Henry, William. 1956. *The Analysis of Fantasy*. New York: J. Wiley and Sons.

Hollingshead, August B. 1975. "Four-Factor Index of Social Status." Working paper. New Haven, Conn.: Yale University.

Horowitz, Ruth. 1983. *Honor and the American Dream: Culture and Identity in a Chicano Community*. New Brunswick, N.J.: Rutgers University Press.

Kantrowitz, B., and L. Rosado. 1991. "Falling Further Behind," *Newsweek*, August 19, p. 60.

Karrer, Betty M. 1987. "Families of Mexican Descent: A Contextual Approach." In *Urban Family Medicine*, edited by Richard B. Birrer. New York: Springer-Verlag.

Keefe, Susan E., Amado M. Padilla, and M.L. Carlos. 1979. "The Mexican-American Extended Family as an Emotional Support System," *Human Organization* 38:144–52.

Lindzey, Gardner. 1961. *Projective Techniques and Cross-cultural Research*. New York: Appleton-Century-Crofts.

Matute-Bianchi, Maria E. 1991. "Situational Ethnicity and Patterns of School Performance among Immigrant and Nonimmigrant Mexican-descent Students." In *Minority Status and Schooling: A Comparative Study of Immigrant and Involuntary Minorities*, edited by Margaret A. Gibson and John U. Ogbu. New York: Garland.

McClelland, David. 1961. *The Achieving Society*. Princeton, N.J.: Van Nostrand.

McClelland, David, John W. Atkinson, R.H. Clark, and E.L. Lowell. 1953. *The Achievement Motive*. New York: Appleton-Century-Crofts.

Montiel, Miguel. 1970. "The Chicano Family: A Review of Research," *Social Work* 18 (3): 22–31.

Murillo, N. 1971. "The Mexican American Family." In *Chicanos: Social and Psychological Perspectives*, edited by Nathaniel Wagner and Marsha Haug. St. Louis: C.V. Mosby.

Ogbu, John U. 1978. *Minority Education and Caste: The American System in Cross-cultural Perspective*. Orlando, Fl.: Academic Press.

———. 1987. "Variability in Minority School Performance: A Problem in Search of an Explanation," *Anthropology and Education Quarterly* 18 (4): 312–34.

Padilla, Amado M., M. Alvarez, and Kathryn J. Lindholm. 1986. "Generational Status and Personality Factors as Predictors of Stress in Students," *Hispanic Journal of Behavioral Sciences* 8 (3): 275–88.

Pathey-Chávez, G. 1993. "High School as an Arena for Cultural Conflict and Acculturation for Latino Angelinos," *Anthropology and Education Quarterly* 24 (1): 33–60.

Rodriguez, Richard. 1983. *Hunger of Memory: The Education of Richard Rodriguez— An Autobiography.* New York: Bantam Books.

———. 1992. *Days of Obligation: An Argument with My Mexican Father.* New York: Viking.

Rogler, Lloyd, D. Cortés, and Robert Malgady. 1991. "Acculturation and Mental Health Status among Hispanics," *American Psychologist* 46 (6): 585–97.

Rogler, Lloyd H., Robert G. Malgady, and Orlando Rodríguez. 1989. *Hispanics and Mental Health: A Framework for Research.* Malabar, Fl.: Robert E. Krieger.

Sabogal, Fabio, Gerardo Marín, Regina Otero-Sabogal, Barbara V. Marín, and Eliseo Pérez-Stable. 1987. "Hispanic Familism and Acculturation: What Changes and What Doesn't?" *Hispanic Journal of Behavioral Sciences* 9 (4): 397–412.

Sluzki, Carlos E. 1979. "Migration and Family Conflict," *Family Process* 18 (4): 379–90.

Suárez-Orozco, Carola. 1993. "Generational Discontinuities: A Cross-cultural Comparison of Mexican, Mexican Immigrant, Mexican American and White Non-Hispanic Adolescents." Ph.D. dissertation, California School of Professional Psychology.

Suárez-Orozco, Carola, and Marcelo Suárez-Orozco. n.d. "The Cultural Psychology of Hispanic Immigrants." In *The Handbook of Hispanic Cultures in the United States,* edited by T. Weaver. Houston: Arte Público Press. In press.

Suárez-Orozco, Marcelo. 1989. *Central American Refugees and U.S. High Schools: A Psychosocial Study of Motivation and Achievement.* Stanford, Calif.: Stanford University Press.

Suárez-Orozco, Marcelo, and Carola Suárez-Orozco. 1993. "La psychologie culturelle des immigrants hispaniques aux Etats-Unis: implications pour la recherche en éducation," *Revue Française de Pédagogie* 101 (4): 27–44.

Trueba, Henry T. 1989. *Raising Silent Voices: Educating Linguistic Minorities for the 21st Century.* Cambridge: Newbury House.

Trueba, Henry T., C. Rodríguez, Yali Zou, and José Cintrón. 1993. *Healing Multicultural America: Mexican Immigrants Rise to Power in Rural California.* London: Falmer.

Vega, William A. 1990. "Hispanic Families in the 1980's: A Decade of Research," *Journal of Marriage and the Family* 52 (11): 1015–24.

Vernon, S.W., and R.E. Roberts. 1985. "A Comparison of Mexicans and Americans on Selected Measures of Social Support," *Hispanic Journal of Behavioral Sciences* 7:381–99.

Vigil, James D. 1988a. *Barrio Gangs: Street Life and Identity in Southern California.* Austin: University of Texas Press.

———. 1988b. "Group Processes and Street Identity: Adolescent Chicano Gang Members," *Ethos* 16 (4): 421–45.

8

Testing the American Dream: Case Studies of At-Risk Southeast Asian Refugee Students in Secondary Schools

Kenji Ima

Introduction

American schools, and especially schools in California, are currently in catch-up mode, endeavoring to design services that will meet the needs of their continually changing newcomer student population. This chapter reports on a study of one such student group—Southeast Asian refugees— and their schooling context. Just as for earlier immigrant groups, success in school—and eventually in the workplace—will determine whether or not these students are able to live the American Dream.

Immigrant ethnic student populations do not all attain the same levels of success in school. Some excel; some fail.[1] Ambert (1991) argues that efforts to understand the academic difficulties of linguistic-minority children should extend beyond linguistic and cultural factors to encompass social, political, and economic considerations: racism, social status, social isolation, majority attitudes toward minorities, lowered teacher expectations and curricular tracking, cultural discontinuities between the home and the school, and educational segregation which stems from segregation and discrimination in society. Several of these factors have the potential to shape schooling outcomes for newcomer youths. This chapter examines specific community and schooling conditions in San Diego city schools that have the potential to alternately help or doom these refugee youths.

---

[1] Various explanations have been offered for the differential success of immigrant ethnic students, including the concepts of cultural capital and immigrant-versus-castelike social status. However, overarching these considerations about resources or the lack thereof is the question of how schools can make a difference.

Background

A panel at a recent conference on education was entitled "Why Asian American Students Succeed Academically." Caplan, Choy, and Whitmore (1992) are among the researchers who have explored the implications of this predication. Caplan and his associates documented high performance among a group of Indochinese refugee students and identified the underlying factor that explained that performance—family support. The implication often drawn from this study is that other groups should work to strengthen families. Thus poor schooling outcomes occur not because schools are inadequate but because families are "dysfunctional."

This interpretation suggests that schools may not be a proper focus for policy and that the emphasis should go to improving families. For researchers like myself, who work with Asian American students, this and similar findings undercut our efforts as advocates for Asian immigrant students. Since the stereotype holds that Asian families are the key resource and that schools simply provide Asian students the opportunity to utilize that resource, it would logically follow that there is no need to pursue fundamental school reforms. However, this argument is seriously flawed, as will be demonstrated below.

The assertion that Asian American students are succeeding (despite evidence to the contrary, presented below) does not exist in a void. This statement sits within a context, and the implicit assumptions of that context raise some questions: Who is making the assertion? What does the assertion imply? Is there a hidden agenda? Should we be looking at the issue differently? If our concern is the well-being of newcomer Asian students in U.S. schools, then this assertion is not neutral. The fact that many Asian immigrant students are failing in U.S. schools despite what appears to be an overall successful adaptation leads me to wonder what agendas lie behind the broad assertion that Asian immigrant students succeed, and what implications these have for the resulting policy of benign neglect directed toward this group of students.

There are two possible approaches to the issue. The first is the scholarly, or generalizing, perspective. It asks, What predicts or explains schooling success? The second, the educational, perspective asks, How do we best educate students? This is a particularizing perspective. We can see the tensions between the two perspectives in educational policy makers' long-standing ambivalence toward Ogbu's generalizing perspective on the systematic differences between immigrant and caste-like minority students (Ogbu 1993). Gibson (1991), who has adopted Ogbu's framework, argues for a distinction between immigrants and caste-like minorities as a major predictor of school success, but she also recognizes that this distinction creates the potential for inappropriate stereotyping. Therefore, she advocates investigating variations in schooling adaptation among immigrants along the dimensions of such factors as age upon admission to the host country, proficiency in the home language, discontinuities between home and school cultures, inappropriate curriculum, socioeconomic situation, and discrimination. This recognition of other factors raises questions about how to contextualize the students' status within larger social and cultural contexts (see Weisner, Gallimore, and Jordan 1988). Furthermore, it speaks to the need to ascertain the relative weights of factors that affect immigrant students' schooling success and to identify the interaction effects between culture/student characteristics and schooling context.

Mehan (1992) considers the role of individual action as mediated through culture and concludes that social actors are not just passive participants directed by structural forces beyond their control. His perspective lends some credence to the idea that the high value that Asian cultures place on education might prompt some Asian immigrant students to modify structural conditions in order to achieve success. However, the Asian immigrant population is not homogeneous, which leads me to conclude that the "model minority" thesis is grossly overgeneralized. Therefore, to ascertain how educational outcomes are produced, we must look not only at the impact of culture but also at various alternative explanations for student success and failure, such as the nature of teachers and schools themselves.

Among those advocating such a contextualized analysis are Sue and Okazaki (1990), who criticize the cultural explanation as failing to take account of an immigrant group's specific experiences as possible factors influencing not only the acquisition of English but also progress in learning academic subject matter. Wong (1987: 206) concurs and offers the following factors, based on Schumann's acculturation model of second-language acquisition: (1) experience of immigration (struggle for survival); (2) Asian ethnicity (racial relations); (3) linguistic and cultural baggage (home-country ways); (4) the adoption of unproductive responses when acquiring English; and (5) distinct language needs (unique linguistic differences). Here she delineates some relevant factors frequently ignored by educators and juxtaposes them with other factors that affect East Asian students (especially Chinese immigrant students), including (1) financial considerations; (2) unrealistic pressures in schoolwork; (3) physically confined residential areas; (4) disjuncture between home and school—culture and language shock; (5) negative views of Asians—accent, textbook images, lack of attention paid to students who are quiet; (6) de-emphasis on language skills while emphasizing quantitative skills; and (7) differences between foreign and immigrant students in age and learning histories (Wong 1988: 210 ff). What we find in her analysis is an attempt to specify the historical as well as the cultural conditions that shape the context within which Asian immigrant students learn.

If Wong's analysis is correct, how is it relevant to our understanding of the academic progress of these students? And how can teachers and schools address these matters within their domain—for example, in lesson plans, intergroup relations on the school grounds, etc.? Wong's interpretation, with its focus on details in the learning environment, challenges those social scientists who argue from a generalizing perspective. In the face of these contrasting views, can we come to some practical conclusion? As suggested above, we should think about what weights to assign to the various factors that influence academic outcomes. We might ask ourselves what weight to assign to ethnicity versus social class resources, for example, and to what extent we should defend the use of primary-language programs as a means to prop up the self-concept of language-minority students and hence their motivation to progress academically. In short, we should look at the schooling context to identify contextual features that affect schooling successes and failures. The study of students from the so-called model minority who are at risk of school failure is a strategic approach to these concepts.

The Underside of the Model-Minority Success Story

Using Wong's observations as a starting point, let us review some evidence from San Diego, California, that corroborates the influence of factors she identified for assessing the education of Asian immigrant students.[2] Despite the fact that Asian immigrant students are frequently held up as a model minority that does well in school, among these youths there are significant pockets of students who are at risk of school failure. Though many Asian refugees are high academic achievers, many fail to finish school and never attain English language fluency. In San Diego city schools, Cambodian students drop out of school at about the same high rate as Latinos. The dropout rate for Cambodian students in grades 10 through 12 was 13.6 percent, and for Latinos, 14.1 percent; in contrast, the rate for Asians was 6.2 percent (Rumbaut and Ima 1988: 53). At the secondary level, two-thirds of Southeast Asian students are limited-English-proficient (LEP), which means that they are excluded from mainstream classes. Their families tend to be poor: approximately 65 percent of San Diego's Southeast Asian immigrant families live at or below the poverty line, and 24 percent receive some form of public assistance. On average, refugee parents have seven years of formal schooling, far less than the average of twelve years or more found among U.S.-born adults.

While it is true that a higher proportion of Southeast Asian students remain in secondary school and graduate than youths from other communities of color, what happens after high school is another story. Far more Southeast Asians enter postsecondary schooling than African Americans

---

[2]Much of what follows is extracted from Ima 1991a, 1991b.

and Latinos, but Southeast Asians as a group are more likely to be neither employed nor in school three years after graduation from high school. The situation of Southeast Asian graduates is similar to the bimodal pattern we find elsewhere among Asians—many make it, but many do not.

Alongside these statistics we find an upsurge in Asian gang activity in San Diego. Over the past five years, the number of Asian refugee youths with delinquency records has increased approximately 500 percent, and refugee gang membership increased fivefold between 1988 and 1992. During the past two years, Southeast Asian gang-related activities in San Diego resulted in 625 arrests and fifteen known deaths. Among all ethnic groups, Southeast Asians have the highest rate of gang-related homicide. The San Diego Police Department conservatively estimates that there are five Southeast Asian gangs in the city, with a membership of approximately nine hundred youths. These numbers reflect the fact that an increasing proportion of Asian newcomer youths get into trouble with the law, and also that schools have generally failed to retain them in classes.

Because immigrant and refugee children tend to adapt more easily than do their parents to the new language and culture of the host country, a generation gap is opening in newcomer families. Many parents undergo role reversals when they are forced to depend on their children to act as interpreters in communication with outsiders. Many Asian parents, overcome with a sense of helplessness, have given up parenting their children. In conjunction, immigrant and refugee children are increasingly alienated from their parents. Some are embarrassed by their parents' lack of English proficiency and are losing their respect for adult authority.

Exacerbating the situation are educators' misperceptions about newcomer families. Asian students now make up approximately 19 percent of enrollment in San Diego city schools, twice the level ten years ago. Approximately two-thirds of the Asian student population are foreign born. This rate of increase has given the schools little breathing space in which to develop adequate responses to newcomers. There is an overall reluctance to address these students' needs—to implement bilingual programs, hire bilingual personnel, upgrade ESL (English as a Second Language) teachers, support the acquisition and development of primary-language materials, monitor and assess the progress of Asian language-minority students, and address problems that are unique to Asian newcomer students. This reluctance stems from the fact that such measures would require a fundamental reorganization of schools, including retraining and recruitment of new personnel (Ima 1991b).[3]

---

[3]Despite the 19 percent Asian and Pacific Islander student enrollment in San Diego city schools, less than 5 percent of teachers have the same background and even fewer administrators come from these communities.

The schooling context for many of San Diego's Southeast Asian refugee youths is far removed from the conference session mentioned earlier, which sought to explain why Asian students do so well in school. The evidence not only casts doubt on the appropriateness of the conference topic, but it also documents conditions that produce poor educational outcomes for at-risk Asian immigrants, despite the contention of many teachers that Asian students will do well regardless of the quality of the school or the teacher. In the following sections I present two case studies of Asian newcomer students and the schools they attend, outlining not only the problems the students have experienced in schools but also the contextual factors that may have influenced their response to schooling.

Case 1: Washington High School

Washington High School was initially designed as a specialty school for U.S.-born, monolingual English speakers, providing a continuation program to students who, for one reason or another, could not complete their studies in a regular comprehensive high school. Washington teachers were prepared to educate students referred from other high schools because of delinquency, pregnancy, etc.

Washington now has a small but growing number of newcomer students. Refugee students rarely begin their schooling at Washington and generally have been in San Diego public schools prior to entering Washington. The student body represents the main ethnic groups, although Latinos and African Americans are overrepresented (at 30 percent each), and whites, Filipinos, and Southeast Asians are underrepresented (30, 4, and 4 percent, respectively). Washington's teachers admit that they have little or no familiarity with the home languages of Asian students. Although Washington has four Spanish-speaking aides and several Spanish-English bilingual teachers, the school does not have a single staff member who speaks a language spoken by other newcomer students and their parents.

Washington's philosophy is that all students deserve an education and that it is better to keep students in school than to allow them to drop out. This philosophy differs from comprehensive, academically oriented high schools, which teach content matter rather than survival skills. At Washington the emphasis is on process and individual personal development.

Many students are transferred to Washington because of attendance problems at their home schools. Some come because of the nursery program, where students can leave their children while they themselves attend classes. Some students are transferred from their home schools because of their membership in gangs. Regardless of why they are at

Washington, most of the students share two characteristics: they have attendance problems, and they lack high school credits. Newcomer students attend Washington for the same reasons as old-timer students; most have had attendance problems in their previous school or lack credits commensurate with their grade level.

From the Teachers' Perspective

Washington's teachers report that their particular strength is personalized instruction. There are about 32 teachers for 450 on-site students and 400 once-a-week students: a 1:20 teacher/student ratio and usually fewer than 20 students per class. Thus, despite little capacity to deal with any languages other than English and Spanish, the teachers feel that the high level of individual contact that they provide counterbalances their lack of skill in addressing second-language acquisition and literacy. These teachers view themselves as especially well equipped to deal with students who are rejected by comprehensive secondary schools because of delinquency, drug abuse, pregnancy, suspension, truancy, and an inability to maintain grade level—in effect, students who do not fit regular schools.

Although there were only twenty-six Southeast Asians at Washington in 1993, teachers expressed concern about their own lack of knowledge about these students' home culture. In a sense, their lack of resources and preparation for dealing with limited-English-proficient students is forcing Washington teachers to implement a bilingual policy of submersion (using English as the only language for instruction, with little attention to the students' primary languages or to how second languages are acquired). This pattern of "backing into" a submersion policy is commonplace at schools with very small populations of any one non-English-speaking language group.

Given their lack of training in language acquisition, particularly second-language acquisition, teachers make mistakes in assessing the language skills of newcomer students. One teacher may focus on the students' ability to speak idiomatic English; another may look only at reading skills. For example, one teacher at Washington High was struck by the newcomer students' oral language facility, from which he inferred (incorrectly) that the students were also skilled in reading and writing. On the other hand, some teachers assume that a student with poor oral English language performance will have poor reading and writing skills. Although students tend to be more proficient in speaking than in reading or writing, either way there is general inability among teachers to assess the newcomers' language competence and needs.

Washington's teachers generally view Southeast Asian students as more responsive to teacher authority, an observation made at other schools as well. However, because the prevailing style of instruction emphasizes helping students make their own choices, when working with Southeast Asian students, teachers must put this philosophy aside and adopt a more directive instructional style. Asking students about options, about their reasons for choosing particular options, and about the consequences of their choices does not work well with Southeast Asian students, who prefer explicit and detailed directions.

Thus the culture gap between Washington's teachers and newcomer students often extends beyond language differences to touch the heart of the philosophy of teaching. In the tradition of the alternative school ideology, Washington's teachers believe that their role is to help students learn how to make decisions, not to fill them with information. These teachers impart the information necessary to meet district requirements, but they are clearly more interested in the affective aspects of learning, with a focus on personal development. Newcomer students have yet to be acculturated to the American tradition of individuality which underlies this educational philosophy, and they therefore find themselves at a cultural distance from teachers. Some newcomer students are just now beginning to speak the new vocabulary of personal development.

Moreover, individualized instruction is based on a contract system, which is based, in turn, on reading competence. Many newcomer students do not have enough background information to handle these contracts. At some schools, incoming students are placed in "newcomer" programs that explain concepts most teachers would consider common sense but which are often beyond newcomer students' understanding.

The difficulties that some Washington students exhibit in school often are rooted in part in problems in the home. School counselors note that many students do not have functional families. In an illustrative case, a Vietnamese student who was failing to attend school had been arrested for burglary. He lives with four older brothers; both parents are still in Vietnam. Like many unaccompanied Vietnamese youths, this student is particularly vulnerable to school and social adjustment problems (see Nidorf 1985). He does not care about school; he attends school occasionally, and then only to ensure that he will continue to receive child support payments.

Though cases such as this are well known to social workers, school counselors are as yet largely unaware of the dynamics of maladjustment often found among unaccompanied Vietnamese minors. Because Washington's faculty prides itself on its ability to deal with individuals, counselors here are much less defensive about their lack of knowledge than are teachers from traditional comprehensive high schools.

Washington is clearly an exceptional school. Its dedicated corps of teachers emphasizes individualized attention and emotional development to help students whose previous schools did not address their needs. Nevertheless, at-risk students often fail to fully engage at Washington. Washington is not yet equipped to deal with language-minority students (other than Spanish speakers). It lacks bilingual staff members and materials and in-service training for monolingual English teachers in the cultures of newcomer students. Although many newcomer students enter Washington with a positive attitude, they are discouraged by the mismatch between their needs and the school's teachers and curriculum. This often results in truancy, even delinquency, as students forgo their commitment to education in order to concentrate on material goals or personal problems. Some teachers suggest that newcomer students are no different from the rest of Washington students, but this view ignores the language and cultural gaps that newcomer students continue to experience.

Talking with Students at Washington High

Many Vietnamese students in San Diego schools confirm research findings that document the academic success of Southeast Asian students (Caplan, Choy, and Whitmore 1992). Yet there are in these same schools Vietnamese and other newcomer students who are at risk of school failure (Rumbaut and Ima 1988). The following pages give voice to the failing Southeast Asian students at Washington High.

During the course of my research, I talked with five Vietnamese and two Lao students about their school experiences at Washington. Though these youths have not been identified as gang members, their troubles with the law and their poor school performance are illustrative of the experiences of many newcomer youths who join gangs.

All seven students would have dropped out of school were it not for Washington's continuation program. All were about seventeen years old, and all had had negative school experiences. Some were at risk of dropping out of school because of a combination of family/personal problems and problems in school. All began withdrawing from school by being tardy and truant, and they often spent their days with other Southeast Asian students who were skipping school or had already dropped out. Two of the students I interviewed had been suspended for fighting. Some had criminal records, including arrest for car theft. In appearance they did not differ from other Vietnamese and Lao youths: they wore conventional clothing and had short hair. None had identifiable gang markings.

They spoke about their problems, including truancy, suspension, dislike of teachers, dislike of classes, conflict with other students, and bad peer influences. In their rare positive statements about school, they mentioned girls or said that going to school was better than staying at home. Only one mentioned the importance of education for a career. To gain an insight into their views of school, I asked what changes they would like to see made at Washington. These are their responses: "nothing," "pick my own teacher," "easier work," "no one tell me what to do," "I shouldn't be in same school as gang bangers," "good-looking teacher," "get rid of the school fence, it looks like a jail," "teacher babbles too much," and "more comfortable chairs."[4]

These students do see some of the benefits that Washington offers: "Here they don't boss you around," and "you can smoke." However, one complained, "Not many female teachers here." Another commented about the dynamic vice principal: "That vice principal does too much control." Though they do appreciate some aspects of Washington High, they have little reason to like school generally and their images of students as prison inmates seem appropriate.

Some of these students had had early success in school, receiving high grades in elementary school and in their early middle-school period. Their troubles with schooling began at about the age of fourteen. They attribute their academic downturn and anti-school attitudes to outside sources, such as "boring teachers," rather than accepting that they may be at least partially responsible for their difficulties.

In contrast, achieving Vietnamese students, such as two outstanding students in another San Diego school, approach schooling proactively; instead of withdrawing, they seek alternative solutions that can advance them toward college. They do not comment on whether a class is boring or a teacher too controlling. They want, they demand, the courses and grades that will enable them to enroll in a prestigious college. They will accept boredom and hard work as part of the cost of "making it."

On the other hand, the Washington students I interviewed not only expressed little tolerance of school, but they had difficulty visualizing a future. When asked what they wished for their future, they responded: "having a nice car," "living a good life," "having money," "winning a million dollars," and "having a nice house and a beautiful wife." All talked about money and material goods, but only two of the seven mentioned needing to earn money in order to obtain these possessions. Instead, most focused on winning the lottery or finding a windfall, all measures of chance rather than effort.

Most surprising was the fact that not one of the seven students envisioned a future that included parents or family members. (This contrasts with successful refugee students, who always mention family as a part of their futures. A typical statement from a successful refugee student would be, "I want my parents to be proud of me.") The at-risk refugee students at Washington have accepted only that portion of the American Dream that involves the accumulation of material possessions. They do not see how their future is related to schooling and work. They are disconnected from the wider community and can only find

---

[4]These comments are noteworthy for the absence of observations commonly offered by high-achieving Southeast Asian students, such as appreciating schooling opportunities, having someone who can speak their language, or having a teacher who cares.

companionship with other youths who share their situation. Simply put, they have little trust in conventional cultural patterns and have turned to a youth subculture that promises short-term gratification.

The fact that Asian newcomer students are usually enthusiastic about living in the United States and about the prospects for a better future in the host country raises a number of questions when counterposed with the experiences of students such as those described above. Why do these youths lose hope? How profound is their loss? Is it temporary, or does it suggest serious, long-term adjustment consequences?

Case 2: McKinley High School

The central theme at McKinley is "keeping order." This preoccupation with keeping students under control is recorded in my research notes:

> I arrived [at McKinley] approximately fifteen minutes before the end of the school day. There were security officers in front and police officers on the street. The vice principal walked toward me with a two-way radio. I also noticed other adults carrying two-way radios. Additionally, while attempting to talk with a student on the other side of a fence, I realized I couldn't enter the school grounds without going through the office. This is indeed a security-conscious campus.

During another visit at lunch hour, I was struck by the fact that school supervisors used bullhorns to address students involved in disorderly conduct. Overwhelmed by the need to keep order among the students, the staff has fallen into a near-prison mentality.

McKinley is located in a neighborhood dominated by multifamily rental units whose low rents make the area a point of first residency for many immigrants and refugees arriving to San Diego, especially Ethiopians, Vietnamese, and Middle Easterners. With 2,000 students, the school has significantly exceeded its maximum capacity of 1,500, and classes are forced to share space. Latinos account for about 40 percent of McKinley's student body. Asian students make up approximately 24 percent; most are them are Vietnamese, with smaller numbers of Cambodians and Laotians (Hmong and Lao). Both newcomers and long-settled resident students (U.S.-born whites, African Americans, and Latinos) at McKinley tend to come from low-income families. The neighborhood has a high rate of residential mobility, and this is reflected in the turnover rates in the local schools. High residential mobility keeps the neighborhood from becoming identified with a single ethnic community. The fact that the neighborhood is "up for grabs" generates conflict between the different ethnic groups whose members attend McKinley. In trying to keep these conflicts out of the school, teachers find that their need to keep order edges out other educational considerations.

From the Teachers' Perspective

To deal with this priority concern of maintaining a semblance of order in the classroom, one McKinley teacher has adopted a severe approach, reprimanding students who get out of line and reminding the class that he is "boss." He defended his approach as follows:

> At this school, with diversity and constant conflict between kids, you've got to be especially aggressive to defuse negative energies. . . . Many teachers are hesitant to respond to bad behaviors and they confuse behavior, culture, and race. They don't want to be seen as racist and therefore ignore misbehaviors which should be directly addressed. However, in this troubled area, with racial and cultural diversity, you have to establish common grounds which are acceptable to all students. I must establish classroom order; to do otherwise is to accept disorder and classroom conflict. Without order, how can you teach?

Another teacher, recently hired, also noted that much of the conflict in the school reflected the overflow of conflict from the surrounding community into the school:

> This community is in crisis. Both parents and kids are hurting—physically, economically, and emotionally. Many of my students do not have breakfast. I find many of my students absent because of illness. This affects me as a teacher because I then must deal with crowd control and conflict resolution. In class, students are constantly on top of each other, which means I spend less time teaching than controlling.

This teacher has not yet learned the techniques of keeping order, and her students suffer because of time lost from teaching and individualized attention.

On one of my research visits to McKinley a male student asked me for a sip of my soda. That a student would make such a request of an adult surprised me, and I gave some consideration to what this incident might indicate about the school environment. The short supply of money in a lower-class community often provokes confrontation between individuals competing for limited resources, producing prey-predator relationships in which people continually jostle for positions of dominance. The student's request for a sip of soda may well have been part of the ritual of establishing dominance. If he could get me to accede, he could dominate. Images of this encounter stayed with me as I saw students vie with one another for positions in line.

Contending for positions of dominance continues in the classroom. McKinley's principal recently dismissed a Vietnamese teacher who was unwilling to teach U.S.-born youths. This individual feared that he would not be able to keep classroom order among non-Vietnamese students (especially African Americans and Latinos) who, unlike Vietnamese students, are disrespectful to teachers and challenge their authority.[5]

When the struggle for dominance occurs between groups of students at McKinley, Vietnamese students, who tend to be smaller, are more likely to be victimized. In cases where such conflict erupts between Vietnamese students and other groups, Vietnamese students feel they are punished more severely than students of other ethnicities— often with suspension—even when they are not the instigators of the conflict. Southeast Asian students are under the impression that the criteria for suspension are less strictly applied to African Americans than to other groups. Even though staff members deny this, the claim may have some basis; while teachers try to be evenhanded, they are also under pressure to reduce the number of suspensions of African Americans, the group with the highest suspension rate of all groups at McKinley. Ironically, each group views the others as aggressors, and each group feels that teachers favor the other groups: in addition to the Asian students' viewpoint, outlined above, African American students complain that teachers favor the Asian students, and Latino students often portray themselves as the victims of other groups. The theme of racial bias recurs with regularity among all the groups at McKinley.

In response to the interethnic conflicts at the school, McKinley has begun holding advisory lessons and assemblies on how to prevent assaults, and it has increased efforts to contact parents about the problem. Another school initiative to diffuse interethnic conflicts and rivalries has been to celebrate the school's ethnic diversity by highlighting cultural events such as Chinese New Year. McKinley's principal feels that these efforts have paid off. The campus is cleaner and safer, and, he claims, there are no hard-core gang members at the school (troublemakers having been transferred elsewhere). However, although the

---

[5]This fear is common among foreign-born teachers, especially those from Asian countries, and it is not infrequently found among U.S.-born teachers as well.

faculty is able to control conflicts on the school grounds, it cannot be responsible for what happens beyond the school's boundaries. McKinley's principal feels strongly that the police department and other agencies are responsible once students leave the school.

The most recent actions to address the violence at McKinley seem to have produced very positive results in further reducing overtly disruptive behaviors. The school hired a consultant to help teachers develop classroom management techniques, now keeps students in class for two consecutive hours rather than having them move between classes every hour, reduced their staff by over 30 percent to drop the teachers with management problems, and moved to a year-round schedule which gives students more frequent relief from the school routine. The faculty notes that these changes have produced a significant turnaround at the school. There are fewer suspensions. Attendance is up. Classes spend more time on learning. And student conflict has decreased.

Listening to Cambodian Students at McKinley High

Six at-risk Khmer (Cambodian) students at McKinley have been meeting as a group with the school's counselor, who hoped to avert these students' withdrawal from school. In fact, one of these six young men has already dropped out of school, and the counselor fears that four more will quit, leaving the prospect of only one of the six graduating from high school. Such numbers would accord with district figures on Cambodian students, whose dropout rate is the third highest among ethnic groups, exceeded only by Latinos and Pacific Islanders.[6]

Five of the Cambodian students who participated in the group sessions with the school counselor have been associated with a local Cambodian gang, and the sixth was a member of a rival gang. All have had trouble with school and have been suspended for fighting, truancy, and failure to do homework. Nevertheless, they rarely create problems in class; they prefer to remain silent rather than be ridiculed for their lack of English language fluency. Although they can articulate the reasons why education is important, they do not really believe that schooling will make a difference in their lives. One of the students mentioned that he would like to be an engineer, but he had no idea what it took to become one. When he learned that it involved doing well in math and graduating from high school, he changed his mind and said it was an unlikely

---

[6]This high dropout rate contributes to a perception among teachers that Cambodian students are "losers." Though there are instances of personalized attention to Cambodian students, they are rare. When Cambodian students are identified as gang members, the administration's response is generally to transfer them to another school or have the police watch them more closely. When the San Diego Police Department recently began monitoring Cambodian student gang members and jailing key leaders, the number of killings and other violent incidences dropped from the preceding year.

career anyway. According to the counselor, experiences such as this contribute to the fact that these students view themselves as "worthless."

The McKinley counselor encourages these youths to imagine their future and how education could make a difference. She has asked them to imagine a peace solution in Cambodia, suggesting that with college degrees these students could play a role in the reconstruction of their home country. The students immediately rejected the possibility because "the Khmer Rouge will come back anyway." They see any hope of returning to Cambodia as a futile dream and devote their attention instead to day-to-day survival.

The McKinley counselor, who herself survived the Pol Pot period (one of history's most tragic events, certainly among the most tragic genocides since the Holocaust and a period that continues to haunt Cambodian refugee students and their families) and speaks the students' home language, has been able to establish an exceptional rapport with the students; they are surprisingly open with her about their feelings. For example, one student talked freely about his home situation. His mother, abandoned by her husband, now neglects her children, leaving them alone and without food. This student, the oldest of four children, feels responsibility for both his mother and his siblings, yet he feels the responsibility is more than he can handle. By rejecting school and associating with gang members, he gains a sense of control and efficacy he cannot find elsewhere. This same feeling of needing to regain control frequently comes into play among Cambodian students, particularly those who are gang members.

The Cambodian students' interactions with other students tend to be fractious, and this sometimes colors attitudes not only among students but also within the faculty and staff. For example, in an incident at another San Diego high school, non-Asian students (blacks, Latinos, and whites) attacked Asian students; several hundred youths eventually joined in and at least a dozen were injured. A Cambodian aide at the school noted that students and teachers became less friendly toward her after the incident:

> The teachers got prejudiced. . . . Before the incident they were appreciative, but afterwards they ignored me. They made comments like "You're in this country and you should be learning the rules," implying that Cambodians don't know how to be civil. . . . They put down Asians for fighting, even though it was the other kids who started the incident.

This aide noted that the youths who were suspended were mainly Asian students, especially Cambodians, and that the non-Asian students involved were not suspended. The incident reinforced the belief among

Cambodian students that their safety lies in banding together in gangs, and, in fact, many Cambodian male students dropped out of school as a result of this incident.

The negative experiences that the Cambodian students brought away from the race riot at the school tend to reinforce what they hear from their parents, many of them survivors of the Pol Pot period: that their world is dead and there is no future except in association with other Cambodians. Although the McKinley counselor advises the students to talk about their past experiences as refugees in an attempt to put the Pol Pot period behind them, the students refuse. This is particularly surprising given their degree of openness in talking about other issues which also influence their current situation. This may tie back into the students' desire to avoid the appearance of being weak. They and their families were victims under Pol Pot, and recollecting this period also brings back memories of powerlessness. However, if they unite in gangs (so goes these youths' mythology), they can project an image of strength which contrasts with their feeble hopes for educational and occupational success.

Conclusions

The paramount trait shared by our two case study schools is their inability to provide equitable schooling for newcomers, despite their different educational settings and approaches. Washington High School—unable to identify any other alternative for dealing with its influx of refugee students, constrained by lean budgets, unfamiliar with teaching strategies designed for use with language-minority students, and locked into a teaching strategy that does not mesh with the cultures and needs of students who arrive at Washington already alienated from the education system and even their own futures—has "backed into" an English submersion strategy. McKinley has sought to respond to its refugee students by turning the student body's cultural diversity into an advantage and viewing the recognition of that diversity as essential to the students' survival, even though this strategy must be embedded within the overriding concern at McKinley—keeping order.

What is clear is that these efforts, however well designed and well intentioned, are failing to meet the needs of a significant group of students—at-risk Asian youths who had heretofore remained relatively invisible behind their more successful Asian classmates. These at-risk students generally perform well during their early educational years but then begin to reject their educational goals during adolescence, as they move into secondary school. This change in orientation may respond to problems at home, as well as to the long-term trauma associated with their histories as refugees. This is especially true of Cambodian youths (see Smith-Hefner 1990). This description accords with Weisner, Gallimore, and Jordan's (1988) argument about "unpackaging cultural effects," which asserts the need to contextualize the analysis of minority achievement and failure in assessing the impact of global factors such as culture or social class by examining teachers, student motivations, school tasks, and the goals/beliefs of school participants.

What do our case studies tell us about schools and their surrounding communities? The students have identified a number of shortcomings in their schools: inadequate materials and teachers, teachers' negative stereotyping of students, and unsafe school environments. As students disengage from school, many also begin to get in trouble with the law. This trajectory is probably explained by a complex series of factors: violence that groups of youths direct against one another, weak home environments or support systems, home-country trauma, and poor schooling experiences, all compounded by the usual problems of adolescence and those that are specific to adjustment to a new country. The fact that schools do not respond adequately to newcomer students' needs leads newcomer students to lose their initial positive attitude toward the school.

What relevance do these students' observations have for teachers and educators? We know there are gaps between teachers and students in language, culture, life experiences, and socioeconomic conditions, and teachers must scramble to deal with the overwhelming newcomer diversity. The result is lower-quality education. All too often, teachers have a deficit model of their students, and they lower their standards for teaching and performance in ESL and bilingual classes. This is compounded by ineffective educational practices and a multiplicity of language groups. This delivery-of-service problem, especially in urban schools with large proportions of low achievers, makes teaching very difficult.

The at-risk Southeast Asian refugee students considered in this chapter certainly belie the stereotype of the ever-successful Asian student. The Asian student population is far from homogeneous. In their efforts to respond to these students' needs, schools must look more closely at the lives of their individual students and be prepared to sort out the complexity that they will find there. What is gained will have application to all newcomers—Southeast Asians, Mexicans, Somalis, and so on. We can help these students realize the American Dream; to rest our analysis on overly global explanations or stereotypes is to abandon them.

References

Ambert, Alba M. 1991. "The Education of Language Minorities: An Overview of Findings and a Research Agenda." In *Bilingual Education and English as a Second*

Language: A Research Handbook 1988–1990, edited by A.M. Albert. New York: Garland.

Caplan, Nathan, Marcella H. Choy, and John K. Whitmore. 1992. "Indochinese Refugee Families and Academic Achievement," *Scientific American,* February, pp. 36–42.

Gibson, Margaret. 1991. "Minorities and Schooling: Some Implications." In *Minority Status and Schooling: A Comparative Study of Immigrant and Involuntary Minorities,* edited by M. Gibson and John U. Ogbu. New York: Garland.

Ima, Kenji. 1991a. *A Handbook for Professionals Working with Southeast Asian Delinquent and At-Risk Youth.* San Diego, Calif.: SAY San Diego, Inc.

————. 1991b. *What Do We Know about Asian and Pacific Islander Language Minority Students? A Report to the California Department of Education's Bilingual Education Office.* Sacramento, Calif.: California Department of Education.

Mehan, Hugh. 1992. "Understanding Inequality in Schools: The Contribution of Interpretive Studies," *Sociology of Education* 65:1–20.

Nidorf, Jeanne. 1985. "Mental Health and Refugee Youths: A Model for Diagnostic Training." In *Southeast Asian Mental Health: Treatment, Prevention, Services, Training, and Research,* edited by Tom Owan et al. Washington, D.C.: U.S. Department of Health and Human Services.

Ogbu, John. 1993. "Variability in Minority School Performance: A Problem in Search of an Explanation." In *Minority Education: Anthropological Perspectives,* edited by Evelyn Jacob and Cathie Jordan. Norwood, N.J.: Ablex.

Rumbaut, Rubén G., and Kenji Ima. 1988. *The Adaptation of Southeast Asian Refugee Youth: A Comparative Study.* Washington, D.C.: Office of Refugee Settlement.

Smith-Hefner, Nancy J. 1990. "Language and Identity in the Education of Boston-area Khmer," *Anthropology and Education Quarterly* 21:250–68.

Sue, S., and S. Okazaki. 1990. "Asian-American Education Achievements: A Phenomenon in Search of an Explanation," *American Psychologist* 45:913–20.

Weisner, Thomas S., Ronald Gallimore, and Cathie Jordan. 1988. "Unpackaging Cultural Effects on Classroom Learning: Native Hawaiian Peer Assistance and Child-Generated Activity," *Anthropology and Education Quarterly* 19:325–53.

Wong, S.C. 1987. "The Language Learning Situation of Asian Immigrant Students in the U.S.: A Socio- and Psycholinguistic Perspective," *NABE Journal* 11:203–34.

————. 1988. "The Language Situation of Chinese Americans." In *Language Diversity: Problem or Resource?* edited by S. McKay and S.C. Wong. Cambridge and New York: Newbury House.

9

School Restructuring and the Needs of Immigrant Students

Laurie Olsen

Introduction

This chapter presents findings from research conducted throughout 1992 to determine whether school restructuring is responsive to the needs of immigrant students. The research was designed to answer two questions: (1) What is the outcome when a school restructures to better meet the needs of its culturally, racially, and linguistically diverse student population? (2) To what extent is school restructuring focusing attention on cultural, racial, and language diversity, and to what extent is this reform movement producing outcomes that are more equitable than traditional school practice?

The project is rooted in the conviction that schools must be fundamentally restructured if they are to correct inequities in school experiences and outcomes among children of different cultural, linguistic, and racial backgrounds and ensure that all children have access to quality public education. This project framed the problem not only as one of immigration but also of race, culture, and language.[1] Immigrants to the

The research on which this chapter is based was conducted by California Tomorrow's "Education for a Diverse Society/School Restructuring" project team. In addition to myself as the project director, the research team included Hedy Chang, Cecelia Leong, Gregory McClain, Zaida McCall Pérez, Catherine Minicucci, Lisa Raffel, and Denise De la Rosa Salazar. Funding for this research was provided by the Pew Charitable Trusts, Charles Stewart Mott Foundation, San Francisco Foundation, ARCO, and the Mellon Foundation.

[1] "Race" has no biological basis as a category. The term is used here not to legitimate the concept of race, but instead as reference to the social reality in our society. We are assigned to one or another "race" based on skin color and are thereby accorded differential access, experiences, and resources. Thus, "racial experience" has meaning, while "race" does not.

United States do not enter a pluralistic society of different but equal cultural and ethnic groups. Instead, they enter a culturally and ethnically diverse society shaped by historical relationships of inequality and stratified by race, language group, and culture. Immigrant children attend schools that are structured to provide differential access and experiences to the foreign born.

Research over the past decade has produced disturbing documentation of the structural inequalities that affect racial and ethnic "minorities" and cultural and linguistic "minorities" in the public schools. Research findings portray an educational system that provides differential access to groups on the basis of language, national origin, culture, and race. Grouping practices track students by race and language (in fact, if not by intent). This produces a situation in which "lower-tracked" students (disproportionately African Americans, Filipinos, Southeast Asians, and Hispanics) receive a curriculum that has been watered down by teachers' low expectations; teacher inexperience; inequitable financing formulas which assign immigrant children in urban areas to overcrowded, underfinanced, and ill-equipped schools; barriers to a close and appropriate relationship between the school and parents of children of minority cultures and experiences; inflexible, lockstep age-grade relationships and expectations that cannot accommodate immigrant children coming from foreign school systems or with interrupted schooling; a shortage of teachers with the language skills and cultural knowledge needed to teach children from cultures other than the dominant culture; and exclusionary disciplinary policies and practices which produce disproportionately high expulsion and suspension rates for children of racial minority communities.

While these patterns of structural inequity persist from kindergarten through twelfth grade, they are compounded at the secondary level by increasingly fragmented and rigid institutional structures which mediate against meeting the needs of immigrant students. Policy concerns in bilingual education have focused historically on the elementary level. The emphasis was understandable. There were more limited-English-proficient (LEP) students at the elementary level than at the secondary level, and most of the early research on second-language learning also focused on the elementary school years.[2]

By 1990, however, almost one-third of California schoolchildren identified as limited-English-proficient were enrolled in grades 7 through 12. Lacking information about what services were available to students at the secondary level, the California state legislature requested an evaluation of

---

[2]"Limited-English-proficient," or LEP, is a category formally used by schools as a designation of little or no English language fluency, which carries with it the right to special educational services designed to "overcome the language barrier." It thus has both a legal and an educational meaning. Despite my objection to labeling children in terms of deficiencies, I use the term LEP when it is necessary for clarity with regard to designation for educational services.

services for LEP students in California schools. Minicucci and Olsen conducted an exploratory investigation into secondary LEP programs in the state (Olsen and Minicucci 1992) which found that LEP students in secondary schools generally lacked access to core required-content classes. At precisely the point when adolescent LEP students faced the combined academic challenges of learning English, learning content areas, and overcoming academic gaps due to absences or lack of prior schooling, they were given short schedules because schools could not provide the courses they needed. This lack of access to core courses derives largely from a shortage of trained and willing teachers and fragmented, departmentalized decision making.

The study found that LEP students are increasingly isolated from mainstream students, due primarily to the grouping of LEP students in sheltered-content classes. And it found disturbing indications that the sheltered approach most often places LEP students in classes with the least experienced, least trained teachers, and with few appropriate materials and little primary-language support or instruction.

Further, Minicucci and Olsen found a mismatch between the traditional structure of secondary schools and the needs of immigrant students. The school structure lacks the flexibility to allow immigrant students to accumulate credits toward graduation and fails to provide a coherent educational approach. The researchers found, in short, no comprehensive policy on the education of immigrant students in secondary schools and little policy or research attention to the pressing challenges facing secondary schools. This work corroborated previous research findings on immigrant student programs in secondary schools (Olsen 1988; Lucas, Henze, and Donato 1990) which together make clear that there are *structural* pressure/tension points in serving immigrant students in secondary schools and that there is a profound mismatch between traditional secondary school structures and the needs of certain students. The structural mismatches at the secondary level derive from departmentalization, which inhibits a comprehensive strategy for educating immigrant students; a standard four-year high school model which presupposes levels of skill development and academic knowledge that are not applicable to students immigrating from other nations; inflexible systems of earning credits which lock in a specified age-grade norm; a lack of support services; and inflexible school schedules to which immigrant students with significant out-of-school responsibilities cannot adhere.

The Education for a Diverse Society/School Restructuring Project

Given these mismatches between school structures and the needs of immigrant and language-minority students, California Tomorrow became interested in identifying attempts to create new schooling structures that would accommodate the needs of the immigrant population. The policy context for the project was the "restructuring" movement, an approach at the core of educational reform both in California and nationally. At the national level the movement has been driven by a combination of the push for site-based management and national restructuring reform projects such as the Coalition for Essential Schools, Comer, Accelerated Schools, etc. In California, the primary force behind the restructuring movement was Senate Bill 1274, which invited proposals from schools for seed grants to support restructuring efforts (212 schools received funding).

The California Tomorrow project looked at the restructuring movement with a skeptical eye, asking: Is this just another rearrangement of the furniture that will leave structures of inequality intact? Will restructuring, like other reform waves, leave immigrant students largely out of the loop? Or are there serious efforts to create new structures of schooling that offer novel and more appropriate solutions to the challenges of designing schools to serve culturally, linguistically, and ethnically diverse students equitably and well?

Methodology

To answer these questions, we developed a two-pronged research strategy. In-depth telephone interviews were conducted with forty-one randomly selected schools in California—schools engaged in "restructuring" and with diverse student populations. The "restructuring" schools in our study included many which did *not* receive SB 1274 funding. We also conducted thirty-two on-site, in-depth case studies of schools selected through a statewide nomination process and screened through interviews. The schools selected for in-depth study were chosen because they appeared to be engaged in exciting, meaningful restructuring which gave serious attention to issues of diversity. The populations of the selected schools range from 5 percent to 89 percent LEP. The schools include ten high schools, seven middle schools, and fifteen elementary schools. At one end of the range are schools that are wholly Hispanic, and at the other are schools with a rich mixture of major ethnic groups. Only one is a white-majority school.

In order to determine to what extent schools are addressing the needs of culturally and linguistically diverse student populations, we needed to define what aspects of the restructuring process and the school program would tell us the most about how the school is responding to issues of culture, language, and race. This led to the development of a field guide which extrapolated from the literature on effective elementary-level programs for racial and cultural minorities and LEP programs, to the secondary level. Through the literature we identified ten crucial areas to examine in detail in each school, in addition to general information about the history and process of the restructuring effort.[3] The following are the ten areas of specific concern.

- We first asked: Whose school is this? What is the governance and decision-making process like? Whose voices are heard in the re-shaping and running of the school? We understood from the literature (Chan 1987; Cistone, Fernández, and Tornillo 1989; Comer 1984; Cummins 1986; Henderson 1987; Lindquist and Mauriel 1989; Lomotey and Swanson 1989; Malen, Ogawa, and Kranz 1990) that a school addressing issues of diversity and equity would need to create ways to open up the school-shaping process to teachers, parents and students, other staff, and community members. We wanted to see how each school would ensure widespread ownership of and involvement in the program, with particular regard to the bilingual program and the immigrant community.

- Based on the literature, we anticipated finding an emphasis on building strong models of home-school relationships (Chan 1987; Chavkin 1989; Comer 1984; Cummins 1986; Epstein 1984; Greenberg 1989; Haynes, Comer, and Hamilton-Lee 1989; Johnston and Slotnik 1985; Leler 1983; Lueder 1989; Tizard, Schofield, and Hewison 1982). We wanted to see if and how parents, community members, and advocates became involved in major decisions affecting the children's education. And we examined the extent to which schools, particularly secondary schools, have institutional practices and mechanisms that allow students themselves to present their needs. We also wanted to see ways in which schools become active players in the communities where their students live: a softening of the boundaries between school and community, more movement back and forth, and a sense of the school as part of the outside world.

- We expected that a school restructuring with diversity in mind would focus on student grouping and placement systems to ensure that all students learn in integrated, heterogeneous settings responsive to different learning styles, abilities, and needs, and that the program would put supports in place to enable all students to participate fully in the core academic program (Children's Defense Fund 1985; Dawson 1987; Dentzer and Wheelock 1990; Green and Griffore 1978; Johnson and Johnson 1982; Moore and Davenport 1988; Oakes 1985; Slavin 1987; Wheelock 1992).

---

[3]The ten areas of concern discussed in this paper, and which formed the basis for our field guide, derive from the work of the National Coalition of Advocates for Students. California Tomorrow is a member organization of NCAS, and we participated with twenty-two other member groups in the development of ten student entitlements which comprise "The Good Common School: Making the Vision Work for All Children." The work of NCAS was a crucial departure point for California Tomorrow's restructuring project.

- We anticipated that a school restructuring for diversity would develop an academic program that provided all students with a comprehensible, accessible, culturally supportive curriculum and teaching strategy (J.A. Banks 1987; F.F. Banks 1988; Baptiste 1986; Comer 1984; Cummins 1986; First et al. 1983; LaFontaine 1987; Lucas, Henze, and Donato 1990; Olsen 1988; Olsen and Mullen 1990; Phillips 1988; Reyhner and García 1989; Schmidt 1991; Snow and Hakuta 1987; Suzuki 1984). This meant that we were concerned with the strength of the ESL program, the primary-language program, and a multicultural, inclusive curriculum. We also were interested in efforts to develop ethnic, cultural, and/or community-specific curriculum and pedagogy.

- We surmised that a school restructuring with concerns for diverse student populations would utilize a broadly based assessment of student academic progress which would allow maximum flexibility in movement through the system (FairTest 1990; Hoover, Politzer, and Taylor 1987; Loewen 1980; Oakes and Lipton 1990; Taylor and Lee 1987; Williams 1979).

- We wanted to observe how schools were working toward restructuring their relationships with other agencies serving youths and families so that students and their families would have access to a well-coordinated, broad range of linguistically and culturally appropriate services (Chang 1992; Gardner 1989; Melville and Blank 1991; Olsen 1988; Orum 1988; Packard Foundation 1991; Podemski and Childers 1987).

- We were concerned with school safety, school attractiveness, and the facilities' appropriateness to learning (Kaeser 1984; Kozol 1991; Lawton 1991; Wayson 1984).

- We were seeking to determine how schools create a climate that combats prejudice, racism, and separation, and what kinds of affirmative efforts connect students across lines of culture, language, and race (Caldwell 1989; Davis 1986; Derman-Sparks 1989; Grant 1988, 1990; Nieto 1992; Olsen and Mullen 1990; Pine and Hilliard 1990; Pollard 1989; Suzuki 1984).

- We supposed that teachers' jobs and work roles would be restructured to give them an opportunity to participate in a full range of professional development activities that would help them meet the challenges of diverse classrooms (Ashby, Larson, and Munroe 1989; Lambert 1988; Little 1984; Olsen and Mullen 1990; Valencia and Killion 1989).

- Last, we expected that schools concerned about educating all students and aware of institutional and historical patterns of exclusion would put in place data systems to identify which groups of students are benefiting from the educational programs in place and which are not.

And we sought to establish how schools measure and monitor "success" and how they verify their progress in creating schools that work for all students.

Put in general terms, our aims were to document the restructuring process, to understand the development of school visions and mission statements, to observe the dialogue process about schooling goals and reform choices, to note the awareness of diversity issues, to witness the obstacles to program implementation, and to discern what steps schools are taking toward creating new schools that address our ten identified areas. As a backdrop, we also set out to collect hard data on the differential experiences of various groups of students as a counterpoint to what schools perceive as their challenges and priorities.

Research Findings

It is obvious that schools hold vastly different assessments of what it means to restructure and what problem or challenge the restructuring is intended to address. There are schools where the "problem" is perceived as located outside of the school program: something is wrong with the students and/or their families, and this is inhibiting the students' full involvement in school. Such schools hold a deficiency view of families' and children's "cultures" and direct restructuring toward developing collaborative services arrangements with health and mental health agencies and toward facilitating the provision of support services to students within the school. They emphasize parent education and encourage "advisories" as a means to enhance close, sustained adult-student contact. Since they do not view the situation as an educational problem, they do not seek an educational solution.

Other schools see the problem as a matter of safety and discipline: students are unruly; the school cannot provide an adequate atmosphere for learning because of external forces affecting life on campus. These schools focus on strategies such as reorganizing students into smaller groups. They emphasize the development of schoolwide assertive discipline, the creation of a sense of stability and consistency, and mechanisms for shielding the campus from the world beyond.

Still other schools define the problem in educational terms from the start: our kids are not doing very well on tests; we know we aren't reaching all our kids. These schools emphasize the educational program and focus their restructuring on changing curriculum and instructional strategies.

Finally, the remaining schools define the problem as a lack of teacher control/empowerment. What is at the heart of restructuring is not a specific educational direction or student needs issue. Rather, it is giving teachers more control over their work environment and work tasks. These schools welcome all new ideas. Teachers are encouraged to try anything that seems promising. These schools support dozens of projects, although they often become fragmented and there may be little cohesion in the school change effort.

In every school we found hardworking and enthusiastic teachers committed to reshaping their schools. Restructuring schools are full of hope; their staffs believe that restructuring will make a difference. Yet the great majority of schools in our sample are paying little or no heed to issues of culture, language, and race, despite ample evidence (from interviews and from our data collection on outcomes) that inequities in access and in appropriate curriculum were present in all schools. In a rare few elementary schools, and in no secondary school, however, were the LEP program, differential access, or the needs of immigrant students mentioned as central to the impetus to restructure.

The exceptions were elementary schools where, *prior to restructuring*, there had been a strong history of bilingual programs, a large population of immigrant and language-minority students, a faculty trained in working with language-minority children and families, and strong administrative leadership with knowledge of and commitment to the LEP program. In most schools, LEP programs exist because they are required by law, not because of teacher commitment, and these programs fall outside of the reform enthusiasm in restructuring schools.

Why is this so? A fundamental facet of restructuring is broadening the dialogue about the school vision, mission, and program. The quality and content of that dialogue determine what occurs in the school. But the teachers involved in this dialogue have a history with each other that is embedded in the traditional school structure (which has often included distance and hostility between the ESL and mainstream departments). In all of the schools we studied statewide, the great majority of the faculty is white and monolingual English-speaking. In most schools, the great majority have no history with second-language programs or with the cultures or languages of their minority students.

Moreover, issues of race and differential treatment of students from diverse racial and cultural groups are explosive and difficult. Teachers who act as advocates for these communities of ill-served or marginalized children often report getting little or no support when they raise these issues within a professional group that has strong norms mediating against "criticizing" one another's work. Other teachers fear that they will be labeled racist because of their ignorance of other cultures; thus they avoid discussions of race and culture and may be defensive about their intentions and efforts. They either *do not* see or are reluctant to admit that they *do* see differences in terms of treatment and outcomes between groups of students. The result is that faculty are not addressing the differential experiences of students of different races, cultures, and language groups. There is, in short, a failure to address precisely the issues with which our project is concerned. This silence is rooted partly in ignorance and partly in resistance. Privately, teachers would tell us how other teachers who emphasize ethnic pride are turning students against each other. Privately, teachers lament that the Latino students are being treated unfairly by other teachers. Privately, we heard bitterness about the elimination of an ethnic studies class. But these issues are not made public.

As one principal, a woman who already had considerable experience in intergroup relations/race relations prior to taking a principalship in a restructuring school, told us:

> Issues of race and gender equity are still so volatile in our society. I like to think we've come a long way since the 1960s and early integration, but there is still so far to go. I came to this school wanting to take my theoretical orientation about race relations and put it into practice, but I've had to find a way to do it that didn't bombard and frighten teachers. I can't take the direct approach. It just brings out defensiveness, and everyone is afraid of being called a racist. So we don't talk about race issues separate from general issues of overall achievement or overall behavior that is expected. I looked for teachers who like kids, who could work in this community. But beyond that, I don't push it. I don't dare. I am hoping that the international perspective in our curriculum is a way to couch diversity issues as positive, and a way in to beginning someday to look at some of our own issues of diversity. But we haven't really gotten there yet. I think it will be a long road. It's just too difficult to bring those issues up.

We found that outside coaches, consultants, or advocacy groups sometimes could facilitate discussion by taking responsibility for putting these issues on the table. In one school, for example, a community group had publicized data on the unequal suspensions of African American students. The vice principal described the effect on her faculty.

> It came to our attention, it was really forced before us actually, that there was a problem with suspension rates. We took a look at that data, and we began working on discipline approaches here. I think everyone was glad to. But that came about partly because we *had* to talk about it. We didn't bring it up, it came from outside . . . and I think that actually made it feel safer. I presented the data to the staff and there it was—

clearly—and so every year we continue to look at suspension rates by ethnic group. But we don't look at
other indicators by race. Just suspension.

The point is that unity is fragile in a newly restructuring school. The
process is not yet really tested, and faculty seem most willing to bring up
and take on issues that do not threaten to divide them or challenge each
other's autonomy. The teachers we interviewed seem anxious to find
areas of consensus. Issues of bilingual education, the use of the primary
language for instruction, and attitudes toward immigrants, culture, and
ethnic experience are *not* areas of easy consensus.

Perhaps in this context we should not have been surprised to find
that LEP issues are not on the table. They are not considered mainstream
issues, they are potentially divisive and explosive, and they would only
come up if someone was deeply committed to them. But who would
bring these issues to the fore? Instructional aides are not included on
restructuring committees and in governance processes, yet they often
are the voices of bilingualism and the major group of adults of color on a
secondary school campus. In many schools, ESL and bilingual program
teachers do not enjoy the same status that mainstream teachers have.
They are often the more recently hired teachers as well. These considerations undermine the school's bilingual staff members' efforts to advance
important issues. Even when an individual teacher who is deeply
involved in restructuring wants to address the school's failure to serve
LEP students, he or she apparently still feels unable to do so because of
lack of support from colleagues.

At one high school, the chair of the ESL Department is also a key
planner and central organizer of the school's restructuring effort. In this
case, restructuring came about district-wide and grew out of a concern
for teacher empowerment. This department chair has done important
research on the ESL students in mainstream classes in her school. In
observing these students, she documented patterns of mainstream
teachers ignoring the lower-level ESL students. She witnessed a lack of
response to students' queries for help and then tracked these students'
records, finding that they were failing these classes. She presented her
findings at a state-level conference but would not present them to her
own faculty. We cannot underestimate how difficult it can be for a
mixed-race, mixed-culture faculty to discuss openly issues of racism,
equity, and differential experiences. This is particularly true where there
are few minority teachers and where there is little support for that
discussion to occur.

Contrast this general pattern found in most schools with the six
schools that did place immigrant students' needs at the center of their
restructuring efforts. One school had a strong tradition of bilingual and
ESL programs prior to restructuring. In this school, discussions of

language policy and issues were not problematic because these issues had been mainstreamed throughout the school years before. Among the first committees established during school restructuring was the "multicultural committee" (focusing on intergroup relationships and curriculum content). And in designing "representational" governance structures, immigrant students and parents were purposely given representation slots. Meetings are multilingual, as are publications sent to students' homes.

Another school decided in the course of restructuring to move from having a bilingual program to becoming a fully dual-language school. The school could reach such a decision because it already had an involved parent body, creative and well-trained bilingual teachers, and a vision of schooling in its heavily migrant neighborhood that was based on a commitment to community empowerment.

However, most schools in our study did not begin their restructuring with a strong ESL/bilingual tradition or such high levels of support for and expertise on bilingual issues. In most cases there is little understanding of LEP programs and immigrant student needs. Thus, when schools face budget cuts which require prioritization, LEP programs may be marginalized or weakened. In two of our case study schools, the LEP programs were discontinued altogether.

Given recent deep cuts to school budgets, every school has had to make hard choices: what to cut, what to preserve. We found evidence that in most cases language and cultural issues have low priority in these decisions. One school has redirected discretionary funds to support library aides instead of bilingual aides because the staff believes the library is of central importance to their integrated thematic instruction program. Another school uses discretionary book money for career materials for their new career pathways program instead of for needed bilingual books. Still another school cut ethnic studies classes in order to create special reading remediation classes; and another cut its bilingual parent liaison positions to fund a computer lab technician because technology was central to that school's vision. Each decision has its own internal logic, but the overall pattern is that programs that serve immigrant students are being eroded.

A strong history of bilingual programs in a school, the presence of a strong core of bilingual/ESL teachers, and a significant concentration of immigrant students seem to be the prerequisites for incorporating language and cultural concerns into the restructuring agenda. In schools where these factors are not present, language-minority and immigrant concerns go unaddressed. This suggests that restructuring alone cannot assure attention to issues of language, culture, and race. Assuming that empowering teachers would, in and of itself, direct attention to issues of equity and diversity is clearly complicated by the fact that in many schools teachers do not share their students' culture and language, and they have little training in culture and language issues. This speaks to a tremendous need to inform decision makers on the issue of educating language-minority students.

Furthermore, schools must create ongoing mechanisms that will include within the decision-making and program-shaping process voices who speak for the needs of racial, cultural, and linguistic minorities. Involving parents who might provide such a voice is the area identified as most problematic by almost every school in our sample. All the schools included "parent involvement" in their restructuring plans. But few have been able to accomplish meaningful parent involvement. Behind the phrase "parent involvement" lies a range of expectations about the role parents should play. In each school, there were differing views on whether parents should be involved, which parents should be involved, and how parents should be involved. And in practice most of the schools chose to use their resources in areas other than parent involvement, to hold their meetings at times and in languages that excluded parent involvement, and to elect governance and committee structures that marginalized parents. Interestingly, the two dual-language immersion schools had the highest levels of parent involvement in our study.

Schools get their ideas on reform from other restructuring schools, from research, and through professional development activities. Most schools claim to be following a standard set of ideas and models, although their understanding and application of a model can vary tremendously. However, very few schools have incorporated research findings about second-language acquisition, effective programs for language-minority students or bilingual education, or the needs of immigrant students into the theoretical and practical restructuring models they have adopted. The highly visible national restructuring models are generic, speaking of education for "all" students. They rely on practices that have also been embraced in the bilingual education field (thematic integrated instruction, houses or tribes, career-oriented programming, cooperative learning, assertive discipline, larger blocks of class time, more project-oriented work, authentic assessment, heterogeneous, nontracked groupings, advisories, etc.), but they are silent on issues of language and culture and immigrant status. Because schools often draw their ideas from other schools, a lack of focus on issues of culture, language, and race at one site is perpetuated in a lack of focus on these issues elsewhere.

In a few districts—specifically San Francisco, Oakland, and San Diego—efforts have been made to introduce a wide range of possible restructuring models. But more often schools are not familiar with the recent literature on education reform and restructuring, and are implementing their own "homegrown" reforms. Nevertheless, most schools are actively seeking information on school reform. Although this presents an opportunity to disseminate new findings about immigrant education, schools generally lack ties with the people and institutions that could provide such expertise. A few schools are working with coaches, university projects, or other restructuring projects which tie them into a network of ideas and resources with other schools, and generally frame their reform efforts around specific principles. While these third-party agents and facilitators help the schools access research on issues identified as being of interest, in only two cases did we document coaches helping schools focus on issues of culture, race, ethnicity, or language.

The good news is that restructuring appears to produce schools with more of a research focus. Restructuring schools are considering a wider range of models, but they are not yet reviewing the research about immigrant education or culture, race, and language issues. If restructuring schools fail to consider how these generic mainstream reform approaches apply to bilingual and multicultural groups, their implementation may proceed in ways that do not benefit immigrant or language-minority students.

For example, we visited a high school that had been obliged to downsize due to budget problems and was using this opportunity to reopen in September with all new teachers (selected through an application process). The teachers—committed, excited professionals inspired by the Coalition for Essential Schools model—were given the autonomy to jointly design the educational program. However, there was not a single ESL or bilingual teacher among them; and when they considered how they were going to implement their restructured educational program, they gave high priority to heterogeneous groupings. Since they could not figure out how to handle immigrant students effectively in that context, they decided to direct LEP students to other schools in the district (schools "better suited to meet their needs"). In the name of creating heterogeneous groupings, the school effectively eliminated its ESL program.

If awareness of the needs of immigrant and cultural- and racial-minority students is not included in the consideration, interpretation, or implementation of mainstream research, the result will often be not only race or culture blind, but also inequitable. In most restructuring high schools, we documented widespread and increasing use of "sheltered-content" classes taught by inadequately trained and prepared teachers, almost no primary-language instruction or support, social isolation of immigrant students, lack of support services in the students' home languages and directed toward the specific needs of immigrant teenagers, great differences in faculty attitudes toward the goals of and approaches to immigrant education—in brief, the same patterns found in traditional high schools.

In most of the elementary schools, we documented business as usual: bilingual programs driven by compliance concerns and passed over in the enthusiasm for reform. In the majority of schools, reforms bypass the bilingual program, either because the bilingual teachers are not part of the committee structure that plans the reforms or because the school does not understand how to serve immigrant and LEP students within the structure of the reforms being attempted. As an example, a large number of middle schools and high schools are restructuring by forming "families" of approximately one hundred students and four teachers, who stay together over several years. These families allow for more integration of curriculum and create more intimate groupings and relationships among students and between students and teachers. But schools do not know where and how to group LEP students within the families. Some simply create bilingual families, a kind of school within a school. Others put newcomer students in temporary classrooms until they have sufficient English skills to join a "family." Still others, convinced that the benefits of intimacy and belonging to a "family" outweigh the disadvantage of having to provide special instruction to address the immigrant students' language and cultural needs, disperse immigrant students throughout the family system in hopes that individualized attention from their core teachers will help them "catch on." Regardless of the approach adopted, in the vast majority of schools we studied, faculty and administrators volunteered that their schools were having difficulty figuring out how to serve immigrant and LEP students within the reform structure.

It becomes essential, therefore, not only that ESL and bilingual teachers play a major role in restructuring design, but also that the research on second-language acquisition and on effective LEP programs become disseminated along with the mainstream restructuring ideas. All teachers in restructuring schools need to know about this research and have access to training on issues of language instruction and culture. The mainstream school reform discourse and the bilingual education dialogues must be combined.

Despite some disappointment over the failure of restructuring to address issues of language and culture, positive changes do appear to be taking place. Several elementary schools boast wonderful family literacy projects; one has a community bilingual publishing center on the school site. An elementary school hosts an immigrant parent-run family services center on the school site which provides dental, health, legal, and parenting services to the families in the school. A small, rural, English-dominant school involves students, teachers, and community members in a Spanish-language learning program to bridge differences with the school's increasing Spanish-speaking migrant population. Nine schools in our sample have implemented exciting small reforms addressing issues of language, culture, and immigration.

Overall, most of the schools we visited had moved toward smaller student groups and more emphasis on adult-student relationships. These schools are attempting to break down departmentalization and do more interdisciplinary teaching. They are instituting longer blocks of learning time for certain combined subjects (most often humanities) and using more cooperative learning strategies. Schools report that with smaller groupings and more adult contact, fewer students are falling through the cracks. Schools are safer, and faculty believe that this makes a difference for immigrant and language-minority students, as well as for others. But can we assume that all students are benefiting equally?

Lack of Data on Outcomes

There is a frustrating lack of data about the experiences of and outcomes for students by language group, ethnicity, race, or LEP status. Not only is there a paucity of data; it appears in most cases that there is no awareness that such data are needed. The data that we set out to collect on educational outcomes and placements by race/ ethnicity and language status were not available. Educators' determination to maintain a color-blind, culture-blind stance—mixed with a healthy distrust of achievement tests—means that they do not ask the questions or collect the data that might tell us whether some groups are falling through the cracks. New methods for assessing student progress, including the portfolio approach to assessment, can clearly enhance the learning and teaching of individual students. However, in the process of developing these approaches, the collection of other kinds of data has fallen by the wayside, and no one in the schools we studied has figured out how to apply portfolio and other individualized assessment approaches to take aggregate looks at groups of students. Only two schools were developing formal ongoing means to monitor the effects of their reforms on the achievement and learning of aggregate student groups.

Schools are dismantling and modifying existing educational programs and experimenting with new approaches, yet in the majority of schools in our survey there are no means of monitoring the effects on students who have traditionally been ill served in our schools. There is no way to tell what is working and for whom. Even data such as suspension rates, discipline rates, attendance, course registration, etc., by race, LEP status, and language group (data that were kept during the era of civil rights vigilance) are no longer compiled.

Creating meaningful assessment and accountability measures for a culturally and linguistically diverse population is an extremely complex task. Nevertheless, developing such measures should be a high priority in the era of reform experimentation. Without concrete data, school sites and the public cannot evaluate whether cultural-, linguistic-, and racial-minority students are being served equitably.

How Restructuring Can Succeed for Immigrant Students

Despite the disturbing tendency of restructuring efforts to sidestep issues relating to immigrant and LEP students, we did identify nine schools whose restructuring efforts focused on immigrant students and on issues of culture, language, and ethnicity. These schools did not share a programmatic agenda, and their specific reforms differed. However, they did coincide in how they have thought about their students and their school program and in how they have pursued their vision of schooling.

- These schools emphasize creating shared time as a school community and as a forum for ongoing assessment and discussion about implementation issues and outcomes. People indicate that conflict and differing viewpoints are to be expected and are welcomed, and that the school community will commit the time and support necessary to talk through those differences.

- The schools devote considerable time and effort to developing communication mechanisms and processes that are multilingual (as appropriate to their communities), continual, and open. There is a lot of access to information. Teachers, paraprofessionals, parents, and students know what is occurring in the school, and communication goes in both directions. That is, it is not just information dissemination but communication as a system of dialogue.

- The school communities are explicit about discussing power relationships and societal inequities and how these affect students, families, and teachers. There is a strong political vision of community empowerment and an ongoing analysis of issues of race, ethnicity, culture, and language. This is evident in multicultural committees, staff development subjects, topics of community forums, programmatic and recruiting efforts aimed at keeping the school diverse, commitment to dealing with prejudice and intolerance, and efforts and structures designed to ensure participation of all members of the school community.

- There is a major emphasis on professional development. Teacher learning and growth is expected and valued. There is follow-up to professional development, with opportunities for teachers to share newly gained information.

- In each of these schools, the restructuring effort is supported by a strong administrator who buffers the reform effort from potentially destructive external forces (e.g., district regulations and bureaucracy), accesses supports and resources for the effort, fosters communication within the school, and manages the school restructuring effort in a manner than ensures smooth operation. The administrator is "up" on instructional issues and strategies, is supportive of new ideas, works actively with parents, and facilitates leadership development among his or her staff.

- The schools with active, energetic change efforts under way have been successful in acquiring resources to support the training and materials needed for restructuring. (Without such additional resources, reform efforts are often doomed to fail, as we found in some of our case study schools.)

- The effective schools closely monitor current research on multicultural education, bilingual education, language development, and other key issues related to the education of immigrant students.

- The effective schools have people of color serving as key planners and/or in key leadership roles.

- There is a strong commitment in these schools' formal plans and proposals, as well as in their ongoing dialogue about the school's mission, to the children of their respective communities. Restructuring encompasses deliberate efforts to connect with the community.

- There is a central concern with developing full human beings, which extends beyond academic outcomes to include self-esteem, self-knowledge, respect for diversity, etc.

- These schools support risk taking. Ideas are encouraged, new approaches are tried. This is coupled with an atmosphere that encourages ongoing self-assessment, program assessment, and discussion about "how are we doing?" and "what isn't working?"

These nine schools appear to be highly effective in addressing key issues relating to their students and their communities.

Restructuring's Impacts on the School District

Of the districts we studied, three have overall district plans for restructuring. However, schools in those districts, just like schools in all other districts, are focusing basically on changing their own individual school site. Our research raises serious concerns about how the present system of voluntary individual school site change will impact the overall school system. We are particularly concerned about some practices we observed in district after district. Some school sites have negotiated with their districts to gain an additional incentive to restructure: the right to select a completely new staff or to press teachers who are less enthusiastic about restructuring to transfer to other schools "voluntarily." Even where this is not formal policy, schools that have developed some restructuring momentum begin to attract change-oriented teachers and to encourage change-resistant teachers to leave. As schools proceed with restructuring, most demand the right to hire new staff. Schools view the right to select faculty as crucial to any attempt to develop a coherent educational program. There is clearly a creaming of the enthusiastic, change-oriented teachers to a few restructuring schools. In those schools where this selection process was at work and there was a strong commitment to the immigrant community, the payoff was significant. The schools were able to attract strong bilingual teachers eager to teach students in that community. But what happens in the schools those teachers left behind? And where do the other teachers—less change-oriented, perhaps less willing to work with "those kind of kids"—end up when they leave the reform-oriented schools? They go to other schools within the district.

This resulting unequal distribution of change-oriented teachers is compounded by the competition for restructuring funding. State grants and foundation grants tend to go to schools with change-oriented teachers and supportive, visionary principals. In this competition, there are a few winners and potentially a lot of losers. The winners of demonstration grants seem to attract even more money and research support and eventually become showcases.

Individual schools are in stiff competition for scarce restructuring funds, in competition for committed, turned-on teachers, in competition for principals who support restructuring. There is a sorting going on, though no one acknowledges it. We are heading toward a system with a few good schools and many inadequate ones.

Where is the line between school site autonomy and an overall system vision? Is this about improving a school or improving a system? Where does the responsibility lie for overall district equity and school change? What is the role of the district? Few districts are thinking through these issues. Yet restructuring within school sites is changing the role of districts, whether by default or by design. Relationships between central district offices and school sites are strained by questions of where the authority to design and implement programs really resides. This becomes increasingly true as the changes that schools wish to make depart from traditional practice. There is a palpable atmosphere in the schools of "anti-statism," of hostility toward intervention from above, including resistance to district employees who feel that it is *their* job to run programs and ensure compliance on issues like bilingual education.

Districts need to switch from a role of program implementation and compliance to a service and enabling role, from a monitoring role to a role of supporting change processes designed at school sites. This can entail tremendous friction between school sites and districts, but it would help resolve some cloudy issues regarding the strategy and intent of the restructuring reform effort. How much autonomy should school sites be given? Who has the right to determine what is done? What is the mechanism by which individual school sites can be held accountable for meeting the needs of all students? And where is the reform vision that insists upon system-wide change, that can applaud the achievements of individual schools but still recognize that the role of policy ought to be to insist on the achievement of all schools?

Summary

The restructuring reform movement offers a potential, but not a guaranteed, mechanism for meeting the needs of immigrant students and of cultural-, linguistic-, and racial-minority students. In the majority of schools studied in this project, restructuring reforms were bypassing the needs of immigrant students—and in some cases eroding programs that had been designed to meet their needs. Based on an analysis of those schools that were using restructuring to create schools that better address issues of culture, language, and ethnic experience, this study draws the following conclusions.

The needs of immigrant students will only be addressed in the restructuring reforms if the people designing those reforms have experience and training in working with language-minority and cultural-minority students and have a strong commitment to that community of students. The critical shortage of bilingual teachers and the lack of professional development in second-language acquisition and in the cultures and backgrounds of the students enrolled in our schools are major barriers to effective restructuring reforms. These concerns must be addressed in teacher education, in the schools' recruitment practices, in the professional development of the teaching force, and in the construction of governance bodies and committees.

Restructuring schools are, in most cases, eager for information. In addition to fostering dialogue between teachers of immigrant students and mainstream reformers, researchers on immigrant education should make every effort to disseminate knowledge directly to schools that are in the process of restructuring.

State and district policy, as well as foundations that award restructuring reform grants, should require schools to collect and analyze data and to institute accountability mechanisms that can track educational experiences and outcomes by students' race/ethnicity and language status.

The immigrant education movement should take the lead in designing such data systems and in urging their adoption.

Strong administrative leadership is needed to support the arduous task of school change. Schools that are restructuring need consistent, supportive, active administrators who can create a climate in which the needs of a culturally, linguistically, and racially diverse student population are placed at the core of the reform effort. Therefore, district policies should support the stable tenure of effective principals in school sites that are in the process of restructuring and provide professional development to help administrators shape school programs to meet the needs of the immigrant population. These needs are in addition to the obvious need for financial resources to support any restructuring effort.

One additional element is crucial if schools are to address the needs of all students: ongoing dialogue about issues of power inequities with regard to racial, cultural, and linguistic groups within the school community. Gaining the skills to facilitate such discussion must be a central goal in the training and preparation of teachers, administrators, third-party change agents, and coaches. Moreover, district and state leaders must take the initiative for placing these issues on the school reform agenda.

References

Ashby, S., R. Larson, and M.J. Munroe. 1989. "Empowering Teachers: The Key to School-based Reform." Paper presented at the Annual Meeting of the Association of Teacher Educators, St. Louis, Mo., February. ERIC Document Reproduction Service No. ED311 004.

Banks, F.F. 1988. "Factors Which Affect the Academic Achievement of Black Students." In *Equity in Secondary Schools: New Perspectives*, edited by C. Glenn. Report to the Massachusetts Board of Education. Quincy, Mass.: Massachusetts Department of Education.

Banks, J.A. 1987. "The Social Studies, Ethnic Diversity, and Social Change," *Elementary School Journal* 87 (5): 531–43.

Baptiste, H.P., Jr. 1986. "Multicultural Education and Urban Schools from a Sociohistorical Perspective," *Journal of Educational Equity and Leadership* 6 (4): 295–312.

Caldwell, J. 1989. "The Need for 'Anti-Racism' Education," *Education Week* 9 (3): 32.

Chan, Y. 1987. "Parents: The Missing Link in Education Reform." Prepared Statement before the House Select Committee Hearing on Children, Youth, and Families, Indianapolis, Ind., November.

Chang, H.N. 1992. "Diversity: The Essential Link in Collaborative Services," *California Perspectives*, Fall, pp. 55–61.

Chavkin, N.F. 1989. "Debunking the Myth about Minority Parents," *Educational Horizons*, Summer, pp. 119–23.

Children's Defense Fund. 1985. *Black and White Children in America: Key Facts.* Washington, D.C.: The Fund.

Cistone, P.J., J.A. Fernández, and P.L. Tornillo. 1989. "School-based Management/Shared Decision Making in Dade County," *Education and Urban Society* 21 (4): 393–402.

Comer, J.P. 1984. "Home/School Relationships as They Affect the Academic Success of Children," *Education and Urban Society* 16 (3): 323–37.

Cummins, J. 1986. "Empowering Minority Students: A Framework for Intervention," *Harvard Educational Review* 56 (1): 18–36.

Davis, A.M. 1986. "Dispute Resolution at an Early Age," *Negotiation Journal*, July.

Dawson, M.M. 1987. "Beyond Ability Grouping: A Review of the Effectiveness of Ability Grouping and Its Alternatives," *Social Psychology Review* 16 (3): 348–69.

Dentzer, E., and A. Wheelock. 1990. *Locked In/Locked Out: Tracking and Placement Practices in Boston Public Schools.* Boston, Mass.: Massachusetts Advocacy Center.

Derman-Sparks, L. 1989. "Challenging Diversity with Anti-Bias Curriculum," *School Safety*, Winter, pp. 10–13.

Epstein, J.L. 1984. *Home and School Connections in Schools of the Future: Implications of Research on Parent Involvement.* Baltimore, Md.: Center for the Social Organization of Schools, Johns Hopkins University.

FairTest. 1990. *Standardized Tests and Our Children: A Guide to Testing Reform.* Cambridge Mass.: FairTest.

First, J., J.B. Kellogg, J. Wilshire Carrera, and B. Clamants. 1983. "Improving Classroom Management: An Experiment in Elementary Classrooms," *Elementary School Journal* 84: 173–88.

Gardner, S. 1989. "Failure by Fragmentation," *California Tomorrow* 4 (4): 18–26.

Grant, C.A. 1988. "The Persistent Significance of Race in Schooling," *Elementary School Journal* 88 (5): 561–69.

———. 1990. "Desegregation, Racial Attitudes, and Intergroup Contact: A Discussion of Change," *Phi Delta Kappan* 72 (1): 25–32.

Green, R.L., and R.J. Griffore. 1978. "School Desegregation, Testing and the Urgent Need for Equity in Education," *Education* 99 (1): 16–19.

Greenberg, P. 1989. "Parents as Partners in Young Children's Development and Education: A New American Fad? Why Does it Matter?" *Young Children* 44 (4): 61–75.

Haynes, N.M., J.P. Comer, and M. Hamilton-Lee. 1989. "You Like School-based Power, but You Wonder if Others Do," *Executive Educator*, November, pp. 15–18.

Henderson, A.T. 1987. *The Evidence Continues to Grow. Parent Participation Improves Student Achievement.* Columbia, Md: National Committee for Citizens in Education.

Hoover, M.B., R.L. Politzer, and O. Taylor. 1987. "Bias in Reading Tests for Black Language Speakers: A Sociolinguistic Perspective," *Negro Educational Review*, April/July, p. 81.

Johnson, D.W., and R.T. Johnson. 1982. "The Effects of Cooperative and Individualistic Instruction on Handicapped and Non-handicapped Students," *Journal of Social Psychology* 118: 257–68.

Johnston, M., and J. Slotnik. 1985. "Parent Participation in the Schools: Are the Benefits Worth the Burdens?" *Phi Delta Kappan*, February, pp. 430–33.

Kaeser, S. 1984. *Citizen's Guide to Children Out of School: Issues, Data, Explanations, and Solutions to Absenteeism, Dropouts and Disciplinary Exclusion.* Cleveland, Oh.: Citizen's Council for Ohio Schools.

Kozol, J. 1991. *Savage Inequalities: Children in America's Schools.* New York: Crown.

LaFontaine, H. 1987. "At Risk Children and Youth—The Extra Educational Challenges of Limited-English-Proficient Students." Paper prepared for the 1987 Summer Institute of the Council of Chief State School Officers, Washington, D.C.

Lambert, L. 1988. "Staff Development Redesigned," *Phi Delta Kappan*, May, pp. 665–68.

Lawton, M. 1991. "California Educators Take Stock of Efforts to Ensure Schools Are Safe, Secure," *Education Week* 10 (27): 1–19.

Leler, H. 1983. "Parent Education and Involvement in Relation to the Schools and to Parents of School-aged Children." In *Parent Education and Public Policy*, edited by R. Haskins and S. Addams. Norwood, N.J.: ABLEX.

Lindquist, K.M., and J.L. Mauriel. 1989. "School-based Management: Doomed to Failure?" *Education and Urban Society* 21 (4): 402–16.

Little, J.W. 1984. "Seductive Images and Organizational Realities in Professional Development," *Teachers College Record* 86 (1): 84–102.

Loewen, J. 1980. "Possible Causes of Lower Black Scores on Aptitude Tests." Burlington, Vt.: University of Vermont. Manuscript.

Lomotey, K., and A.D. Swanson. 1989. "Urban and Rural Schools Research: Implications for School Governance," *Education and Urban Society* 21 (4): 436–54.

Lucas, T., R. Henze, and R. Donato. 1990. "Promoting the Success of Latino Language-minority Students: An Exploratory Study of Six High Schools," *Harvard Educational Review* 60 (3): 315–40.

Lueder, D.C. 1989. "Tennessee Parents Were Invited to Participate—and They Did: A Statewide Effort to Strengthen Parent/School Partnerships Has Generated an Enthusiastic Response," *Educational Leadership*, October, pp. 14–17.

Malen, B., R.T. Ogawa, and J. Kranz. 1990. "Site-based Management: Unfilled Promise. Evidence Says Site-based Management Hindered by Many Factors," *School Administrator*, February, pp. 32–59.

Melville, A.A., and M.J. Blank. 1991. *What It Takes: Structuring Interagency Partnerships to Connect Children and Families with Comprehensive Services.* Washington, D.C.: Education and Human Services Consortium.

Moore, D.R., and S. Davenport. 1988. *The New Improved Sorting Machine.* Chicago, Ill.: Designs for Change.

Nieto, S. 1992. *Affirming Diversity: The Sociopolitical Context of Multicultural Education.* New York: Longman.

Oakes, J. 1985. *Keeping Track: How Schools Structure Inequality.* New Haven, Conn.: Yale University News.

Oakes, J., and M. Lipton. 1990. *Making the Best of Schools: A Handbook for Parents, Teachers, and Policymakers.* New Haven, Conn.: Yale University Press.

Olsen, L. 1988. *Crossing the Schoolhouse Border: Immigrant Students and the California Public Schools.* San Francisco, Calif.: California Tomorrow.

Olsen, L., and C. Minicucci. 1992. "Programs for Secondary Limited English Proficient Students: A California Study," *Focus* (National Clearinghouse for Bilingual Education) 5 (Spring).

Olsen, L., and N. Mullen. 1990. *Embracing Diversity: Teachers' Voices from California's Classrooms*. San Francisco: California Tomorrow.

Orum, L.S. 1988. *Making Education Work for Hispanic Americans: Some Promising Community-based Practices*. Los Angeles, Calif.: National Council of La Raza.

Packard Foundation. 1991. *The Future of Children* 2 (1).

Phillips, C.B. 1988. "Nurturing Diversity for Today's Children and Tomorrow's Leaders," *Young Children*, January, pp. 42–47.

Pine, G.J., and A.G. Hilliard. 1990. "Rx for Racism: Imperatives for America's Schools," *Phi Delta Kappan*, April, pp. 593–600.

Podemski, R., and J.Childers. 1987. "The School Counselor's Role: Reexamination and Revitalization," *Planning and Changing*.

Pollard, D.S. 1989. "The Resurgence of Racism. Reducing the Impact of Racism on Students," *Educational Leadership*, October, pp. 73–75.

Reyhner, J., and R.L. García. 1989. "Helping Minorities Read Better: Problems and Promises," *Reading Research and Instruction* 28 (3): 84–91.

Schmidt, P. 1991. "Three Types of Bilingual Education Effective, E.D. Study Concludes," *Education Week* 10 (22).

Slavin, R.E. 1987. "Ability Grouping and Its Alternatives: Must We Track?" *American Educator*, Summer, pp. 32–48.

Snow, C., and K. Hakuta. 1987. "The Cost of Monolinguism." Cambridge, Mass. Unpublished monograph.

Suzuki, B.H. 1984. "Curriculum Transformation for Multicultural Education," *Education and Urban Society* 16 (3): 294–322.

Taylor, O., and D.L. Lee. 1987. "Standardized Tests and African-American Children: Communication and Language Issues," *Negro Educational Review*, April/July, p. 67.

Tizard, J., W.N. Schofield, and J. Hewison. 1982. "Collaboration between Teachers and Parents in Assisting Children's Reading," *British Journal of Educational Psychology* 52:1–15.

Valencia, S.W., and J.P. Killion. 1989. *Implementing Research-based Reading and Writing Programs Overcoming Obstacles to Teacher Change: Three Case Studies*. ERIC Document Reproduction Service No. ED 305 595.

Wayson, W.W. 1984. Prepared Statement before the House Subcommittee on Elementary, Secondary, and Vocational Education, Hearing on School Discipline, Washington, D.C., January.

Wheelock, A. 1992. *Crossing the Tracks: How Untracking Can Save America's Schools*. New York: New Press.

Williams, D. 1979. "Black English and the Stanford-Binet Test of Intelligence." Ph.D. dissertation, Stanford University.

10

Are Our Schools Really Failing?

Richard Rothstein

Introduction

There is a conventional wisdom about public schools which holds that:

- Graduates do not have the skills needed in a technologically advanced economy.

- We have doubled funds for public education since the mid-1960s, but the additional money has not improved schools.

- Academic achievement is stagnant or declining.

- Public schools cannot improve because teachers are smothered by bureaucracy.

- To address this system failure, structural reform like site-based decision making or parental choice of schools is imperative.

Liberals and conservatives share these views, parting only when the left proposes radical decentralization while the right insists this does not go far enough—and calls for privatization with vouchers. Yet despite the broad popular consensus, each assertion contained in the conventional story is incorrect or misguided. The *truth* is that:

- Public schools now produce the academic skills demanded by employers, and they probably already produce the skills needed even if industry adopted more flexible production methods.

- While it is true that public education funding has more than doubled since 1965, little new money has gone to improve academic outcomes. Instead, added funds have pursued social goals like education of the handicapped, nutrition programs, and busing for integration. Teacher salary increases and class size reductions have been insufficient to produce educational effects.

- Despite the meager increases in regular education funding, progress has been achieved in reduced dropout rates, higher test scores for white and especially for minority students, improved minority college attendance, and increased output of scientists and engineers.

- Bureaucracy does stifle creativity but school administration consumes few dollars, mostly to prevent favoritism or fraud in purchasing, to ban discrimination, or to maintain minimum academic standards.

- Consequently, systemic reforms like decentralization and school choice mostly address nonexistent problems. Choice programs will increase race and class segregation and depress academic achievement for disadvantaged students. Radical decentralization could waste teacher time with routine administrative tasks.

- Schools need incremental reforms like improved evaluation and training of teachers and principals and more curricular emphasis on conceptual and verbal skills. But the most important reform remains more money. Results are most likely to come from investments in health care for pregnant mothers, education of preschoolers, improved teacher pay, drastic class size reductions for disadvantaged students, and workplace training for the non-college bound.

- Public education advocates miscalculate when they attempt to mobilize support by attacking school outcomes. The strategy likely to enhance support for public schools is to highlight schools' accomplishments, suggesting that even greater gains are likely with additional resources.

The "Jobs-Skills Mismatch"

At President Clinton's December 1992 "Economic Summit" in Little Rock, Apple Computer chairman John Sculley claimed that "we're still trapped in a K–12 public education system which is preparing our young people for jobs that just don't exist anymore" (Sculley 1992). After Sculley was seconded by Princeton economist Alan Blinder, Clinton challenged them: "Only about 15 percent of the employers of this country report difficulty finding workers with appropriate occupational skills. Does that mean the employers don't know what they're talking about, or that we're wrong?" (Blinder 1992).

Blinder evaded Clinton's probe, claiming there is no skills shortage only because of the recession; when hiring picks up, "skills are going to be in short supply." But Blinder was mistaken. The employer survey to which Clinton alluded was conducted by the Commission on the Skills of the American Workforce in *prerecession* 1989. Sponsored by a bipartisan group led by Ira Magaziner (now a staff adviser to President Clinton) and former labor secretaries Ray Marshall (under Carter) and Bill Brock (under Reagan), the survey found that over 80 percent of American employers were satisfied with new hires' education. Only 5 percent expected future increases in skill requirements (NCEE 1990). Nonetheless, illustrating the power of ideology over experience, employers who find little fault with their own workers' preparation frequently complain that public schools are failing, just as the public consistently tells pollsters that schools fail although the schools their own children attend are doing just fine.

Academics, politicians, journalists, and business leaders seem to agree that schools' failure is confirmed by growing "returns to education"—each additional year of school boosts earnings (Rasell and Appelbaum 1992). In 1979, adults over the age of twenty-five who had graduated from college earned 38 percent more than high school graduates of the same age group. That figure is now 57 percent (Hecker 1992).

If employers pay relatively increasingly more for college degrees, it seems reasonable to conclude that employers must find it harder to fill jobs that require higher education. And if the premiums paid to college graduates indicate a shortage, it seems reasonable to demand an increase in the number of graduates. This can be done by focusing policy attention on the shortcomings of a public school system that seems to produce too few students qualified for college studies.

But a recent report by Daniel Hecker in the Department of Labor's *Monthly Labor Review* challenges this logic. It is true that college graduates earn increasingly more than high school graduates. But it also seems that many college graduates take jobs that do not require degrees. In 1990, twenty-nine million Americans had college degrees, but 20 percent of them had jobs that do not require a degree or they could not find work at all. The number is growing: in 1979 only 18 percent of college graduates were unemployed or had jobs not requiring degrees, and in 1968 it was only 11 percent (Hecker 1992).

There are now 644,000 college graduates working as retail salespersons (with 75,000 selling door to door). There are 83,000 graduates who are maids or janitors; 166,000 of today's truck and bus drivers have college degrees. Blue-collar workers include 1.3 million college graduates, twice as many as fifteen years ago. Even *before* the current recession began, 400,000 college graduates were unemployed despite their credentials (Hecker 1992).

Of course, not all college graduates want professional or technical work, and some young graduates seek blue-collar jobs when they first graduate, settling later on professional careers. But it is unlikely that voluntary blue-collar work explains much of these data because the number of jobs in technologically sophisticated occupations is not increasing nearly as rapidly as is popularly believed. The oft-cited conclusion of the Department of Labor's *Workforce 2000* report (Johnston and Packer 1987) that jobs of the future will require more education was based on a misinterpretation of the data: the report failed to weight its conclusion about increased educational requirements by the number of new jobs in each occupational category, failed to offset increases in educational requirements for some jobs with decreases in educational requirements for others, and neglected to consider the growth of low-skill industries as well as those needing higher skill levels. In their reanalysis of *Workforce 2000's* projections, Mishel and Teixeira (1990) conclude that probable industrial shifts (and occupational shifts within industries) will require only that those entering the workforce at the turn of the century have one-fourth of a grade level more education than those who leave the workforce at that time. In other words, students entering the workforce in the year 2000 will need only one-fourth of a grade level more schooling than students who entered in 1955.

Examination of the Bureau of Labor Statistics' 1988–2000 occupational projections illustrates the dangers of a too hasty conclusion that changing occupational requirements will include substantially greater skills. The Bureau expected paralegals to be the nation's fastest-growing occupation, with employment increasing by 75 percent from 1988 to 2000. But growth in this small group means only 62,000 new jobs. A 48 percent increase in computer programers will only include 250,000 additional jobs. Meanwhile, there are substantial vacancies in more populous occupations with slower growth rates: while representing an increase of only 19 percent, there are expected to be 730,000 additional retail salespersons by the year 2000. Also with only a 19 percent growth rate, janitors and maids will add 556,000 jobs. There will be 551,000 additional waiters and waitresses, a 31 percent increase in their number (Silvestri and Lukasiewicz 1989).

With no shortage of educated workers, college graduates' high relative earnings stem not from premiums paid for more education but rather from penalties exacted from those with less. The oversupply of college graduates is confirmed by a 10 percent drop in wages of college-educated workers since 1973. But high school graduates' earnings have dropped even more, by 16 percent (Mishel and Bernstein 1992). Greater returns to education suggest, not a need to increase schooling, but rather a need for trade and labor market policies to reverse the earning losses among industrial and service workers.

Despite this evidence, to conclude that schools now adequately prepare youths for expected job openings seems counterintuitive. Notwithstanding general employer satisfaction with their own new hires' academic preparation, a barrage of public opinion surveys and employer anecdotes reinforce a view of failing education.

Examination of these surveys reveals that schools are condemned mostly when questions focus on the respondents' view of schooling in general. When, on the other hand, questioners focus on executives' experience with *their own new hires* or with the public's experience with schools *their own children* attend, responses are more favorable. The surveys' condemnation of public schools, therefore, tends to be a circular ideological exercise: business executives or the public are asked if schools fail to prepare youths for economic success; respondents' answers reflect the conventional wisdom and are then cited as proof of this wisdom; meanwhile, answers reflecting respondents' own experience, which tend to contradict convention, are downplayed or ignored in the surveys' public releases.

The Gallup Organization, for example, conducts an annual poll of the public's attitude toward the public schools. Respondents are asked to give the schools a "grade": A = 4, B = 3, C = 2, D = 1, F = 0. Consistently, public school parents give the schools with which they have experience—schools in their own local community—a higher grade than they give schools in the nation as a whole. In 1990, public school parents gave their local community schools an average 2.44 grade, while schools in the nation as a whole were given a grade of only 2.03 (NCES 1992: table 20).

A Business Week/Harris Poll conducted in September 1992 reports similar results. Only 39 percent of Americans consider public schools "excellent" or "pretty good," and 23 percent consider them "poor." But when those with a child or grandchild in the public schools were asked about the schools their children attend, 50 percent rated them "excellent" or "pretty good," and only 10 percent rated them "poor" (*Business Week* 1992: 85).

In 1990, the National Association of Business (NAB) conducted a survey of Los Angeles businesses. NAB's press release claimed that two-thirds of Los Angeles firms were dissatisfied with workers' educational preparation. According to NAB president William Kolberg, the results underscore the need to "reform the nation's education system" because "employers have lost faith in the value of the high school diploma" (NAB 1990; Greene 1990).

Yet the workforce survey on which Kolberg's claims were based showed nothing of the sort. The NAB had asked Los Angeles business executives if they agreed with the statement, "education has not kept up with the nation's technological growth," and two-thirds assented. But when asked specifically about "educational training of entry-level employees" in their own businesses, 75 percent of those very executives rated it 3 or higher, on an "unsatisfied to satisfied" scale of 1 to 5 (Fairbank, Bregman, and Maulin 1990).

Shortly thereafter, the California Business Roundtable reported that 80 percent of the state's business executives support a comprehensive restructuring of public education to improve job skills. In presenting this finding to California governor Pete Wilson, Pacific Telesis (PacTel) chairman Sam Ginn complained that his company gave a seventh-grade-level reading test to 6,400 applicants for the job of "operator," and more than half failed. This, according to Ginn, was proof of business's need for improved public education to provide "workers with skills that will allow us to be competitive into the next century" (Akst 1991; Weintraub 1991).

What Ginn failed to mention in his public statement was that for the 2,700 who passed the test, there were only 700 job openings, paying wages of less than $7 an hour (author interview with Joe Richey, of the PacTel corporate office, 1991). A more telling conclusion would have been that schools provided PacTel with nearly four times the number of qualified candidates it needed, even at low wages. If the company offered wages above the poverty line, even more successful test takers might have applied.

Some critics—like Ray Marshall and Marc Tucker in their recent book, *Thinking for a Living*—acknowledge that schools prepare youths for today's jobs and even for the more sophisticated jobs expected to evolve in the future. But this is no cause for complacency, they add. Skills are now adequate only because we maintain outmoded assembly lines where workers follow detailed instructions to perform repetitive, unskilled tasks. We will never accelerate productivity with these assembly lines, Marshall and Tucker claim. High-productivity organizations of the future (already common in Japan and Germany) require flexible workers able to perform many tasks, work together, and diagnose production problems. Were American companies to adopt high-productivity structures, skills would be insufficient (Marshall and Tucker 1992).

These authors' argument is impressive, but it overestimates the schooling required even for high-performance work organizations. Consider the investigation of Mexican automobile manufacturing conducted by Harley Shaiken (Shaiken 1987 and author interview, December 1992). Ten years ago Shaiken began to study Ford Motor Company's new engine plant in Chihuahua, Mexico. Initially, Shaiken believed that Ford's Mexican gamble to save on labor costs would fail. Of all manufacturing, automobile engine production is most sophisticated. Crankshafts, for example, must be machined with tolerances of one ten-thousandth of an inch. Equipment for one production line can cost $30 million. Close coordination between production workers and more highly skilled technicians is essential. Surely, Shaiken conjectured, workers in Mexico (where six years of schooling is the norm [Lustig 1992: table 3-11]) could not meet an engine plant's high-performance requirements.

He found otherwise. Within two years, Chihuahua's facility achieved 75 percent of the labor productivity at Ford's North American engine plant in Lima, Ohio. After eight years, Chihuahua became the world's most productive engine plant. Having displaced the Lima facility, it is now Ford's sole source of North American engines.

In Mexico, Ford required a minimum of a ninth-grade education for new hires. The average was 10.2 school years for engine block workers, 11 years on the crankshaft line, and 12 years for skilled technicians and maintenance workers. In U.S. auto plants, "we take a guy off the street, show him which button to push, and he's a production worker," according to an auto executive Shaiken interviewed. In Chihuahua, on the other hand, Ford enrolled high school dropouts in a four- to twelve-week technology institute program covering gasoline engines, mechanical drawing, and mathematics. Before beginning work, each employee was able to tear down and reassemble an engine. Once at work, employees were rotated every three to six months to different jobs within the plant so that skills would be broadened further. As the Chihuahua plant matured, Ford hired workers with even less schooling and relied even more on its own training. As skilled technicians left, Ford replaced them with production workers promoted and trained from within, as required by Ford's Mexican union contract.

It is not evident that our schools do not now produce workers qualified to staff such a system. Even if American school standards are lower than those of some other nations, we have a plethora of underemployed graduates whose skills are at least equal to those of Mexican dropouts. When General Motors implemented a high-performance work system at its Tennessee Saturn plant, American schooling was no impediment. But unlike other GM plants, Saturn gave ten weeks of formal training to new hires and required ongoing classroom work for permanent employees (Shanker 1993). Most American corporations, however, make few training investments, so their claim that public schools cannot provide qualified workers rings hollow.

School Funding Growth since 1965

Irving Kristol recently attacked President Clinton's social spending plans by asserting, "Look at the spending on public schools. It goes up and up and up, and the results go down and down and down" (DeParle 1993). When Benno Schmidt resigned Yale's presidency in 1992, he denounced public education to justify a new national for-profit private school chain:

> We have roughly doubled per-pupil spending (after inflation) in public schools since 1965. . . . Yet dropout rates remain distressingly high. . . . Overall high school

students today are posting lower SAT scores than a
generation ago. The nation's investment in educational
improvement has produced very little return (Schmidt
1992).

With near unanimity on these points, it is understandable that
aerospace executive Joseph Alibrandi justifies his sponsorship of California's private school voucher ballot initiative by declaring, "our schools
are worse today than they were five or ten years ago. No one denies this,
not even the education Establishment" (Alibrandi and Teasley 1992). In
1990 we spent $5,521 per pupil in the public schools, more than double
the $2,611 (in 1990 dollars) spent twenty-five years earlier (NCES 1992:
tables 3, 32, 38). More money for schools won't do any good, critics
assert; it's just pouring good money after bad.

The truth, however, is that little new money has been invested in
regular educational improvements since 1965. The option of spending
more hasn't failed. It hasn't been tried. Nearly 30 percent of new
education money has gone for "special education" of children with
disabilities.[1] Since 1975, federal law has required public schools to
provide "a free appropriate education" to each child, no matter how
seriously handicapped. Schools must design an "individualized education program" for each child with a learning, emotional, or physical
disability. Publicly financed medical diagnoses, special transportation
arrangements, personalized instruction, tiny class sizes, specially
trained teachers, and the purchase of special equipment may be required to place a child in the "least restrictive environment." Parents
dissatisfied with an individualized program are entitled to a hearing.
The Supreme Court has ruled that cost cannot be an excuse for failing to
design an appropriate program from which a disabled child can benefit
(Bartlett 1992).

The result has been an explosion of costs associated with special
education. By 1989–1990, over 4.5 million children (11.5 percent of all
U.S. public schoolchildren) were being taught in conformity with their
own individualized education programs (NCES 1992: table 50). In about
one-third of these cases, the program involves a special teacher who
visits children in their regular classrooms. In another third, children are
pulled out of their regular classes for several hours to work with special
teachers in resource rooms, sometimes individually and sometimes with
a handful of other children, but these teachers work with no more than
twenty-eight children in the course of a day. About one-fourth of the
children are in a full-day special class where, by law, class size cannot

---

[1]This and subsequent estimates of the share of added school funds devoted to various
programs were made by the author using available national data, supplemented by
estimates based on budgets of the Los Angeles Unified School District. The author will be
pleased to share his detailed methodology with interested scholars.

exceed thirteen. The remaining special education students (about 6 percent of the total) are placed in separate public facilities—or private facilities, if no public facility is available—where the children reside or to which they are transported (NCES 1992: table 51). Where school districts do not have appropriate facilities, they must pay private tuition for each child with special education needs.

Education of the handicapped is worthwhile, but it is dishonest to suggest that special education funds should produce academic gains for regular students, and when they do not, to claim this as proof that money spent on public schools is wasted.

Nearly one-third of new school money has gone for smaller classes. Pupil-teacher ratios have declined by about 30 percent since 1965 (NCES 1992: table 62). Average class size is now about twenty-four (close to thirty in California), requiring more teachers and extra classrooms. It seems reasonable that this investment should produce academic gains. Yet while reducing class size to twenty-four creates better working conditions for teachers and may be needed for discipline—as education becomes more universal and society's authority norms weaken—it is not enough to improve academic outcomes. Unless class sizes get small enough (about fifteen) so that the method of teaching can change to individualized instruction, smaller classes have no measurable academic effect (Slavin, Karweit, and Wasik 1992).

School breakfast and lunch programs have absorbed nearly 10 percent of increased expenditures. In 1965, nutrition programs were mostly self-supporting and were basically limited to selling milk and ice cream. Today, 35 percent of all students get free or reduced-price meals, costing over $6 billion a year (NCES 1992: tables 347, 360). Providing meals to needy children should improve academic achievement since nutrition is necessary for learning.

However, the expectation of academic improvement from meal programs assumes that children are better nourished as a result. If, on the other hand, school food subsidies only offset the deterioration in children's health since 1965, expecting academic gains from this program would be unrealistic. Fourteen percent of Americans lived in poverty in 1992, the highest rate since 1964 (Pear 1992; Risen 1992). And this growth of overall poverty masks an even more drastic growth in child poverty. In 1990, nearly one-fourth of American children under age six were poor, an increase from 18 percent in 1979 (Mishel and Bernstein 1992). With a probable deterioration in the nutritional condition of children when they come to school, it is questionable whether educational improvement can be expected from today's breakfast and lunch programs. Nor is it appropriate to suggest that maintenance of such expenditures would, from an educational point of view, be throwing good money after bad.

Teacher salaries have grown 21 percent—less than 1 percent a year—from an average $27,221 in 1965 (1990 dollars) to $32,977 in 1990 (NCES

1992: tables 38, 73). This increase is responsible for another 8 percent of increased education costs. This added expenditure should result in improved student achievement if higher salaries attract more highly qualified graduates to teaching. But if other professional salaries grew more, higher teacher pay would not enable school districts to maintain teacher quality in the face of greater competition from other professions.

Since 1975, pay increases for starting teachers have lagged behind pay increases for other beginning professionals with bachelor's degrees. Starting teacher salaries have grown by 149 percent since 1975, less than the rate of inflation. For beginning engineers, the increase was 153 percent; for marketing representatives, 169 percent; for business administration graduates, 171 percent; for mathematicians and statisticians, 163 percent; for economists and finance personnel, 161 percent; for liberal arts graduates, 183 percent. Teachers did better than chemists (144 percent) and accountants (130 percent) (U.S. Bureau of the Census 1992a: table 234).

Teacher salaries increased faster from 1965 to 1975 than afterward (NCES 1992: table 73). But over twenty-five years, the overall increase in real teacher pay at best maintained schools' ability to attract candidates. If anything, the increase has been inadequate to maintain teaching's competitive standing, since more professions have welcomed women since 1975. Highly qualified female college graduates are no longer captives of the teaching profession, so the same relative teaching salary now attracts less-qualified teachers than before. All told, we can't expect teachers' pay gains since 1965 to produce higher student achievement. For this result we would need bigger pay boosts to attract higher-quality college graduates to teaching.

Transportation has consumed 5 percent of increased expenditures. In 1965, 40 percent of public school students were bused, at an average individual cost of $214 (1990 dollars). By 1989, 59 percent were bused, and the cost had jumped to $390 (NCES 1992: tables 38, 49).

Some new spending stems from keeping more students in school. The oft-repeated worry that more students are dropping out has no factual basis. Since a student dropping out of one school may move to a new community and enroll there, the most accurate measurement of dropouts is not schools' own records but census information on young adults who have completed twelve years of school.

In 1970, 75 percent of youths twenty-five to twenty-nine years old had completed high school. By 1990, 86 percent had done so. Minorities' dropout rates have declined steadily. In 1940, only 12 percent of blacks between the ages of twenty-five and twenty-nine had completed high school. In 1950, the black completion rate rose to 24 percent; in 1960, to 39 percent; in 1970, to 58 percent; in 1980, to 77 percent. The rate continued to rise in the 1980s, to 83 percent in 1990 (NCES 1992: table 8).

A series on Hispanic dropout rates is less accessible because the 1980 decennial census was the first with separate data on Hispanics and because many so-called Hispanic dropouts (young adults who have not completed high school) are immigrants, some of whom came too old to enroll in school. They shouldn't be considered "dropouts"—many never "dropped in." In 1990 only 58 percent of Hispanics aged twenty-five to twenty-nine had completed high school. But for Hispanics in their forties (in their twenties in 1970), the rate was less—52 percent. And for those in their sixties (in their twenties in 1950), the rate was only 38 percent (NCES 1992: table 9). Thus it seems that Hispanic dropout rates are declining as well.

If the typical dropout completes 10.5 years of school, then the higher completion rate is responsible for an increase of 1.3 percent in total education costs since 1965. This added spending does not improve graduates' average academic achievement. While preventing dropouts is important, lower dropout rates will also reduce average test scores, since a broader base is now tested, including those less academically motivated than earlier groups that did not include potential dropouts. Fewer dropouts will also generate more anecdotes about high school graduates who can't read or compute well. So, paradoxically, expenditures for more schooling can appear to reduce academic achievement while contributing to an improved overall education level for society.

In sum, special education, smaller classes, school lunches, increased teacher pay, more buses, and fewer dropouts account for over 80 percent of new education money since 1965. That these produced few academic gains is no surprise. Indeed, since teachers' salaries have not kept pace with those in other professions and school nutrition programs have not fully offset the growth of child poverty, greater spending may not even have been enough to support the maintenance of 1965's academic standards. It is to the credit of the public schools and of the teaching profession that real gains have occurred at all.

Improved School Outcomes since 1965

Yet there have been real gains, partly due to higher academic standards and curricular reforms implemented in the last fifteen years. In many if not all classrooms, for example, conceptual math has embellished arithmetic and literature has replaced basal readers. The 1983 report entitled *A Nation at Risk* accelerated a curricular reform movement which was already gathering steam. Heightened consciousness of the ways in which low teacher expectations for working-class and minority students become self-fulfilling has also helped boost student academic progress. New spending related to these curricular reforms, though modest in scope, has made a difference. Some new money has gone for education of the disadvantaged through Chapter I and bilingual programs. Computers have been added to classrooms: 54 percent of elementary schools (including 43 percent of those in the lowest family income quartile) now use computers in the classroom (NCES 1991). Thus, with limited new investment, academic performance has improved, especially for minority students. This is one reason why schools' skills production has outpaced industry's ability to absorb educated workers.

It does seem that academic performance declined in the late 1960s and 1970s, to rebound dramatically in the last decade. School achievement, certainly for minority youths and most likely for whites as well, today exceeds not only 1970s standards but those of twenty-five years ago. True, average Scholastic Aptitude Test (SAT) scores have declined to 899 (math and verbal combined) in 1992 from 937 twenty years ago. Yet this favorite fact of headline writers tells a very partial story. Last year, 29 percent of SAT takers (students planning to go to college) were minority, more than double the 13 percent twenty years earlier. In 1992, 43 percent of test takers ranked in the top fifth of their high school classes. In 1972, 48 percent were in the top fifth, a more elite group (ETS 1992a; College Board 1974). In California, where over half the test takers were minority students, only 66 percent came from homes where only English was spoken, and 20 percent spoke English as a second language, up from 13 percent just six years earlier (ETS 1986, 1992b). These shifts unsurprisingly produce lower average scores. Declines in average SAT scores stem mostly from expansion in the test takers' base, adding more disadvantaged students to a pool that earlier included mostly privileged students.

While average scores have gone down, minority scores have gone up. From 1976 (when the College Board began tracking racial and ethnic group scores) to 1992, black students' scores went from 686 to 737; Mexico-origin students' scores went from 781 to 797; and Puerto Rican students' scores went from 765 to 772. White students' scores declined, but this is due, at least in part, to the broadened social class base of this subset of test takers. In 1976, the number of white test takers was equal to only 19 percent of the seventeen-year-old white population. In 1992, it was 25 percent, a less elite group (ETS 1975, 1992a; U.S. Bureau of the Census 1992b).

The best way to improve average SAT scores would be to encourage only the best middle-class students to take the test. We used to do just this, which is why average scores were higher. Today we prepare more minority and lower-middle-class students to take college entrance exams. It is a sign of accomplishment, not failure.

A more accurate evaluation of SAT trends comes from examining, not average scores, but the percentage of all youths in the seventeen-year-old cohort (both test takers and non-takers) who do well on the test. Last year, test takers equal in number to 2.2 percent of all seventeen-year-olds had verbal scores of at least 600 (good enough to get into top-ranked universities), better than the 1.9 percent with such scores in 1976. In math, test takers equal in number to 5.4 percent of all seventeen-year-olds got at least 600 in 1992, up from only 3.8 percent who scored that well in 1976. The number of students who scored over 500, good enough for admission to academically respectable four-year colleges, also grew (ETS 1975, 1992a; U.S. Bureau of the Census 1982, 1992b). These data suggest improved grade school and high school performance.

Reports of the National Assessment of Educational Progress (NAEP), a federal attempt to test student achievement, mostly confirm this conclusion. White students' reading levels have been stagnant, for example, but growth in minority scores has closed much of the gap in the last twenty years. The same is true for math and, to a lesser extent, science. Absolute scores still leave great room for improvement: the average thirteen-year-old, for example, reads adequately to "search for specific information, interrelate ideas, and make generalizations"; but only 11 percent of thirteen-year-olds can "find, understand, summarize and explain relatively complicated information" (ETS 1990: table 1.1).

SAT tests measure the abilities of high school seniors who consider attending college. Actual enrollment data provide more evidence of improvement. White student college enrollment has jumped from 27 percent of all 24-year-olds in 1970 to 34 percent in 1991. In 1970, 16 percent of black 18- to 24-year-olds were enrolled in college. In 1991, 24 percent were enrolled. In 1972 (the earliest year for Hispanic census data), 13 percent of Hispanic 18- to 24-year-olds were enrolled in college; 18 percent were enrolled by 1991. Immigration, however, confounds this statistic; if we consider only those who graduated from high school, the proportion of Hispanic youths enrolled in college jumped from 26 percent in 1972 to 34 percent in 1991, not all that much below whites' 42 percent (ACE 1993).

From 1980 to 1991, the number of black students enrolled in four-year colleges jumped by 20 percent nationwide, despite the fact that blacks between the ages of eighteen and twenty-four in the population declined by 6 percent. Hispanic enrollment in four-year colleges increased by 76 percent nationwide, far outpacing a 41 percent population gain (including immigrants) for this age group (ACE 1993).

In California, gains have been especially strong in recent years. In Los Angeles, for example, 8 percent of Hispanic high school seniors in 1985–1986 enrolled in four-year programs at either California State University or the University of California the following academic year. An additional 28 percent of Hispanic seniors enrolled in public community colleges. Four years later, in 1989–1990, 12 percent of Hispanic seniors enrolled in four-year institutions the year following graduation, with an additional 27 percent enrolling in community colleges.

African American students' college-going rates also improved in this period, with 17 percent of 1989–1990 seniors going to four-year public colleges, up from 12 percent in 1985–1986. Community college enrollment also climbed, from 33 percent to 38 percent (IAU 1992).

These data are no reason to be self-satisfied; minority participation rates in higher education still fall below white rates. And enrollment gains do not necessarily translate into college completion, which is affected as much by joblessness, tuition costs, and the declining availability of financial aid as it is by academics. But enrollment data are also no basis for condemning the preparation for college in public schools. On the contrary, we should look at what schools do right so that we can do more of it.

Education critics often seize on two aspects of recent African American experience to support a view that schools are failing. First, they note that the percentage of black high school graduates who attend college has declined—from a high of 35 percent in 1976 to a low of 25 percent in 1988 (rebounding to 32 percent by 1991). Second, they note that the gap in college attendance of white and black youths is growing. In 1980, the share of 18- to 24-year-olds in college was 26 percent for whites and 19 percent for blacks, a 7-point difference. By 1991 it had jumped to 34 percent for whites but only 24 percent for blacks, a 10-point gap (ACE 1993; Koretz 1990).

Yet the apparent decline in the rate at which blacks attend college relative to the number of black high school graduates is entirely due to the fact that black high school graduation rates have been climbing faster than college attendance, though both have been going up. And the growing gap between white and black college attendance rates has been due almost entirely to the explosion in college attendance by white females, a consequence of the feminist revolution of the last several decades. Neither of these factors justifies condemnation of our public schools.

American science and engineering performance surpasses our competitors. Of every 10,000 Americans, 7.4 have bachelor's degrees in physical science or engineering. Japan has 7.3 per 10,000, and West Germany has 6.7. American performance continues to improve: in 1987, 7 percent of 22-year-olds had a science or engineering degree, up from less than 5 percent in 1970. Only 6.5 percent of Japan's 22-year-olds and 4 percent of German 22-year-olds had science or engineering degrees in 1987. Our advantage stems from greater commitment to educating women: in the United States, 35 percent of new scientists are women, compared to Japan's 10 percent (Carson, Huelskamp, and Woodall 1991a).

During the Cold War, Sandia National Laboratories in Albuquerque, New Mexico, produced nuclear weapons components. With demand for warheads declining and a belief that production of scientists was declining as well, the Bush administration asked Sandia to plan how "to pick up our society by its bootstraps and find a new mechanism to obtain science and math literacy" (Carson, Huelskamp, and Woodall 1991a). Sandia gave the assignment to three "systems analysts" with experience in nuclear weapons, a subject too dangerous to approach with preconceptions. They took pride in their ability to examine facts dispassionately. In early 1991, the Sandia team prepared a report asserting that "evidence of decline used to justify systemwide reform is based on misinterpretations or misrepresentations of the data" (Carson, Huelskamp, and Woodall 1991b). Sandia researchers have since been muzzled. The Department of Education complained that the report was biased because "data shown are consistently supportive of a picture of U.S. education in a positive light." The report, Secretary of Energy James Watkins charged, "is a call for complacency at a time when just the opposite is required. The Department of Energy will not permit publication of the study as presently drafted" (Watkins 1991). It has still not been released.

School Bureaucracy

Conventional wisdom has an explanation for deteriorating education: schools spend inordinate resources on administration, teacher creativity is stifled by centralized control, and funds for educational improvement are diverted to bureaucracy. These claims, however, do not withstand scrutiny. In Los Angeles, typical of other California districts, schools spend 65 percent of their own resources (excluding state and federal programs) on "instruction," including salaries, benefits, and training of teachers and paraprofessional aides, textbooks, classroom equipment, and supplies. School counselors, psychologists, and nurses take 4 percent. Security and maintenance consumes 11 percent. School administrators (principals, deans, attendance officers, and school clerical personnel) account for 7 percent. Busing is 6 percent. Miscellaneous expenses (including librarians, library books, educational television) is another 3 percent. This leaves central administration (the "bureaucracy")—including superintendents, accounting, payroll and purchasing, property and liability insurance—with only 5 percent of the annual budget. Its peak in the last decade was 6.6 percent (Rasmussen 1992). Although category definitions may vary, national data also show schools spending approximately 61 percent of their budgets on instruction and 5 percent on administration (NCES 1992: table 153). Yet even these relatively modest bureaucratic expenditures are often characterized as wasteful, lending support to calls for decentralization, "school-site autonomy," or "school-based management."

Twenty years ago, New York gave parent- and teacher-dominated community boards finance and hiring power. The relaxation of controls spawned scandals like loans of school funds to employees; theft of school property; hiring of politicians' relatives as teacher aides; solicitation of bribes; ethnic-based hiring; and extortion of political contributions from teachers. Despite his commitment to school-site decision making, New York's former school superintendent Joseph Fernández expanded the central bureaucracy's role in monitoring finances and appointments.

Schools' bureaucratic rules (like centralized textbook selection, detailed curriculum requirements including the number of minutes spent on specified subjects, demands for attendance accounting and ethnic surveys, and restricted telephone or copying machine use) inhibit teacher creativity and should be reformed. But behind classroom doors, teachers are still the most autonomous and unsupervised of all professionals. Rarely acknowledged in school debates is that bureaucracy results from compromises made between spontaneity and creativity, on the one hand, and eliminating discrimination, corruption, and incompetence, on the other.

Decentralization cannot stimulate creativity without also risking corruption. Schools with flexibility to buy classroom computers without cumbersome bidding also have opportunities to solicit bribes. A principal who can select unconventionally qualified candidates, ignoring credentials and test scores, can also discriminate in hiring teachers or custodians.

Centralized school systems restrict flexibility, yet districts have mostly been freed of the corruption that once prevailed. Bureaucratic mazes have roots in earlier reforms to curb graft. After employees are caught in a kickback scheme, multiple signatures are required to make purchases. Years ago, hiring relatives was routine in school employment. To avoid this abuse, school hiring is now governed by cumbersome civil service rules. The most egregious exception is New York City's system of school building custodians. Reform will require more bureaucracy, not less.

If decentralizing school bureaucracies proceeds, there will be calls for re-centralization when inevitable scandals follow. The trade-off is most stark when academic standards become an issue. Bilingual teaching for non-English-speaking students is now national policy. School administrators train faculty and inspect schools to ensure that students get native-language instruction while gaining English fluency. Data clerks track student progress to assure that appropriate tests for transition to English are administered. Without central monitoring, some schools might ignore language-minority students. Indeed, prior to 1978 many did, until the courts ordered bilingual teaching.

Special education requires tests to identify handicapped children, as well as specialists who investigate whether special education is provided. Without watchful bureaucrats, some schools might ignore these expensive requirements, as many schools did before courts mandated these programs in 1974. Demands for less bureaucracy imply a willingness to risk that such a situation might reappear.

Bureaucrats review applications to determine which students get free lunch, which are eligible for subsidy, and which must pay full cost. It would be simpler, and more expensive, to provide meals to all. But few business or political leaders are prepared, despite antibureaucratic rhetoric, to commit additional tax funds to such administrative streamlining.

Simultaneous calls for greater school autonomy and higher national standards put two drives for education reform in direct conflict. One wants higher standards, the other less administration. Yet bureaucracy must enforce mandates unless we allow each school to decide if it will teach math, science, or American history. Indeed, higher standards demand more bureaucracy, not less. Many leaders say they want school-based decision making, but they don't really mean it. What they really seek is a chimera: all schools deciding to do the "right" thing, without administrative enforcement.

Bureaucracy stifles, and school reform should reduce inefficient bureaucratic structures performing redundant or useless tasks. But without willingness to abandon common standards and tolerate more corruption, calls for radical dismantling of school bureaucracies are mostly demagogic. It is no surprise that school-based management experiments have mostly floundered. The new incarnation, "charter schools," will likely meet a similar fate. Good school principals normally involve teachers in school planning. But when, in contemporary reforms, teachers get formal powers to run schools, they often balk at the time demands of administrative tasks. Good teachers, reformers have been discomfited to find, want to teach. They don't want to attend committee meetings, entertain textbook publishers, solicit low bids for supplies, or calculate race and ability distribution for classroom assignments.

Reform Proposal: School Choice

Led by aerospace executive Joseph Alibrandi and other business leaders, a group called EXCEL (Excellence through Choice in Education League) obtained sufficient signatures to put an education voucher initiative on California's spring 1994 ballot. Had this initiative passed, any student accepted by a private school would have received an annual tuition voucher worth about $2600 from the state treasury. The initiative would have saved the state money because for each voucher granted, state spending on public education would have been reduced by about $5200 a year. Despite this fiscal advantage, Alibrandi claimed that his sole objective was "to improve public schools" because, he argued, "educrats" would only respond to the threat of students leaving. "The thing we're trying to accomplish is to really change the incentives in the public system" (Alibrandi and Teasley 1992; Trombley 1991).

Supporters of both private school vouchers and public school choice argue that competition between schools can improve academic performance by forcing schools to be more responsive to their "clients." Using a free market model, they claim, if the security and employment of education producers (school staffs) depended on consumers' (parents') satisfaction, quality would improve. If parents could choose which school their child attends, quality schools would expand and multiply, while unselected schools that lose enrollment would be forced to attract new students or close.

But the model doesn't work in theory or in practice. It assumes that the "consumers" of education are the parents of schoolchildren. While this is partly true, the education consumer is also the nation's economic competitiveness, its democratic values, and its moral fiber. Parents are part of the citizenry who make decisions about effective schooling, but not the whole part.

Since, as public opinion surveys demonstrate, parents tend to be more satisfied than social critics think they should be with the public schools their children attend, few parents take advantage of the choice programs that do exist. In Minnesota, students have been permitted since 1987 to transfer to any district in the state, but only 1.8 percent of students opt to leave their home districts. Other states with choice programs have similar experiences. In Arkansas, less than one-half of 1 percent of students opt to transfer; in Massachusetts, this figure is one-tenth of 1 percent and in Iowa 1 percent (Carnegie 1992).

Parents may be satisfied with schools that still need to be improved, or the security of having children in the school closest to home may be more important to parents than educational advantages of schools farther away. If, as it seems, this is the case, even if market competition worked it might not improve schools.

Indeed, we have some experience with giving too much weight to consumer choice in education, without balancing that choice with the expertise of professional educators or the public at large. The well-documented deterioration of American public schools' academic standards in the early 1970s was propelled by a belief that schools should be responsive to clients—in that case, students—whose opinions about "relevant" curriculum were given extraordinary and undue weight in the design of American high schools. In response to the dramatic decline in test scores that consumer-driven education produced, professional educators and the public demanded that schools reestablish academic standards. Since professional educators and the public began demanding higher standards in the early 1980s, student test scores have consistently improved.

A related assumption of school choice promoters is that if parents had the right to choose their child's school, they would choose the school with the best academic program. One flaw in this assumption is that many parents with the opportunity to choose make their decisions on nonacademic grounds. In fact, this happens more than half the time in actual school choice systems, according to the Carnegie Foundation for the Advancement of Teaching. For example, Iowa's open enrollment application asks parents why they chose to leave their neighborhood school. Only 32 percent said "educational benefits," and another 10 percent referred to "school philosophy." The rest chose to move because of factors like the proximity of a school to a parent's job. In Arizona, only one-third of school choosers who were surveyed said that academic reasons motivated their selection. The others chose new schools because they liked the athletic program, proximity to parents' work or to day care, or the availability of a special education program. In a number of states where school choice is available, a common reason for switching to a smaller school is a better chance to make the varsity team (Carnegie 1992). These may be good reasons to switch schools. But a school that is chosen because it is located along a convenient commuting route or because it has less competition for the baseball team cannot be expected to improve academically because of its accountability to parents.

More troubling evidence comes from studies indicating that parents who choose to leave neighborhood schools do so for racial or status reasons, not academic ones. UCLA professor Amy Stuart Wells studied the St. Louis choice plan, where inner-city African American students were permitted to choose to attend county schools outside the city. She interviewed seventy-one students and parents and found that many of those who chose to leave their neighborhood schools did so in the belief that county schools were better because they were white and suburban, not because of any actual information about comparative academic programs. And she also found that many of those who chose *not* to leave did so because they felt more comfortable in their own community and within their own racial group, not because of a studied conclusion that their neighborhood schools were academically superior (Wells n.d.).

A free market assumes that consumers have full information and can distinguish between quality products and inferior ones. But in education, no matter how many pamphlets schools send home with children, parents' information will vary by their educational level, social class, and sophistication about schools. It will also depend on the validity of the information itself. A school's test scores, for example, may be high because it has more students from wealthier backgrounds, not because of effective teaching.

Relatively affluent Montclair, New Jersey, has a choice plan in which there are no neighborhood schools—all parents must list two choices from Montclair's eight elementary schools. The district is able to honor parent preferences 90 percent of the time, making adjustments only if space is unavailable or for racial balance. How do parents make these choices? Eighty-four percent of the parents with family income over $100,000 visit the schools, but only 53 percent of the parents with income under $50,000 do so. Seventy-four percent of the wealthier parents attend an informational program on the schools, but only 45 percent of the less wealthy parents do so. Seventy-six percent of the wealthier parents read written information sent home by the schools, but only 35 percent of the less wealthy parents do so (Carnegie 1992). The percentage of parents seeking out information would likely be lower in a less wealthy district.

In Minnesota, which has the longest existing statewide school choice program, a recent study found that parents who choose schools outside their districts have more education than the state population as a whole (Carnegie 1992). Milwaukee, Wisconsin, is the only city in the country that presently permits private schools to accept publicly funded vouchers. The private schools that participate in the program are not permitted to charge tuition in addition to the voucher. The program was designed to give the most at-risk inner-city students (families earning less than $22,000, or 1.75 percent of the poverty line for a family of three) an opportunity to have a private school education. Yet Professor John Witte of the University of Wisconsin, who has been studying the Milwaukee experiment, found that 52 percent of the mothers who used the vouchers for their children had some college education, compared to only 40 percent of all mothers in Milwaukee and 30 percent of all low-income mothers like themselves. For those who have used the vouchers to attend private schools, academic achievement is no better than for those who stayed behind (Witte n.d.).

The most widely publicized school choice program is that of District 4 in East Harlem, New York City. Like the Montclair program, all parents must choose—there are no neighborhood schools. For many years, choice advocates pointed to the East Harlem experience because reading scores went up after choice began. But now, with choice still in place, scores are in decline. When choice first began in 1972–1973, only 16 percent of District 4 students were reading at or above grade level, compared to 34 percent of all students citywide. In the late 1970s and 1980s, when all New York City students benefited from tightened standards and other curricular reforms, District 4 students seemed to gain the most. By 1987–1988, 63 percent of East Harlem students were at grade level, almost equal to the 65 percent of students at grade level citywide. But by 1991–1992, New York City scores had fallen, and District 4 scores had fallen even further: 46 percent of New York's students were at or above grade level, but only 38 percent of District 4 students were reading satisfactorily (Carnegie 1992).

When investigators from the Carnegie Foundation asked District 4 officials to explain their declining reading scores, the educators cited children who were runaways, physically or sexually abused, or from families with problems of drug and alcohol abuse (Carnegie 1992). These are certainly factors that impede District 4's ability to educate. But choice advocates can't have it both ways. If choice is not responsible for the decline in reading scores in the late 1980s, it may not be responsible for the earlier gain in reading scores either.

Parent choice plays a limited role today in many urban school systems. Specialized theme "magnet" schools, for example, give ambitious minority students a chance for integrated education and entice whites to stay in the city system. These are worthy goals, but they have little to do with the fantasy that the whip of competition will force schools to improve. In fact, "choice" schools, like magnet schools, may make neighborhood schools worse. Despite careful admissions restrictions, magnet programs attract the most highly motivated students, draining neighborhood schools of students and parents who could spur higher achievement levels. Controls cannot be subtle enough, for example, to prevent counselors from giving greater encouragement to middle-class magnet applicants than to poor students. While magnets have better academic records than neighborhood schools, this is because the motivated students they attract do well in any setting. Magnets provide no evidence for the free market idea that a need to be selected forces schools to improve. Analysis of student outcomes shows that magnet students generally do no better than neighborhood school students who applied to magnets but, because of space limitations, could not get in.

The possibility that choice, public or private, may increase race and class segregation if parents choose schools attended by children like their own is suggested by other nations' experiences.

- Since 1978, the Canadian province of British Columbia has subsidized private schools. Wealthier and better-educated parents took these subsidies, leaving public school students in a less advantaged milieu (Brown 1991; Erickson 1986).

- The French government has since 1959 paid the salaries of all teachers, public and private. Though France attempts to limit inequality by requiring comparable public and private class sizes, rich students are disproportionately enrolled in subsidized private schools, leaving immigrant students concentrated in the public system (Fowler 1991).

- Israel recently established alternative schools with differing philoso-
phies and curricula. They are academically superior to neighborhood
schools; parents who choose them are wealthier and more educated
(Goldring 1991). Choice schools offer islands of excellence to the rich
while Israel struggles to assimilate immigrants from North Africa and
Russia.

- Holland's choice system is eighty-five years old. The government pays
for buildings and teacher salaries for any school that parents establish;
two-thirds of all schools are privately run. School choice in Holland
has enabled "white flight" from Turkish and Moroccan neighborhood
schools. Recent Dutch studies show that Muslim students in segre-
gated classrooms do worse than those who are integrated. Meanwhile,
most Dutch parents choose schools based on the socioeconomic status
of students already enrolled, not on the school's academic performance
(James 1984; Louis and Van Velzen 1990).

- In Australia, government funding of private schools, begun in 1973,
has increased race and class segregation. There are no limits on extra
tuition that schools can charge and no restrictions on private school
admissions procedures. Most upper-middle-class Australian students
now attend government-supported private schools; public schools
have less status and lower academic standards (Goldring 1991).

- Scotland got school choice in 1982; parents can send children to public
schools outside their local district. Data reveal that 12 percent of
children whose parents are professionals choose to escape neighborhood schools, but only 5 percent of children whose parents are manual
workers do so. During the 1970s, Scotland had reformed public
secondary schools, making academic programs available to all, not just
to students attending elite academies. After mixing students from
social classes in comprehensive schools, academic achievement of
blue-collar students rose more rapidly than achievement of students
from professional families. Scotland's choice program reversed this
trend (Echols, McPherson, and Willms 1990).

There is little doubt that wealthier parents believe their children gain
advantage by attending schools with other privileged children. But the
consequence of honoring their option to choose is diminished opportunity for less advantaged children. Historically, however, we have
honored such choices. White middle-class parents once moved to homogeneous suburbs to seek "better" schools. Today this method of exercis-
ing school choice is less available. Urban areas, with their impoverished
minority populations, are now too large to permit easy escape within
commuting distance of central cities. The incorporation of professionals
into upper income strata has expanded elite private school options,
previously reserved for the hereditary or corporate elite. As a result, this

class's desire to restore the segregation it once enjoyed has been transformed into a demand for school choice. Cloaked in a faulty assessment of schools' academic decline, the demand for choice is presented as a necessity for broad school reform to benefit all children.

Reforms That Could Work

If the foregoing is true—that increasing returns to education are deceptive and we have a skills surplus rather than a shortage; that expanded educational resources since 1965 have not been dedicated primarily to academic improvement; that public schools' academic achievement has risen nonetheless; that bureaucracy is not stifling American education; and that the most popular contemporary reforms (decentralization and choice) address the wrong problems and could do great damage—then it is hard to avoid an iconoclastic conclusion: the public school system is mostly on the right track and the best way to improve its results, especially for minority children, is to pour more money into it.

An increase in resources is not the only improvement needed. Better systems for hiring and evaluating principals and improved teacher training—for undergraduates as well as teachers already on the job— could contribute to better academic achievement. So too would a satisfactory method of removing poor teachers from the profession. But design of this reform is difficult; results produced by individual teachers are hard to measure statistically, so sustaining the removal of poor teachers through civil service or union procedures is improbable unless child abuse or other criminal behavior is present. Also, within rather broad curriculum guidelines, teachers have great freedom to design programs. There is no other profession where possibilities for peer or adult client review are so limited.

Most teachers are competent, as the performance of our schools indicates. We could not claim improved outcomes without a teaching force which, on the whole, is dedicated, prepared, and increasingly creative. This is why, while weeding out uninspired teachers would be worthwhile, the most useful reform of public education remains more money. Here is how more resources could most productively be spent:

- *A comprehensive national prenatal health program.* It is a shibboleth of the education establishment, overcompensating for generations of contempt for poor and minority children, that all children can succeed if only their teachers communicate high expectations. This has an element of truth but also an element of denial. Low-birthweight babies or infants addicted to drugs, nicotine, or alcohol before birth cannot mature into successful students to the extent that healthy babies can. Giving all babies a healthy start in life would contribute to improved academic outcomes.

- *Full funding of Head Start.* Preschool children exposed to books, manipulative toys, and literate adults are better prepared to succeed than those who are not so exposed. Quality school experiences cannot fully compensate for deprivation in preschool years. Yet Head Start funding is sufficient to enroll only 30 percent of eligible low-income children. While Head Start children's test scores surpass those of nonenrolled children in grades 1 through 3, the advantage seems to be lost by the fourth grade. While further investigation is needed to understand this loss, other evidence supports full funding. Head Start graduates are less frequently retained in grade, have better school attendance, lower dropout rates, higher employment rates, fewer criminal arrests, and less welfare dependency than those of similar backgrounds without benefit of a preschool program (Rasell and Appelbaum 1992).

- *School funding equalization.* In states that have not equalized funding between rich and poor districts, students continue to attend dilapidated schools without adequately paid teachers or necessary equipment. As Jonathan Kozol (1992) has pointed out, if money made no difference in education, wealthy districts would not be so determined to hoard it.

- *Improved teacher salaries.* The highest-achieving college students don't always make the best teachers, but teachers are too often recruited from among college graduates whose grades or ambitions are not high enough to win places in more remunerative professions. Higher teacher salaries will improve the competitive position of education vis-à-vis law, accounting, engineering, medicine, and nursing. To attract good teachers, salaries need not be higher than in other professions, but improving relative teacher pay will improve schools' ability to attract more highly qualified graduates.

Despite the importance of winning more funds for teacher salary increases, the role of some teachers' union leaders in education debates has been curious. Each Sunday a paid *New York Times* advertisement by American Federation of Teachers president Albert Shanker analyzes American education, often denouncing school performance and contrasting the illiteracy of American youths with academic achievements of other nations' children. If a teachers' union goal is to mobilize support for public education and its employees, denunciation of school performance is a questionable strategy. The public is more likely to increase tax support for systems that perform well than for those that fail. Campaigns to highlight teachers' extraordinary accomplishment—the advance of universal education in a social system hostile to economic equality—could do more to mobilize opinion on teachers' behalf. Nonetheless, teachers' unions around the country follow Shanker's lead, mounting attacks on their own school systems in the vain hope that the public will blame only administrators, and not teachers, for schools' purported failures.

- *Reduction of class size to fifteen or less.* Educational research shows that class size reduction has little effect if classes remain so large that teaching is mostly to large groups. Reductions of class size to fifteen or less, on the other hand, can have academic results. This is the most expensive school reform imaginable (reducing class size from twenty-four to fifteen doubles the marginal costs of education), and it should perhaps be restricted to schools with the most disadvantaged students. But if we want to close the gap between minority and white students more quickly, lowering class size could be effective.

- *Improved apprenticeship and workplace training.* Schools presently send students with adequate numeric and literacy skills into the workforce. But their work habits may not be adequate, and curricular reforms should, therefore, emphasize team building and cooperative skills. But schools cannot be expected to provide the kind of practical technical training that Ford offers to Mexican dropouts in Chihuahua. The Clinton administration may propose requiring business to fund worker training, with the further mandate that training funds be expended on frontline as well as supervisory workers. Ongoing workplace training is needed to preserve the fruits of improved schooling.

The prevailing consensus that schools need radical systemic reform is at odds with economic and academic data. But it derives support from a political culture surviving from the Reagan era—a suspicion of all public institutions and the conviction that if public bureaucracy is responsible, performance must be deficient. The school failure myth also derives support from the nation's corporate leadership, anxious to find a scapegoat for high unemployment, racial division, and income inequality. Blaming the schools avoids confronting business's deindustrialization strategies, failure to invest in high-wage jobs, and shortsighted trade policies. Faulting public education also excuses business's desire to reduce tax support of schools. The myth of school failure derives support from liberals and minority group activists who too easily assume that youth unemployment must stem from lack of preparation, not lack of decent jobs. And the myth derives support from the right's privatization agenda; it is easier to mobilize support for private school subsidies if belief in public school failure gains currency—thus, the suppression of Sandia National Laboratories' school performance report because it sent a message of "complacency."

Finally, the school failure myth is reinforced by experiences of many in the professional middle class who have their own anecdotes about ill-prepared (usually minority-group) high school graduates. In some cases, the stories suffer from an idealized memory of how much better prepared graduates once were—discounting realities that not only did fewer students graduate in past decades, but many graduates had "general" or "vocational" diplomas in which carpentry or metal shop, not algebra, dominated the curriculum. Today all graduates are in academic programs, both because our expectations of universal education have expanded and because jobs no longer exist for which vocational programs once trained.

There are still too many dropouts and too many high school graduates who can't read or compute at appropriate levels. Almost invariably, however, these are students without a consistent school experience, who have moved frequently, have no stable home support, or come from environments dominated by violence, drugs, or alcohol. School reforms, no matter how creative, cannot substitute for a full employment program with jobs at good wages in minority communities.

Schools have done less well in developing work-world disciplinary habits in students from social strata which, in earlier generations, dropped out. As the Commission on the Skills of the American Workforce put it, while few businesses find a lack of academic skills in entry-level workers, "the primary concern of more than 80 percent of employers was finding workers with a good work ethic and appropriate social behavior—'reliable,' 'a good attitude,' 'a pleasant appearance,' 'a good personality'" (NCEE 1990). Conventional critiques of school performance, however, have little to say about this problem, nor do popular systemic solutions to education's alleged academic failures address it.

We have no reason to be complacent about schools' performance. That school output may be adequate for industrial needs does not suggest that a more literate and mathematically sophisticated workforce would not be even more productive. Industry should invest more in workplace training, but training can be more effective if workers bring greater literacy and numeric skills to their jobs. Academic achievement is steadily improving, but it is still too low. No democratic society should tolerate adults who cannot interpret bus schedules or newspaper articles. When job applicants can't pass a seventh-grade-level employment exam, we have a problem, even if the promise of jobs for those who pass is a false one.

But when schools are doing better than ever before, the best way to encourage continued improvement may not be a concerted attack on school governance and organization. More effective would be praise for accomplishment, provision of additional resources to programs whose results justify support, and reforms on the margin to correct programs and curricula shown to be ineffective. Unfortunately, the crusade for school reform eclipses the true causes of youth unemployment and declining wages for those who graduate from high school but do not proceed to college. Industrial, trade reform, and labor market policies hold more promise for income growth than does school reform.

References

ACE (American Council on Education). 1993. *Minorities in Higher Education, 1992, Seventh Annual Status Report*. Washington, D.C.: The Council.

Akst, Daniel. 1991. "Show and Tell? Business Can Bring Reform," *Los Angeles Times*, January 29.

Alibrandi, Joseph, and Kevin Teasley. 1992. "Power to the Parents!" *Los Angeles Times*, March 2.

Bartlett, Larry J. 1992. "The Cost of FAPE: Can LRE Make a Difference?" EDLAW Briefing Paper. Cincinnati.

Blinder, Alan. 1992. "Remarks by Alan Blinder, Professor of Economics, Princeton University, to the Economic Conference, Little Rock, Arkansas." Federal News Service, December 14.

Brown, Frank. 1991. "Dutch Experience with School Choice: Implications for American Education." Chapel Hill: University of North Carolina at Chapel Hill. Photocopy.

Business Week. 1992. "How Americans Grade the School System," September 14.

Carnegie Foundation for the Advancement of Teaching. 1992. *School Choice*. Princeton, N.J.: The Foundation.

Carson, C.C., R.M. Huelskamp, and T.D. Woodall. 1991a. "Perspectives on Education in America. Annotated Briefing." Albuquerque, N.M.: Systems Analysis Department, Sandia National Laboratories, May 10. Draft.

———. 1991b. *Perspectives on Education in America*. Albuquerque, N.M.: Systems Analysis Department, Sandia National Laboratories, September 24.

College Board. 1974. *College Bound Seniors, 1971–72*. Princeton, N.J.: College Entrance Examination Board.

DeParle, Jason. 1993. "Social Investment Programs: Comparing the Past with the Promised Payoff," *New York Times*, March 3.

Echols, Frank, Andrew McPherson, and J. Douglas Willms. 1990. "Parental Choice in Scotland," *Journal of Education Policy*, Paper 372293.

Erickson, D.A. 1986. "Choice and Private Schools: Dynamics of Supply and Demand." In *Private Education: Studies in Choice and Public Policy*, edited by Daniel C. Levy. New York: Oxford University Press.

ETS (Educational Testing Service). 1975. *College Bound Seniors, 1975–76*. Princeton, N.J.: College Entrance Examination Board.

———. 1986. *California Report, College Bound Seniors, 1986 Profile of SAT and Achievement Test Takers*. Princeton, N.J.: College Entrance Examination Board.

———. 1990. *America's Challenge, Accelerating Academic Achievement, A Summary of Findings from 20 Years of NAEP*. Washington, D.C.: Office of Educational Research and Improvement, U.S. Department of Education.

———. 1992a. *National Report, College Bound Seniors, 1992 Profile of SAT and Achievement Test Takers*. Princeton, N.J.: College Entrance Examination Board.

———. 1992b. *California Report, College Bound Seniors, 1992 Profile of SAT and Achievement Test Takers*. Princeton, N.J.: College Entrance Examination Board.

Fairbank, Bregman, and Maulin. 1990. "National Alliance of Business Work Force Survey." Santa Monica, Calif.: Fairbank, Bregman and Maulin, October 26.

Fowler, Frances C. 1991. "One Approach to a Pluralist Dilemma: Private School Aid Policy in France, 1959–1985." Paper presented at the Annual Meeting of the American Educational Research Association, April 3.

Goldring, Ellen B. 1991. "Parents' Motives for Choosing a Privatized Public School System: An Israeli Example," *Educational Policy* 5:4 (December).

Greene, Jay. 1990. "63% of L.A. Employers Unhappy with Quality of Entry-level Workers," *Los Angeles Daily News*, October 30.

Hecker, Daniel E. 1992. "Reconciling Conflicting Data on Jobs for College Graduates," *Monthly Labor Review*, July.

IAU (Independent Analysis Unit). 1992. *Enrollment of LAUSD Seniors in California Public Colleges, 1986–1990*. Los Angeles: IAU, Los Angeles Unified School District, March 16.

James, Estelle. 1984. "Benefits and Costs of Privatized Public Services: Lessons from the Dutch Educational System," *Comparative Education Review* 28:4.

Johnston, William B., and Arnold H. Packer. 1987. *Workforce 2000: Work and Workers for the 21st Century*. Indianapolis, Ind.: Hudson Institute.

Koretz, Daniel, with Elizabeth Lewis and Lenore DeSilets. 1990. *Trends in the Postsecondary Enrollment of Minorities*. Santa Monica, Calif.: Rand Corporation.

Kozol, Jonathan. 1992. *Savage Inequalities: Children in America's Schools*. New York: Harper Perennial.

Louis, Karen Seashore, and Boudewijn A.M. Van Velzen. 1990. "A Look at Choice in the Netherlands," *Educational Leadership*, December 1990/January 1991.

Lustig, Nora. 1992. *Mexico: The Remaking of an Economy*. Washington, D.C.: Brookings Institution.

Marshall, Ray, and Marc Tucker. 1992. *Thinking for a Living*. Washington, D.C.: Basic Books.

Mishel, Lawrence, and Jared Bernstein. 1992. *The State of Working America, 1992–93*. Washington, D.C.: Economic Policy Institute.

Mishel, Lawrence, and Ruy A. Teixeira. 1990. *The Myth of the Coming Labor Shortage*. Washington, D.C.: Economic Policy Institute.

NAB (National Alliance of Business). 1990. "News Release: NAB Poll: LA Employers Not Satisfied with New Workers." Washington, D.C.: NAB, October 29.

NCEE (National Center on Education and the Economy). 1990. *America's Choice: High Skills or Low Wages!* Rochester, N.Y.: NCEE.

NCES (National Center for Education Statistics). 1991. *The Condition of Education, 1991, Vol. 1, Elementary and Secondary Education*. Washington, D.C.: NCES, U.S. Department of Education.

———. 1992. *Digest of Educational Statistics: October, 1992*. Washington, D.C.: NCES, U.S. Department of Education.

Pear, Robert. 1992. "Ranks of U.S. Poor Reach 35.7 Million, the Most Since '64," *New York Times*, September 4.

Rasell, M. Edith, and Eileen Appelbaum. 1992. *Investment in Learning: An Assessment of the Economic Return*. Washington, D.C.: "Investment 21."

Rasmussen, Roger. 1992. "LAUSD Expenditures Compared to Other Districts." Los Angeles: Independent Analysis Unit, Los Angeles Unified School District, July 31.

Risen, James. 1992. "Number of Poor in America Hits a 27 Year High," *Los Angeles Times*, September 4.

Schmidt, Benno C., Jr. 1992. "Educational Innovation for Profit," *Wall Street Journal*, June 5.

Sculley, John. 1992. "Remarks of John Sculley, Chairman and CEO, Apple Computer, to the Economic Conference, Little Rock Arkansas." Federal News Service, December 14.

Shaiken, Harley, with Stephen Herzenberg. 1987. *Automation and Global Production: Automobile Engine Production in Mexico, the United States, and Canada.* Monograph Series, no. 26. La Jolla: Center for U.S.-Mexican Studies, University of California, San Diego.

Shanker, Albert. 1993. "Ninety-two Hours," *New Republic*, February 15.

Silvestri, George, and John Lukasiewicz. 1989. "Projections of Occupational Employment, 1988–2000," *Monthly Labor Review*, November.

Slavin, Robert E., Nancy L. Karweit, and Barbara A. Wasik. 1992. "Preventing Early School Failure: What Works?" *Educational Leadership* 50:4 (December 1992/January 1993).

Trombley, William. 1991. "Major Fight Looms over Initiative on Vouchers," *Los Angeles Times*, December 15.

U.S. Bureau of the Census. 1982. *Preliminary Estimates of the Population of the United States, by Age, Sex and Race, 1970–1981.* Publication P25-917. Washington, D.C: U.S. Government Printing Office.

———. 1992a. *Statistical Abstract of the United States: 1992.* 112th ed. Washington, D.C: U.S. Government Printing Office.

———. 1992b. *Population Projections.* Publication P25-1092. Washington, D.C: U.S. Government Printing Office.

Watkins, James D. 1991. Letter to *The Albuquerque Journal*, September 30. Washington, D.C.: Office of the Secretary, U.S. Department of Energy.

Weintraub, Daniel M. 1991. "Business Gives Public Schools a Failing Grade," *Los Angeles Times*, January 24.

Wells, Amy Stuart. n.d. "The Sociology of School Choice: Maximizing and Satisficing in the Educational Marketplace." In *Choice—What Role in American Education?* edited by M. Edith Rasell and Richard Rothstein. Washington, D.C.: Economic Policy Institute, forthcoming.

Witte, John. n.d. "The Milwaukee Parental Choice Program." In *Choice—What Role in American Education?* edited by M. Edith Rasell and Richard Rothstein. Washington, D.C.: Economic Policy Institute, forthcoming.

Commentary

Politics, Education, and Immigrant Children in New York City: Is Nothing Sacred?

Karen Shaw

Joseph Fernández, while chancellor of New York City's public school system, published a book, *Tales Out of School*, part memoir and part educational blueprint. In one passage he noted:

> I have run the fourth-largest school system in America—Dade County, Florida, which is greater Miami—and am now running the largest, New York City, with almost a million students and a thousand schools. (I don't expect to be running it much longer because you can't separate politics and education in America and the politics in New York City are almost certain to bring me down sooner or later. I say that without rancor. . . . If you make waves in New York, you learn not to lean back in your chair) (Fernández 1993: 13).

As it turned out, Fernández's departure came sooner, not later. Shortly after publication of his book, the governors of the school system, a seven-member Board of Education, voted to terminate his contract.

Why? In his book, Fernández offered possible explanations for the anticipated action by the board. He had balked at board members' attempts to micromanage his office and the school system. He found the board factionalized, too contentious to carry out its mission to advise on policies, programs, and financing for New York's vast and complex system. Further, for months Fernández had fought with numerous critics, both board members and others, to introduce into the schools a "rainbow curriculum," a grade-by-grade guide on diversity. Bitter debates regarding the public schools' obligation to sexually active youths in the era of AIDS also contributed to his ouster. Fernández and his allies wanted the schools to take an active, vigorous role in AIDS education and prevention, including distributing condoms. Opponents, especially in the neighborhoods, felt that this role intruded on the authority of parents and religious figures. Others of his critics objected to discussing new roles for a system seen as failing in its primary mission. After months of intense public meetings on these issues, the board voted 4 to 3 to dismiss the chancellor.

Would that that had been all—just professional disagreements over educational roles and objectives. However, the "politics" that Fernández had alluded to provided less obvious but perhaps equally influential reasons for his dismissal. Sources of these political influences are found throughout the system. Thirty-two local districts, which oversee eleven hundred neighborhood schools, are governed by elected local boards. Each one of them hires a district superintendent, a professional charged with managing the individual schools within the district's borders. Staff of the local schools relate to the local board and superintendent. The chancellor manages a central bureaucracy of some thirty-five hundred employees (no one has an accurate count) who aid him in setting and enforcing pedagogical standards, operating the secondary schools, complying with state and federal mandates, and collecting statistics, among other tasks. In consultation with the mayor, the chancellor and the board propose an annual budget, currently around $8.5 billion, which becomes part of the executive budget but is not managed by mayoral staff.

Members of the central Board of Education are appointed. The mayor designates two, and the five respective borough presidents, elected officials who manage certain funds and services for constituents in the boroughs, appoint one each. When this board was established decades ago, members were prominent citizens, expected to act solely for the benefit of the students. However, political associations have emerged as equally important over the past years.

The governor, members of education-related committees in the state Assembly and Senate, and the city's representatives on the city council and in the state legislature have roles to play. Union executives, watchdog civic groups, media executives, and educational reformers play parts as well. The system is a complicated mix of roles and authorities, beset with conflicting opinions and agendas. Those individuals involved must deal with unprecedented situations. Thousands of sincere, well-intentioned professionals are committed to the best possible education for the million mostly poor or working-class, mostly minority students. There are many others, though, who are ambitious strivers, seekers or donors of patronage, or partisans who find opportunities to exploit the system for personal ends. The interplay is abrasive, relentless, and exaggerated, bringing to mind the tournament jousting scenes in the film *Ivanhoe*. It becomes hard to separate substance from theater and posing from truth, since one actor's position may be a genuine policy initiative or a means to unhorse a foe.

As one example, during Mr. Fernández's tenure, the dynamics of mayoral politics influenced the central board. Then-mayor David Dinkins, up for reelection, had two loyal appointees on the board and a personal ally as board president. Two borough presidents, both with mayoral ambitions of their own, had deferred to Dinkins's candidacy; their two appointees were expected to follow this lead (although one did not). Three other board members were wooed by both Mayor Dinkins and then-challenger (now mayor) Rudolph Giuliani. So, were the contests with Fernández really about educational strategies to help students? Or were they reflections of struggles to build coalitions that would reelect a sitting mayor or elect his rival?

Mayoral politics have continued. A bumpy search process to replace Fernández, marked by debates on the ethnicity of a new chancellor, eventually yielded two outstanding candidates. When then-mayor Dinkins, anxious to strengthen mayoral influence over board decisions, endorsed one candidate, the board quickly selected the other one — Ramón Cortines, former head of San Francisco's school system. Mayor Giuliani, elected on pledges to eliminate a multi-billion-dollar deficit by cutting services, has targeted the public school budget for major cuts on advice from his aides, who assert that only $2,500 of the $7,000 spent per student per year actually reaches the classroom and the students. As of this writing, the mayor, the board, the chancellor, the unions, and the city council are arguing over budget cuts in the millions of dollars. Chancellor Cortines has already resigned once, but he was persuaded to stay by a coalition of key players. Two borough presidents are on the verge of announcing their candidacies for mayor, an election three years hence. The chancellor, two borough presidents, and an adviser to the mayor have all offered plans to restructure the entire education system, with some advocating the elimination of the board.

At the grassroots level, politics within the schools, boards, and community organizations within the thirty-two local districts are just as intense in their way as are those at the top. Good work is being done at the district levels, particularly in the six districts that observers have rated as outstanding. The districts bring multiple viewpoints and experiences to the policy discussions at the central level. Staff and parents of the schools are often the first to see the results of changing demographics and the emerging needs of students. Creative superintendents and teachers have designed model programs such as small-scale intensive schools with innovative curricula, which the chancellor later recommended for systemwide adoption.[1] And Chancellor Cortines has built on the work of his predecessors to implement school-based management as broadly as possible.

Yet some of the rawest abuses have occurred at the local district level. Jobs in the schools—at all levels—are valuable income in the city's neighborhoods, and the appointment power has been abused. Contracts and program budgets are lucrative and tempting. These become important sources of patronage for political clubs and elected officials who can only manipulate public funds in areas with little private investment. Consequently, some districts have been characterized as "corrupt little fiefdoms, complete with cronyism and nepotism, and a depressing sense of mismanagement," with nearly 30 percent "under investigation for everything from selling drugs to selling jobs" (Fernández 1993: 188–89). The chancellors have intervened against corruption wherever and however their legal authority permits, but the local districts still have considerable discretion.

From this description it is clear that the New York City school system is a highly politicized environment, with struggles over policies, resources, contracts, and control occurring at many points. The system is strife-ridden and subject to abrupt changes in direction as managers replace one another at various levels. Local initiatives contend with a resistant bureaucracy. Conflicting ideas prevent agreement on approaches in a system so full of needs and demands that solutions are imperative.

Immigrant children are certainly part of the picture. All levels are recognizing their presence. Some 100,000 immigrant students have been in the city less than three years,[2] and an estimated 40,000 immigrant youngsters, from every nation, enter the public schools each year.[3] The rate of admissions will hold steady or rise as long as current immigration procedures remain unchanged. Impacts of the immigrant students vary by district. Several districts instruct children speaking dozens of primary languages, and others, magnets for a single nationality, are severely overburdened and overcrowded. Formerly underutilized city schools are now full of immigrant newcomers. All of the affected schools need far more resources and trained staff than they now have.

The needs of immigrant children in New York City schools echo those described by several authors in this book. Thousands of refugee

---

[1] See Fliegel 1993. This book describes the work that creative teachers and a district superintendent did for poor children in one district and their battles with the central bureaucracy, which stifled many efforts.

[2] Department of City Planning 1992: 162. This report covers demographic changes found through analyses of the 1990 census; it is very useful for research on New York City.

[3] Author interview with David Jaffee, aide to New York State Senator John Marchi, August 1994. The bicameral state legislature will review and decide on the restructuring plans for the city's schools.

children from Southeast Asia, Eastern Europe, and Central America (including persecuted indigenous youths from Mexico and Central America) attend New York City schools, and their psychosocial profiles fit those observed by Padilla and Durán (this volume). Prior exposure to political violence has marked them in ways that Suárez-Orozco (1989) has discussed. Too, some schools, most often in desolate neighborhoods, generate the climate of fear which these authors mention, with immigrant students subjected to gang intimidation, interracial tensions, and physical violence. And in encouraging environments, immigrant children here also become high achievers; this year, Asian students— from immigrant, refugee, and native-born families—scored higher in math and reading than did African American and Hispanic children.

Would that advocates for the education of immigrant children could tell political figures "Hands Off!" and place the children's needs in the hands of professionals. Although that is not possible, there are ways in which advocates can influence decisions and programs. Advocates should press government officials and educational managers to create structures offering information about immigration and immigrant children. Supporters can then move within these structures, defining needs, promoting and evaluating programs and services, informing policy makers, and keeping the needs of the children in the foreground.

Persistence is required since these efforts seesaw. Even when agreement is reached to create such structures, new political figures or opinions can change them. In New York, for example, the state legislature in 1987 created a Task Force on New Americans, which examined legislation and policies on immigration at the state level. When the founding chairman was replaced in 1992, his successor phased out the office. In 1989, Chancellor Richard Green established a Chancellor's Committee on Immigrant Affairs to review the education system's procedures regarding immigrant children. The committee was continued by Chancellor Fernández, but it faltered as he became caught up in other issues.

Advocates should identify decision makers in educational systems, acknowledging the influence of various actors, and track the implementation of decisions. Who makes a decision? Who interprets it and how? Who obeys it? Conversely, how is a decision eroded, ignored, or blocked as it moves throughout a system? In New York City, a decision made by the chancellor is influenced by hundreds of other actors, and advocates should be watchful that positive efforts are not derailed.

Advocates need to be reliable experts for political actors and decision makers who have roles in the education system. Once beneficial plans are designed by advocates, all of these figures should hear the same information, as a way of guaranteeing universal consideration and eventual adoption of some of the best ideas.

As Richard Rothstein has suggested, education advocates should not be so quick to agree that public schools are failing. His thoughtful analysis recommends sifting actual accomplishments from too encompassing indictments. The questions stimulated by his chapter should be answered by political actors drafting reform proposals. Who is the target for educational reform—the school system or the business community, which uses the schools as a scapegoat for its failures? If educational achievement is not crucial for workers in business settings, why does discrimination in the workplace exist? If on-the-job training programs produce fine results for the Ford Motor Company in Mexico, why aren't similar programs in place in areas where this country's needy youths would relish them? Are so many youths who see no future in the workplace correct, or do these youths fail to see the potential that other more successful students sense? Are we accustomed to thinking that a certain percentage of students in any school system will always fail or be shortchanged? Is there a threshold between those who succeed and those who are lost?

The economic future of many major cities and their nearby suburbs—in California, Texas, Illinois, Florida, New York, and other states—is tied to the education of native-born and immigrant children. In New York City, researchers are finding that, given the current economy, newly arriving immigrant adults start out earning and continue to earn substantially less than their native-born counterparts with equivalent credentials. Immigrant workers no longer reach income parity, and immigrant families may live in impoverished circumstances for some time, needing public services. However, immigrant children who are schooled with native-born children can achieve and demand income parity. Education is still a means to escape or avoid poverty. The potential that education offers should shame anyone, anywhere, who exploits the schools for lesser aims.

References

Department of City Planning. 1992. *The Newest New Yorkers*. New York: Department of City Planning, City of New York.

Fernández, Joseph. 1993. *Tales Out of School*. Boston: Little, Brown and Co.

Fliegel, Seymour. 1993. *Miracle in East Harlem*. New York: Manhattan Institute.

Suárez-Orozco, Marcelo. 1989. *Central American Refugees and U.S. High Schools: A Psychosocial Study of Motivation and Achievement*. Stanford, Calif.: Stanford University Press.

Contributors

Wayne A. Cornelius is Professor of Political Science and Gildred Professor of U.S.-Mexican Relations at the University of California, San Diego. He was founding Director (1979–1994) of the Center for U.S.-Mexican Studies at UCSD and continues to serve as the Center's Director of Studies and Programs. He received his Ph.D. from Stanford University, and for eight years was a member of the Political Science faculty at the Massachusetts Institute of Technology. Since 1975 he has directed six major studies of Mexican migration to the United States, involving fieldwork in Mexican sending communities as well as receiving cities in California and Illinois. He is co-chair of the University of California's all-campus Comparative Immigration and Integration Research Program. His most recent book is *Controlling Immigration: A Global Perspective* (coeditor and coauthor). He is a frequent commentator on immigration issues for the *Los Angeles Times* and other major newspapers in the United States and Mexico. His current research includes a comparative study of the utilization of immigrant labor in San Diego County and two Japanese cities.

David Durán is a doctoral student in the Counseling Psychology Program at Stanford University. He is interested in minority mental health services and treatment interventions for Latinos.

Margaret A. Gibson, a member of the faculty at the University of California, Santa Cruz, is an educational anthropologist. Her research has focused on explaining the variability in immigrant and minority students' school achievements. In her fieldwork she has given particular attention to ways in which ethnicity, gender, and social class interact to shape students' school-adaptation patterns. In addition to ongoing fieldwork in a multiethnic California high school, Gibson has conducted field research in the U.S. Virgin Islands and Papua New Guinea. Her major publications include *Accommodation without Assimilation: Sikh*

Immigrants in an American High School and *Minority Status and Schooling: A Comparative Study of Immigrant and Involuntary Minorities,* coedited with John Ogbu.

Kenji Ima is Professor of Sociology at San Diego State University. He received his Ph.D. from Northwestern University. His work focuses on Asian Americans regarding schooling, child abuse, delinquency, and the professional development and adjustment of refugees. Among his most recent publications is *Myth or Reality: Adaptive Strategies of Asian Americans in California* (with Li-Rong Cheng and Henry Trueba). A forthcoming book, *Between Two Worlds: Southeast Asian Refugee Youth in America* (with Rubén G. Rumbaut) reviews the schooling progress of Southeast Asian refugee youth over a decade of research. Besides his professional work, he is involved locally, California-wide, and nationally in organizations that emphasize policy issues affecting Asian American youth.

Laurie Olsen is Co-Director of California Tomorrow, a nonprofit organization committed to making racial and ethnic diversity work in California. She also directs three California Tomorrow projects: the Education for a Diverse Society project, the Curriculum for a Diverse Society project, and a demonstration project in secondary immigrant education. Ms. Olsen is author of *Crossing the Schoolhouse Border: Immigrant Students and the California Schools; Bridges: Promising Programs in Immigrant Education;* and *Embracing Diversity: Voices from the Classroom;* as well as numerous articles on immigrant education and diversity and equity issues in public schooling. She is a nationally known speaker and consultant on immigrant education and past chair of the National Coalition of Advocates for Students.

Amado M. Padilla is Professor of Education at Stanford University. He received his Ph.D. in experimental psychology from the University of New Mexico. Prior to his appointment at Stanford, he was Professor of Psychology at UCLA and Director of the Spanish Speaking Mental Health Research Center. Currently he is chairperson of the Graduate Training Program in Language, Literacy, and Culture. He has published numerous books, articles, and chapters on Latinos. He is also the founding editor of the *Hispanic Journal of Behavioral Sciences,* which has appeared quarterly for the past fifteen years.

Alejandro Portes is John Dewey Professor of Sociology and International Relations and chair of the Department of Sociology at Johns Hopkins University. He is coauthor (with Rubén G. Rumbaut) of *Immigrant America: A Portrait,* and (with Alex Stepick) of *City on the Edge: The Transformation of Miami.* He has also recently edited *The Economic Sociology of Immigration: Essays on Networks, Ethnicity, and Entrepreneurship,* and a special issue of the *International Migration Review* on "the new second generation."

Richard Rothstein is a research associate of the Economic Policy Institute, specializing in trade, labor, and educational policy. He writes a biweekly newspaper column on economic and social policy issues for the *L.A. Weekly*, the *Sacramento Bee*, and *La Opinión*. His articles also appear in *The American Prospect*, *Dissent*, and other social policy journals. He is the author of *Setting the Standard*, an analysis of the role of labor standards in U.S. international economic policy, and of *Keeping Jobs in Fashion*, a study of international trade in the apparel industry. From 1988 to 1992, he was a program analyst for the Los Angeles City Board of Education, where he studied shared decision making and school-based management, effective elementary education, and budgetary and financial problems.

Rubén G. Rumbaut is Professor of Sociology at Michigan State University. He received his Ph.D. from Brandeis University in 1978 and taught at the University of California, San Diego and San Diego State University from 1978 to 1993. He is the coauthor of *Immigrant America: A Portrait*, with Alejandro Portes; Portes and Rumbaut are now conducting a comparative longitudinal study of over 5,200 children of immigrants in the San Diego and Miami metropolitan areas. Rumbaut has published widely on Asian and Latin American immigrants in the United States, particularly on refugees from Vietnam, Laos, and Cambodia, and is finishing a book, *Between Two Worlds: Southeast Asian Refugee Youth in America* (with Kenji Ima), which is based on a decade of research on the topic. He is coeditor of *Origins and Destinies: Immigration, Race, and Ethnicity*, and currently serves as consulting editor of the *American Journal of Sociology*, as founding chair of the Section on International Migration of the American Sociological Association, and as a member of research initiatives on immigration issues of the National Academy of Sciences and the Social Science Research Council.

Karen Shaw, a political scientist and writer, specializes in immigration and refugee issues. She is the author of numerous articles on immigration and human services, most recently, "Neighborhood-based Immigration Services in New York City," in *In Defense of the Alien*, published in 1993 by the Center for Migration Studies. Dr. Shaw is currently the Associate Director of Videoteca del Sur, working with Latin American and Caribbean filmmakers.

Carola E. Suárez-Orozco completed her Psychology Clinical Internship in the Department of Psychiatry at the University of California, San Diego, and is now a research associate in the Department of Human Development at Harvard University. She is the author of many scholarly publications, including "Hispanic Cultural Psychology: Implications for

Education Theory and Research." Her book *Latino Cultural Psychology* (coauthored with Marcelo M. Suárez-Orozco) is currently in press.

Marcelo M. Suárez-Orozco is Professor of Human Development at Harvard University. Prior to his appointment at Harvard, Dr. Suárez-Orozco was a faculty member in the Department of Anthropology, University of California, San Diego, and a fellow of the Center for Advanced Study in the Behavioral Sciences, Stanford (1992–1993). Professor Suárez-Orozco is the author of many books and articles in the fields of psychological anthropology and anthropology of education. His publications include *Central American Refugees and U.S. High Schools: A Psychosocial Study of Motivation and Achievement*, and "Migration, Minority Status and Education: European Dilemmas and Responses in the 1990s" (*Anthropology and Education Quarterly* 22:2).

Mia Tuan is a doctoral student at the University of California, Los Angeles. Her research focuses on the development of intergroup relations in multiethnic and multiracial schools. These include relations between immigrants and established residents, immigrants and teachers, immigrants and immigrants, and immigrants and their second-plus generation counterparts. She received her M.A. in sociology from the University of California, Los Angeles.